The Clinician's Guide to Oppositional Defiant Disorder

The Clinician's Guide to Oppositional Defiant Disorder

Symptoms, Assessment, and Treatment

Michelle M. Martel
University of Kentucky, Lexington, Kentucky, USA

ELSEVIER

ACADEMIC PRESS
An imprint of Elsevier

Academic Press is an imprint of Elsevier
125 London Wall, London EC2Y 5AS, United Kingdom
525 B Street, Suite 1650, San Diego, CA 92101, United States
50 Hampshire Street, 5th Floor, Cambridge, MA 02139, United States
The Boulevard, Langford Lane, Kidlington, Oxford OX5 1GB, United Kingdom

British Library Cataloguing-in-Publication Data
A catalogue record for this book is available from the British Library

Library of Congress Cataloging-in-Publication Data
A catalog record for this book is available from the Library of Congress

ISBN: 978-0-12-815682-7

For Information on all Academic Press publications
visit our website at https://www.elsevier.com/books-and-journals

Publisher: Nikki Levy
Acquisition Editor: Nikki Levy
Editorial Project Manager: Pat Gonzalez
Production Project Manager: Sujatha Thirugnana Sambandam
Cover Designer: Miles Hitchen

Typeset by MPS Limited, Chennai, India

Dedication

To my DJs

Contents

Preface

This book provides cutting-edge research-based clinical information on oppositional defiant disorder (ODD). ODD is one of the most common childhood disorders, with a prevalence rate of approximately 10% in the general population. Largely propagated by environmental factors such as negative parenting strategies, it is also highly impairing, leading to poor family relationships, increased likelihood of parental divorce, poor peer relationships, and school failure. In addition, untreated ODD increases risk for attention deficit/hyperactivity disorder, conduct disorder (CD), and depression and anxiety. Yet, ODD is one of the most easily and effectively treated childhood disorders once it has been identified. For this reason, early assessment and increased dissemination of treatments for the disorder are critical.

This book provides the latest research information on ODD symptoms, outcomes, causal factors, and assessment and treatment. It is written to be of immediate and applied use to a wide range of professionals including clinicians, from pediatricians to mental health workers, as well as teachers and students in these fields. The current book thus reaches a broader audience than most prior books in this area. Importantly, it provides hands-on, empirically based assessment and treatment guidelines for ODD in children and adolescents. In addition, current online assessment and treatment materials are provided. Such materials will make the current book a quick, go-to resource for clinicians.

In the first several chapters, the book covers the descriptive features of ODD, including information on causal factors and theories. Next, the book has a chapter devoted to assessment materials. Then, overarching evidence-based treatment programs and components are reviewed, and then individual treatment components that cut across different treatment programs are described in detail. Finally, commonly needed adjunct treatment issues are briefly introduced. Relevant online and text resources are provided throughout the book, and easy-to-use assessment and treatment materials are included to make the book maximally useful for clinical professionals and students.

Critically, there is currently no other book that focuses exclusively on ODD with the goal of providing clinicians with key information and assessment and treatment strategies for addressing the disorder. Other existing books generally lump ODD with CD, specifically focus on particular treatment programs, or are simplified to be marketed to parents. The current book adds to existing professional resources by being comprehensive, covering etiology, theory, assessment, and treatment, including treatment information integrated across different treatment approaches. It is also user-friendly, including applied clinician resources such as links to online resources, technological tools such as applications, and clinical assessment and treatment worksheets.

1

CHAPTER

Oppositional defiant disorder dimensions and prediction of later problems

Luis is a 4-year-old Latino male. He was referred by his pediatrician for an evaluation after his parents presented complaining about Luis' aggression. Luis only uses one- to two-word phrases to communicate and is difficult to understand. His parents speak Spanish at home and both work long hours at minimum wage jobs. They have five kids total, ages 1, 4, 8, 10, and 12. Luis' parents report that he was born 1 month premature, weighing 4 lb and 3 oz. Luis' mother had severe hypertension toward the end of her pregnancy. Although his motor milestones were reported to be on time, Luis did not say his first words until age 3. He is still not potty trained and sleeps in bed with his parents. Luis' parents complain that he becomes angry and aggressive with minimal provocation. Luis will hit, kick, bite, and throw a tantrum if he does not get his way. He frequently does things that he knows his parents find annoying (such as yelling and running away at the supermarket). He does not comply with adult commands, yelling no and running away.

The Clinician's Guide to Oppositional Defiant Disorder. DOI: https://doi.org/10.1016/B978-0-12-815682-7.00001-X

He once ran away in a store parking lot and was almost hit by a car. His parents were worried social services would be called. Luis' parents are concerned about him starting school next year, given they cannot currently leave him at home with even a babysitter due to his severe misbehavior.

***

Frederick is a 10-year-old African American male. His mother presents with him to the emergency room after his school called her to come and pick him up during the middle of the day after he threatened to "gut" another 10-year-old boy in his class. The school reported that the provocation for this incident was that Frederick became angry when the other boy asked him to share his colored pencil. More concerning, Frederick was found to have had a knife hidden in his schoolbag and indicated that he planned to use it on the other boy so the other boy would "get what was coming to him." The school has suspended Frederick until his mother obtains treatment for him. Frederick has a history of problems with peers. He has few friends and his peers report being scared of him. Frederick frequently graphically threatens his peers following minor disagreements, telling them he will "cut them open," he "wants to explore their insides," and he will "show them their hearts." He is known to hold a grudge and will wait for a peer following a disagreement after school, threatening them and saying he will hurt them. Frederick lives with his mother, who is single. His biological father has been in jail for armed robbery since he was born. His mother is a mortician with little family in the area. Frederick often spends his afternoons largely unsupervised at the morgue. Frederick's mother acknowledges that she is sometimes scared of him. He reportedly does not listen to her, often argues with her, and she is at a loss as to how to discipline him. Frederick's mother indicated that he has always been difficult to parent. She is worried because his school is insisting she seek some kind of treatment for Frederick; otherwise, they have said they will expel him.

***

Anna is a 15-year-old Caucasian female whose parents present with concerns about possible drug use, sexting, and promiscuous sex. Anna has been diagnosed with depression and has been taking antidepressants since age 13. She was described as irritable and easily annoyed most of the time. She acknowledges frequent marijuana use with friends and being sexually active with several males. She has been grounded for the last 2 weeks after she sent a naked picture to one of these males, and her parents were informed by a friend's mother, who saw the picture on her daughter's Snapchat. Anna acknowledges that her current friend group has not been the best influence. She complains that the girls are all catty and talk about her behind her back. She reports engaging in sexting or sex, as well as impulsivity, without a lot of forethought about the consequences, or while under the influence of alcohol. She indicated that she has no desire to listen to her parents and often argues with them about curfews and rules. She justified her behavior by reporting that she was bullied extensively in grade school and feels the need to fit in with her peers whatever the cost.

***

What is oppositional defiant disorder?

All of these cases are examples of oppositional defiant disorder (ODD). But what exactly is ODD? ODD "ain't [just] misbehaving" (Wakschlag, Tolan, & Leventhal, 2010), although some parents will certainly present with concerns that include that. According to American Psychiatric Association's (APA) (2013) *Diagnostic and statistical Manual of Mental Disorders*, 5th edition (DSM-5), ODD is a disruptive, impulse-control, and conduct disorder (CD) characterized by frequent and persistent angry/irritable mood, argumentative/defiant behavior, and/or vindictiveness. As shown in Table 1.1, DSM-5 lists the symptoms of ODD under three symptom domains: angry/irritable mood (i.e., loses temper, touchy or easily annoyed, and angry and resentful), argumentative/defiant behavior (argues, actively defies or refuses to comply with requests or with rules, deliberately annoys others, and blames others for mistakes or misbehavior), and vindictiveness (spiteful; APA, 2013). Importantly, an individual has to exhibit four or more symptoms in the last 6 months to meet diagnostic criteria. Further, the persistence and frequency of symptoms should exceed age, gender, and cultural expectations, and symptoms do not

TABLE 1.1 ODD symptoms.

Angry/irritable mood
• Often loses temper
• Is often touchy or easily annoyed
• Is often angry and resentful
Argumentative/defiant behavior
• Often argues with authority figures or, for children and adolescents, with adults
• Often actively defies or refuses to comply with requests from authority figures or with rules
• Often deliberately annoys others
• Often blames others for his or her mistakes or misbehavior
Vindictiveness
• Has been spiteful or vindictive at least twice within the past 6 months

ODD, Oppositional defiant disorder.

need to be present in more than one setting. The American Medical Association's *International Classification of Diseases*, 10th edition (World Health Organization, 1992), describes ODD similarly as a pattern of negative, defiant, disobedient, and hostile behavior toward authority figures.

ODD typically begins early, during preschool. The disorder is fairly stable and leads to numerous problems, notably problems in family relationships and later problems with peers (Foster, Jones, & Conduct Problems Prevention Research Group, 2005; Nock, Kazdin, Hiripi, & Kessler, 2007). If left untreated, it dramatically increases risk for school failure and later delinquency and problems with the legal system (Foster et al., 2005). Therefore it is associated with high societal cost in the amount of over $70,000 per child over a 7-year period in the United States alone (Foster et al., 2005).

ODD is also quite common, occurring in about 3%—10% of the population. It affects slightly more boys than girls at a ratio of about 1.5:1 during childhood (APA, 2013; Frick & Nigg, 2012; Kessler et al., 2005a; Kessler, Chiu, Demler, & Walters, 2005b; Nock et al., 2007). Importantly, ODD predisposes to many other types of problems. ODD turns into conduct disorder (CD) in a subset of individuals. Further, it cooccurs with attention-deficit/hyperactivity disorder (ADHD) in approximately 50% of cases (Lavigne et al., 2001). Lastly, it increases risk for anxiety and mood problems, perhaps particularly in females.

ODD is associated with substantial later impairment, including family problems, academic problems, peer problems, self-esteem problems, and even legal problems (Campbell, Spieker, Burchinal, Poe, & The NICHD Early Child Care Research Network, 2006; Foster et al., 2005; Greene et al., 2002; Speltz, McClellan, DeKlyen, & Jones, 1999). Girls, in particular, seem at risk for social problems with peers and anxiety and depression (Burke, Hipwell, & Loeber, 2010). In fact, early physical maturation in girls puts them at particular risk for these problems (Burke, Loeber, & Birmaher, 2002; Graber, Lewinsohn, Seeley, & Brooks-Gunn, 1997; Ullsperger & Nikolas, 2017). In addition, children with disruptive behavior problems are much more likely to engage in risk-taking behaviors such as illegal drinking and drug use, part of the adult externalizing spectrum (Krueger et al., 2002; Krueger, Markon, Patrick, Benning, & Kramer, 2007).

Thus overall, ODD is a fairly common and early-emerging disruptive behavior disorder (DBD) characterized by angry/irritable mood, argumentative/defiant behavior, and/or vindictiveness. It is very impairing, increasing risk for a number of other disorders, predominantly CD, ADHD, and anxiety and mood problems.

Oppositional defiant disorder symptom domains and structure

Theoretical and limited empirical work suggests that the ODD symptom domains are differentially related to concurrent and prospective comorbidity patterns (or commonly cooccurring conditions; Rowe, Costello, Angold, Copeland, & Maughan, 2010). In line with the names of the symptom domains, angry/irritable mood appears to predispose to later anxiety and mood problems (Loeber, Burke, & Pardini, 2009a). Argumentative/defiant behavior appears to be related to ADHD symptoms. Finally, vindictiveness appears to predict later CD (Stringaris & Goodman, 2009a, 2009b).

However, a large study utilizing four different community samples of children ages 5–18 and different measures of ODD symptoms suggests that a bifactor model with an overarching, general ODD factor and more specific factors of irritability and oppositional behavior best characterizes ODD (Burke et al., 2014; see Fig. 1.1). This is perhaps not surprising as the vindictiveness domain in the DSM-5 only utilizes one symptom: spiteful/vindictive (Whelan, Stringaris, Maughan, & Barker, 2013). Further, the specific domains were highly correlated with one another, suggesting that all symptoms hang together well in the overall ODD diagnostic category. Regardless of the best model of ODD, general behavioral ODD symptoms seem to predispose to ADHD, while irritable mood symptoms appear to predispose to later depression and suicide attempts.

Irritability appears to be at the core of ODD and is one of the features that makes ODD so difficult to diagnosis (Burke et al., 2014). Several other conditions share this feature as a core characteristic and must be ruled out or considered in place of, or in addition to, ODD. Disruptive mood dysregulation disorder (DMDD), which used to be known as severe mood dysregulation (SMD; Leibenluft, 2011), is one such condition that must be ruled out, or considered in place of, an ODD diagnosis (APA, 2013). Listed in the

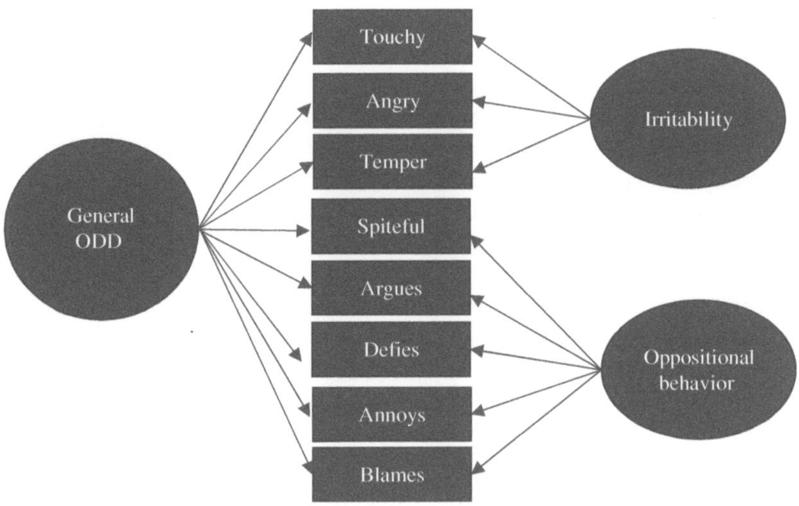

FIGURE 1.1 ODD bifactor model. *ODD*, Oppositional defiant disorder.

depressive disorders category in DSM-5, DMDD is characterized by severe recurrent temper outbursts that are out of proportion to the situation. These temper outbursts must occur, on average, at least three times a week, and mood between temper outbursts must be persistently irritable or angry most of the day nearly every day for at least 12 months. Therefore, in the presence of severe, frequent temper outbursts, DMDD should be diagnosed instead of ODD. Although originally SMD (now DMDD) was conceived as a childhood precursor to bipolar disorder, it is currently viewed more as a childhood manifestation of depression with which it commonly cooccurs (Copeland, Angold, Costello, & Egger, 2013). Therefore for now, DMDD appears to be best thought of as a precursor of depression and should be treated accordingly.

Overall, current work suggests that ODD is best conceptualized as three continuous symptom dimensions that cooccur and appear most largely defined by high irritability. The symptom domains somewhat differentially predict comorbidity such that angry/irritable mood appears to predispose to later anxiety and mood problems, argumentative/defiant behavior appears to predict ADHD symptoms, and vindictiveness is related to later CD.

Associated disruptive, impulse-control, and conduct disorders

ODD most often increases risk for other DBDs, particularly CD and antisocial personality disorder (Loeber, Burke, Lahey, Winters, & Zera, 2000). While ODD symptoms often first appear in preschool and precede the development of CD, CD develops in a subset of children with ODD between middle childhood and adolescence. CD can further be distinguished into subtypes depending on whether symptoms arise in childhood (i.e., prior to 10 years of age) or, more commonly, during adolescence (APA, 2013; Moffitt, 1993). Age of onset is associated with different patterns of symptoms, with childhood-onset CD associated with more aggressive behaviors and adolescent-onset CD associated with more delinquent, rule-breaking behaviors (Lahey, Waldman, & McBurnett, 1999). Therefore, the subset of children with ODD that progresses into CD are a particularly impaired group.

Furthermore, CD includes a specifier of limited prosocial emotions, which includes lack of remorse or guilt, callousness (i.e., lack of empathy), unconcern about performance, and shallow or deficient affect. These limited prosocial emotions, commonly referred to as callous–unemotional traits in the research literature, are seen as a precursor to adult psychopathy (Frick & Nigg, 2012; Loeber, Burke, & Pardini, 2009b), and this feature denotes a more severely impaired and particularly problematic subgroup of children. Luckily, this feature can be quickly and easily assessed as early as preschool, as will be detailed in Chapter 4, The importance and ease of assessment of oppositional defiant disorder.

Just like only some children with ODD will go on to develop CD, only some individuals with CD go on to develop antisocial personality disorder. Antisocial personality disorder was long considered an adulthood disorder because DSM-5 requires the presence of problem behaviors since the age of 15 years. Antisocial personality disorder is defined as a pattern of disregard for and violation of the rights of others, including a failure to conform to social norms, deceitfulness, impulsivity, irritability and aggressiveness, disregard for safety, irresponsibility, and a lack of remorse (APA, 2013). These symptoms are related to, but are broader than, the limited prosocial emotions CD specifier or callous–unemotional traits described above.

Children with these types of externalizing problems are at greater risk of having externalizing disorders during adulthood, compared with children without such problems, and those with childhood-onset (vs adolescent-onset) CD exhibit worse trajectories and outcomes (Moffitt, 1993). Further, in adulthood, externalizing disorders are highly comorbid with substance-related and addictive disorders and, for that reason, are believed to fall on a common externalizing spectrum (Krueger et al., 2002, 2007).

Based on this kind of research, ODD, CD, and antisocial personality disorder are grouped together in a category called disruptive, impulse-control, and CDs in DSM-5 (APA, 2013). Other disorders included in this category include intermittent explosive disorder, pyromania, and kleptomania. These last three disorders are much less studied than ODD, CD, and antisocial personality disorder. Intermittent explosive disorder is characterized by recurrent verbal or physically aggressive outbursts out of proportion to provocation and occurring twice weekly on average over a period of 3 months or resulting in damage to persons or property (APA, 2013). Such outbursts should not be premeditated or committed for gain. Little research has been conducted on this disorder. However, in practice, it is often diagnosed when criteria for another DBD such as ODD is not met, but aggressive outbursts predominate and require treatment.

As mentioned, the other disorders included in the DSM-5 disruptive, impulse-control, and CDs category include pyromania and kleptomania. Pyromania, the deliberate and purposeful setting of fires on more than one occasion, is sometimes suggested clinically as a symptom denoting an especially serious form of conduct problem, particularly in younger individuals. The other problem that is associated with particularly poor outcomes is *deliberately* hurting animals. Kleptomania is the recurrent failure to resist impulses to steal objects. These two disorders are also both relatively understudied.

Yet, in research and practice, all of the aforementioned problems tend to be called DBDs, or DBDs, perhaps particularly when the term is utilized to describe childhood problems. These problems are also, synonymously, called externalizing problems across the lifespan, given they are considered "acting out" behaviors, as contrasted with the internalized affective problems seen in anxiety and mood disorders. Further, these problems can be graded by severity, based on number of settings in which they are manifest and the number of symptoms expressed.

Overall, disruptive, impulse-control, and CDs most commonly cooccur with ODD.

Aggression and delinquency

Disruptive behavior problems during childhood and adolescence often cooccur with associated problem behaviors such as aggression and delinquency. However, aggression and delinquency are not necessary for diagnosis of a DBD. They also do not require such diagnoses be given as they can be behaviors that are part of normal development. For example, as any parent knows, aggression in young children is very common.

Aggression can take different forms and be performed for different functions (Little, Brauner, Jones, Nock, & Hawley, 2003; Marsee et al., 2014; Ostrov & Crick, 2007). Aggression can take the form of physical (or overt) aggression such as when one child hits another. Aggression can also take the form of relational (or covert) aggression such as when one girl starts a rumor about another girl. Although females do not engage in more relational aggression, compared with males, it *is* their preferred form of aggression.

Aggression can serve a reactive or a proactive (or instrumental) function. Reactive aggression is aggression performed instinctively, without much foresight, in response to a provocation. Proactive, or instrumental aggression, is premeditated as, for example, when a teenager sets up a prank to get back at someone with whom they are angry. Reactive aggression is more common and less concerning than habitual instrumental aggression, which is associated with psychopathy and callous–unemotional traits.

Delinquency is the term denoting disruptive behavior problems that lead to legal problems and is typically used in reference to adolescents. Delinquency limited to adolescence can be a normal part of growing up, as long as it is not severe or chronic; individuals with such normal delinquency usually engage in mild, only occasional acts and typically grow out of it.

Therefore aggression and delinquency commonly occur in individuals with ODD, but these problems are not necessary or sufficient for a diagnosis.

Developmental pathways models of oppositional defiant disorder and associated features: problems with language, potty-training, and sleep

Keeping all of this terminology in mind, individuals with ODD can look very different from one another, as our earlier case examples illustrate. In fact, longitudinal work examining trait pathways to CD suggests at least two distinct pathways, shown in Fig. 1.2. The first pathway involves a decreased

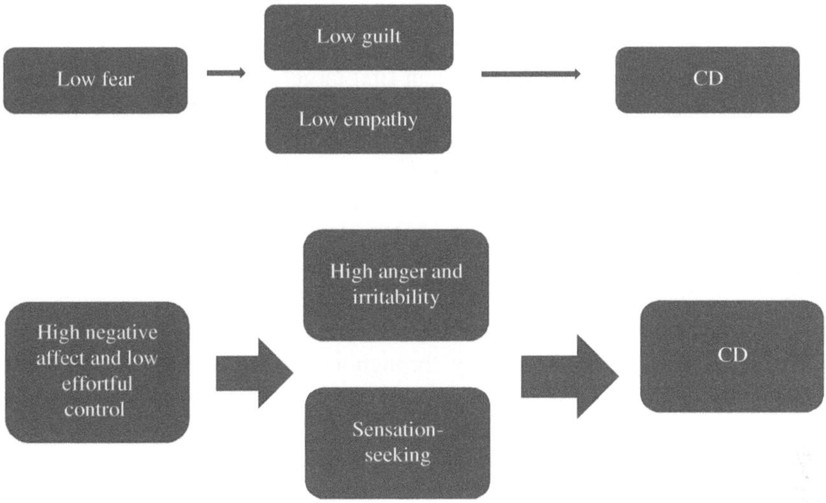

FIGURE 1.2 Pathways to conduct problems.

fear response, predicting later development of CD (reviewed by Nigg, 2006) through low guilt and empathy (Blair, 2001). This is a rarer pathway through callous–unemotional traits, predisposing to later psychopathy and instrumental forms of aggression (Loeber et al., 2009a). The second, more common pathway is through high levels of negative affect and low reactive or effortful control (reviewed by Nigg, 2006) through high anger reactivity, irritability, and high sensation-seeking, leading to the development of behaviors and symptoms consistent with CD (Frick & Morris, 2004). These children are predisposed to poor emotion regulation and reactive aggression.

During early childhood, this second, more common pathway to ODD appears to coexist with many other problems, predominantly ADHD, elimination (or potty-training) problems, and sleep problems. ADHD is, by far, the most common comorbid disorder, cooccurring in about 50% of children with ODD (Egger & Angold, 2006), particularly the symptoms of hyperactivity–impulsivity. Children with ODD and ADHD are frequently impulsive and argumentative. Their parents frequently describe them as "headstrong" and/or "strong-willed." These children also usually exhibit problems across many other regulatory domains that, at early ages, are often best expressed by parents as complaints about elimination (or potty-training) and sleep, sometimes also including language problems.

Children with ODD, often with ADHD, often exhibit problems with language and with elimination, or potty-training (Matthys & Lochman, 2017). Parents with young children with ODD often report that they were delayed in speaking their first words. They often develop language more slowly and speak less clearly once they begin to develop language. Oftentimes, aggression and acting out behaviors in these children may be secondary to problems understanding language or making themselves understood. In these cases, it will be important that treatment first target speech and language problems, discussed briefly in Chapter 12, Related treatment issues: how to address sleep, toilet training, social skills, and learning problems and when to consider medication for comorbid disorders.

In regard to potty-training, parents will often complain that children with ODD are deliberately peeing in bed and/or that they are insensitive to cues of needing to go, urinating on themselves during the day. More rarely, these children will defecate in inappropriate places (e.g., the corner) or even spread feces on the wall. These children also frequently refuse to sleep independently, often waking up frequently throughout the night and crawling into their parents' beds. All of these associated problems also have fairly straightforward treatments, detailed in Chapter 12, Related treatment issues: how to address sleep, toilet training, social skills, and learning problems and when to consider medication for comorbid disorders, and—because they contribute greatly to what is usually already great parental stress—should be tackled as early as possible.

Therefore children with ODD can look very different from one another. Notably, there are at least two different pathways: (1) a more common pathway through low reactive control, associated with other developmental problems such language, potty-training, and sleep problems; and (2) a rarer pathway through high callous–unemotional traits, which predisposes to more stable conduct problems. As detailed in Table 1.2, a careful assessment of ODD requires consideration of a number of different kinds of cooccurring problems.

TABLE 1.2 Other diagnostic considerations.

Disruptive mood dysregulation disorder
ADHD
Conduct disorder
Depressive disorders
Anxiety disorders
Elimination disorders
Sleep disorders
Language disorders
Substance use disorders

Illustration through case examples

Characteristics and cooccurring problems associated with ODD are well illustrated in the case examples at the beginning of the chapter.

Luis

Luis, our 4-year-old Latino male, has preschool ODD given he often loses his temper, is frequently angry, often refuses to comply with adult requests, and deliberately annoys others. An important diagnostic consideration in his case would be DMDD. If his temper outbursts occur three or more times each week, and his mood is persistently angry or irritable between these outbursts, then he might be better diagnosed with DMDD (vs ODD). Yet, clearly, language problems are an important issue in this case and need to be formally evaluated as this will affect both diagnosis and treatment; that is, Luis' language problems may be leading to his aggressive temper outbursts. Luis' parents' use of Spanish at home and his prematurity will be important to consider in such an evaluation. Other diagnostic and treatment concerns include Luis' elimination (or potty-training) problems and his problems sleeping independently. These issues can also be addressed during treatment. Finally, looking into additional avenues of social support for Luis' parents will be important.

Symptoms:

- often loses temper
- frequently angry
- often refuses to comply with adult requests
- deliberately annoys others

Possible cooccurring problems:

- DMDD
- language problems
- potty-training problems
- independent sleep problems

Other considerations:

- bilingualism
- prematurity

Frederick

Frederick, our 10-year-old African American male, has a particularly concerning form of ODD. Although he meets criteria for ODD because he is easily annoyed, often resentful, often argues with authority figures, often defies authority figures, blames others for his misbehavior, and is vindictive, he seems at risk for CD, given his threats toward others and his carrying a weapon. Further, he is exhibiting signs of callous–unemotional traits, given his graphic description of how he would like to hurt others that are often premeditated and well thought out. Given his threatened expulsion, immediate treatment is indicated. Finding additional support for Frederick's mother and his school for providing closer supervision of Frederick will be important for facilitating treatment.

Symptoms:

- easily annoyed
- often resentful
- often argues with authority figures
- often defies authority figures
- blames others for his misbehavior
- is vindictive

Possible cooccurring problems:

- CD

Other considerations:

- callous–unemotional traits

Anna

Anna is our 15-year-old Caucasian female whose parents presented with concerns about possible drug use, sexting, and promiscuous sex. Anna, as you will remember, has already been diagnosed and treated for depression. Although she has reportedly been successfully treated for depression with antidepressants, she still appears to be exhibiting enough significant difficulties to be diagnosed with ODD as well. She is often irritable and easily annoyed; she often argues with or defies adult requests. Other diagnostic considerations will include substance use disorder. Bullying, safe sex, and healthy peer and romantic relationships will also all need to be addressed in treatment.

Symptoms:

- often irritable
- often easily annoyed
- often argues with adult requests
- often defies adult requests

Possible cooccurring problems:

- substance use disorders

Other considerations:

- bullying
- sexual and romantic relationships
- peer relationships

Conclusion

Despite the substantial variations between individuals in these cases, Luis, Frederick, and Anna all meet criteria for ODD. Further, all three cases exhibit different aspects of the substantial impairment associated with ODD. Yet, fortunately, ODD is easy to assess and treat, particularly during early development, as described in subsequent chapters.

References

American Psychiatric Association. (2013). *Diagnostic and statistical manual of mental disorders* (5th ed.). Washington, DC: Author.

Blair, R. J. R. (2001). Neurocognitive models of aggression, the antisocial personality disorders, and psychopathy. *Journal of Neurology, Neurosurgery, and Psychiatry*, *71*, 727–731.

Burke, J. D., Boylan, K., Rowe, R., Duku, E., Stepp, S. D., Hipwell, A. E., & Waldman, I. D. (2014). Identifying the irritability dimension of ODD: Application of a modified bifactor model across five large community samples of children. *Journal of Abnormal Psychology*, *123*(4), 841.

Burke, J. D., Hipwell, A. E., & Loeber, R. (2010). Dimensions of oppositional defiant disorder as predictors of depression and conduct disorder in preadolescent girls. *Journal of the American Academy of Child & Adolescent Psychiatry*, *49*(5), 484–492.

Burke, J. D., Loeber, R., & Birmaher, B. (2002). Oppositional defiant disorder and conduct disorder: A review of the past 10 years, part II. *Journal of the American Academy of Child & Adolescent Psychiatry*, *41*(11), 1275–1293.

Campbell, S. B., Spieker, S., Burchinal, M., Poe, M. D., & The NICHD Early Child Care Research Network. (2006). Trajectories of aggression from toddlerhood to age 9 predict academic and social functioning through age 12. *Journal of Child Psychology and Psychiatry*, *47*(8), 791–800.

Copeland, W. E., Angold, A., Costello, E. J., & Egger, H. (2013). Prevalence, comorbidity, and correlates of DSM-5 proposed disruptive mood dysregulation disorder. *American Journal of Psychiatry*, *170*(2), 173–179.

Egger, H. L., & Angold, A. (2006). Common emotional and behavioral disorders in preschool children: Presentation, nosology, and epidemiology. *Journal of Child Psychology and Psychiatry*, *47*(3/4), 313–337.

Foster, E. M., Jones, D. E., & Conduct Problems Prevention Research Group. (2005). The high costs of aggression: Public expenditures resulting from conduct disorder. *American Journal of Public Health*, *95*(10), 1767–1772.

Frick, P. J., & Morris, A. S. (2004). Temperament and developmental pathways to conduct problems. *Journal of Clinical Child & Adolescent Psychology*, *33*, 54–68.

Frick, P. J., & Nigg, J. T. (2012). Current issues in the diagnosis of attention deficit hyperactivity disorder, oppositional defiant disorder, and conduct disorder. *Annual Review of Clinical Psychology*, *8*, 77–107.

Graber, J. A., Lewinsohn, P. M., Seeley, J. R., & Brooks-Gunn, J. (1997). Is psychopathology associated with the timing of pubertal development? *Journal of the American Academy of Child & Adolescent Psychiatry*, *36*(12), 1768–1776.

Greene, R. W., Biederman, J., Zerwas, S., Monuteaux, M. C., Goring, J. C., & Faraone, S. V. (2002). Psychiatric comorbidity, family dysfunction, and social impairment in referred youth with oppositional defiant disorder. *American Journal of Psychiatry*, *159*(7), 1214–1224.

Kessler, R. C., Berglund, P., Demler, O., Jin, R., Merikangas, K. R., & Walters, E. E. (2005a). Lifetime prevalence and age-of-onset distributions of DSM-IV disorders in the National Comorbidity Survey Replication. *Archives of General Psychiatry*, *62*(6), 593–602.

Kessler, R. C., Chiu, W. T., Demler, O., & Walters, E. E. (2005b). Prevalence, severity, and comorbidity of 12-month DSM-IV disorders in the National Comorbidity Survey Replication. *Archives of General Psychiatry*, *62*(6), 617–627.

Krueger, R. F., Hicks, B. M., Patrick, C. J., Carlson, S. R., Iacono, W. G., & McGue, M. (2002). Etiologic connections among substance dependence, antisocial behavior, and personality: Modeling the externalizing spectrum. *Journal of Abnormal Psychology*, *111*, 411–424.

Krueger, R. F., Markon, K. E., Patrick, C. J., Benning, S. D., & Kramer, M. D. (2007). Linking antisocial behavior, substance use, and personality: An integrative quantitative model of the adult externalizing spectrum. *Journal of Abnormal Psychology*, *116*, 645.

Lahey, B. B., Waldman, I. D., & McBurnett, K. (1999). Annotation: The development of antisocial behavior: An integrative causal model. *Journal of Child Psychology and Psychiatry and Allied Disciplines*, *40*, 669–682.

Lavigne, J. V., Cicchetti, C., Gibbons, R. D., Binns, H. J., Larsen, L., & Devito, C. (2001). Oppositional defiant disorder with onset in preschool years: Longitudinal stability and pathways to other disorders. *Journal of the American Academy of Child & Adolescent Psychiatry*, *40*(12), 1393–1400.

Leibenluft, E. (2011). Severe mood dysregulation, irritability, and the diagnostic boundaries of bipolar disorder in youths. *American Journal of Psychiatry*, *168*(2), 129–142.

Little, T. D., Brauner, J., Jones, S. M., Nock, M. K., & Hawley, P. H. (2003). Rethinking aggression: A typological examination of the functions of aggression. *Merrill-Palmer Quarterly (1982-)*, *49*, 343–369.

Loeber, R., Burke, J. D., Lahey, B. B., Winters, A., & Zera, M. (2000). Oppositional defiant and conduct disorder: A review of the past 10 years, Part I. *Journal of the American Academy of Child & Adolescent Psychiatry*, *39*(12), 1468–1484.

Loeber, R., Burke, J. D., & Pardini, D. A. (2009a). Development and etiology of disruptive and delinquent behavior. *Annual Review of Clinical Psychology*, *5*, 291–310.

Loeber, R., Burke, J., & Pardini, D. A. (2009b). Perspectives on oppositional defiant disorder, conduct disorder, and psychopathic features. *Journal of Child Psychology and Psychiatry*, *50*(1–2), 133–142.

Marsee, M. A., Frick, P. J., Barry, C. T., Kimonis, E. R., Centifanti, L. C. M., & Aucoin, K. J. (2014). Profiles of the forms and functions of self-reported aggression in three adolescent samples. *Development and Psychopathology*, *26*(3), 705–720.

Matthys, W., & Lochman, J. E. (2017). *Oppositional defiant disorder and conduct disorder in childhood*. John Wiley & Sons.

Moffitt, T. E. (1993). Adolescence-limited and life-course-persistent antisocial behavior: A developmental taxonomy. *Psychological Review*, *100*, 674–701.

Nigg, J. T. (2006). Temperament and developmental psychopathology. *Journal of Child Psychology and Psychiatry*, *47*, 395–422.

Nock, M. K., Kazdin, A. E., Hiripi, E., & Kessler, R. C. (2007). Lifetime prevalence, correlates, and persistence of oppositional defiant disorder: Results from the National Comorbidity Survey Replication. *Journal of Child Psychology and Psychiatry*, *48*(7), 703–713.

Ostrov, J. M., & Crick, N. R. (2007). Forms and functions of aggression during early childhood: A short-term longitudinal study. *School Psychology Review*, *36*(1), 22.

Rowe, R., Costello, E. J., Angold, A., Copeland, W. E., & Maughan, B. (2010). Developmental pathways in oppositional defiant disorder and conduct disorder. *Journal of Abnormal Psychology*, *119*(4), 726.

Speltz, M. L., McClellan, J., DeKlyen, M., & Jones, K. (1999). Preschool boys with oppositional defiant disorder: Clinical presentation and diagnostic change. *Journal of the American Academy of Child and Adolescent Psychiatry*, *38*(7), 838–845.

Stringaris, A., & Goodman, R. (2009a). Three dimensions of oppositionality in youth. *Journal of Child Psychology and Psychiatry*, *50*(3), 216–223.

Stringaris, A., & Goodman, R. (2009b). Longitudinal outcome of youth oppositionality: Irritable, headstrong, and hurtful behaviors have distinctive predictions. *Journal of the American Academy of Child & Adolescent Psychiatry*, *48*(4), 404–412.

Ullsperger, J. M., & Nikolas, M. A. (2017). A meta-analytic review of the association between pubertal timing and psychopathology in adolescence: Are there sex differences in risk? *Psychological Bulletin*, *143*(9), 903.

Wakschlag, L. S., Tolan, P. H., & Leventhal, B. L. (2010). Research review: 'Ain't misbehavin': Towards a developmentally-specified nosology for preschool disruptive behavior. *Journal of Child Psychology and Psychiatry*, *51*(1), 3–22.

Whelan, Y. M., Stringaris, A., Maughan, B., & Barker, E. D. (2013). Developmental continuity of oppositional defiant disorder subdimensions at ages 8, 10, and 13 years and their distinct psychiatric outcomes at age 16 years. *Journal of the American Academy of Child & Adolescent Psychiatry*, *52*(9), 961–969.

World Health Organization (1992). *International classification of diseases and related health problems* (10th rev., ICD-10). Geneva.

2

CHAPTER

Causal factors of oppositional defiant disorder

What could cause the types of behaviors exhibited by Luis, Frederick, and Anna, described in Chapter 1, Oppositional defiant disorder dimensions and prediction of later problems? Consistent with the substantial individual differences described in these case examples, it is likely that each individual has a slightly different constellation of implicated causal factors. Unfortunately, however, advanced statistical approaches are just reaching the point where we can examine etiological factors at the level of the individual. Up until recently, most research has focused on large groups, so, as clinicians, we can usually only speak in generalities as to what factors increase risk at the population and group levels.

Behavioral genetic estimates of genetic and environmental influences

Behavioral genetic work has been key in elucidating the relative role of various causal factors in psychopathology. Behavioral genetics uses innovative designs such as studies of twins to estimate the magnitude of genetic versus

The Clinician's Guide to Oppositional Defiant Disorder. DOI: https://doi.org/10.1016/B978-0-12-815682-7.00002-1

environmental influences on behavior at the population level. Such research suggests an almost equal combination of genetic and environmental factors on oppositional defiant disorder (ODD) (Burt, Krueger, McGue, & Iacono, 2001; Dick, Viken, Kaprio, Pulkkinen, & Rose, 2005), as shown in Fig. 2.1. Heritability of ODD is estimated at approximately 50%, while the remaining variance is due to the environment (Burt et al., 2001; Dick et al., 2005; Rhee & Waldman, 2002). Therefore genetic and environmental influences are approximately evenly implicated in risk for ODD.

Behavioral genetics work also allows us to evaluate how much environmental influences on ODD are due to environmental factors that are shared between siblings, called shared environmental influences, compared with those that are not shared, called nonshared environmental influences. Such work suggests that environmental influences on ODD are almost evenly split between shared and nonshared environmental influences. There is no rule about what sort of environmental influences are shared and unshared, and what is considered shared versus nonshared can vary from family to family and individual to individual. For example, although peer group is usually thought of as a nonshared environmental influence because siblings often have different friend groups, obviously, there can be families in which siblings share a common peer group (e.g., two of my childhood friends were twins and shared a number of friends, including me). Likewise, parenting is often thought of as a shared environmental influence because surely parents parent all their children the same way. However, if you were the eldest child in your family growing up, you may beg to differ, arguing that your youngest sibling got away with murder. So, it can be difficult to determine

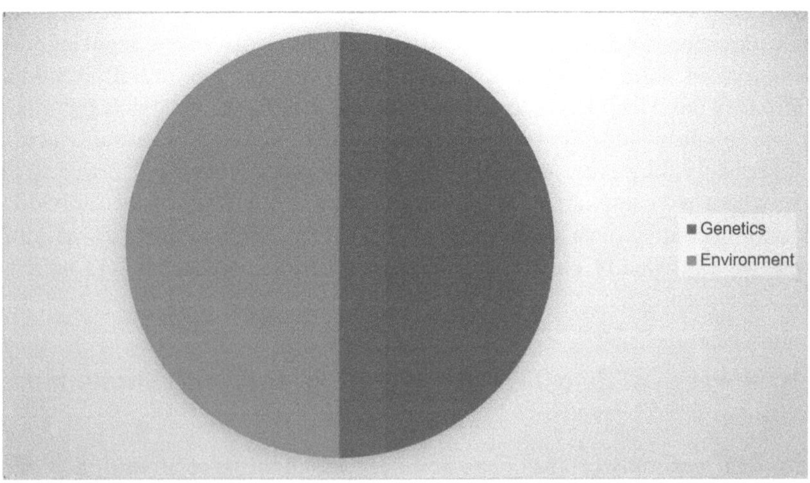

FIGURE 2.1 Estimates of causal influences on child conduct problems.

precisely which environmental factors are shared and nonshared in ODD. Yet, shared and nonshared environmental factors each appear to be about equally important in ODD.

To make matters more confusing, covariation between ODD and other externalizing disorders can be viewed as mostly accounted for by either genetic *or* environmental influences, depending on how symptoms are assessed (Burt et al., 2001; Martin, Levy, Pieka, & Hay, 2006; Nadder, Rutter, Silberg, Maes, & Eaves, 2002; Tuvblad, Zheng, Raine, & Baker, 2009). Shared genetic factors seem to largely account for independent rater reports of externalizing behaviors; that is, for covariation in parent or child reports on externalizing problems, when examined separately. However, shared environmental influences seem to largely account for consistency among multiple informant reports of externalizing behavior, that is, the level of agreement between parents and children about externalizing problems (Burt et al., 2001; Martin et al., 2006; Nadder et al., 2002; Tuvblad et al., 2009). What this seems to suggest is that where parents and children agree about cooccurrence of externalizing problems, factors common to siblings in that family play a large role. However, when individual reports of cooccurring externalizing symptoms are examined, shared genetic factors play a large role.

Overall, ODD is approximately 50% genetic and 50% environmental. Yet, genetic and environmental influences on externalizing problems vary based on child characteristics. Heritability and genetic influences are higher, or stronger, for children with high callous–unemotional or psychopathic traits and for children with childhood-onset conduct problems (Bezdjian, Raine, Baker, & Lynam, 2011; Blonigen, Hicks, Krueger, Patrick, & Iacono, 2005; Larsson, Viding, & Plomin, 2008; Viding, Blair, Moffitt, & Plomin, 2005; Viding, Jones, Paul, Moffitt, & Plomin, 2008).

Gene by environment interactions

Specific genetic risk seems to involve genes influencing serotonergic and dopaminergic neurotransmission or genes influencing those neurotransmitters' availability. Such genotypes can result in difficult temperament types, including high negative emotionality or high impulsivity, for example (Lahey & Waldman, 2017). In fact, theory suggests three distinct temperament profiles that increase risk: callousness–unemotionality (mentioned above, associated with increased genetic risk), high negative emotionality, and high sensation-seeking (Lahey & Waldman, 2017). The latter two temperament profiles in particular may make such children more susceptible to environmental influences.

In fact, most work that has been done on genetic risk for ODD or related externalizing problems has focused on gene by environment interactions, or interplay. That is, research has generally focused on how genotypes and child temperament seem to interact with environmental influences to increase risk for ODD and related conduct problems. The most touted gene by environmental interaction finding has been an interaction between MAOA polymorphisms and child maltreatment. Genes for low MAOA activity (which affects levels of serotonin, dopamine, and norepinephrine) appear to lead to conduct problems in males, particularly for those exposed to childhood abuse (Kim-Cohen et al., 2006). In addition, the short allele of 5HTT-LPR has been associated with ODD in the presence of self-blame related to parental conflict (Martel, Nikolas, Jernigan, Friderici, & Nigg, 2012). Further, parental psychopathology such as criminality has been associated with conduct problems in children, but only for those with dopaminergic risk (Waldman & Lahey, 2013); that is, DRD4 is associated with ODD in families with a history of ODD (Kirley et al., 2004). DRD4 has also been associated with ADHD and sensation-seeking. Such temperament and neurobiological pathways to conduct problems are depicted in Fig. 2.2.

Therefore genetic influences on child conduct problems are likely complex and interact with environmental influences. Further, such effects are likely to be at least somewhat child specific, operating through particular child traits, particularly negative emotionality and sensation-seeking.

Environmental influences

The majority of work on causal factors related to ODD and other externalizing problems has been conducted on environmental influences. Stress, broadly defined, is associated with the later development of externalizing problems and ODD in particular, beginning during the prenatal period. Prenatal stress, low birth weight and complications, and abuse of substances

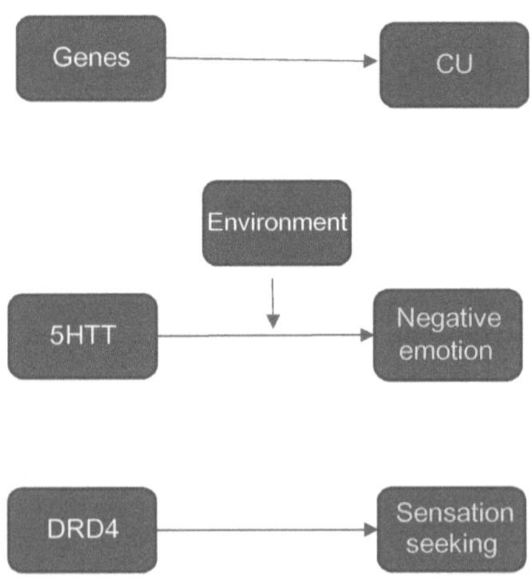

FIGURE 2.2 Causal pathways to conduct problems.

such as alcohol during pregnancy appear to increase risk for child externalizing problems (Boden, Fergusson, & Horwood, 2010; D'Onofrio et al., 2008; Lahey & Waldman, 2017; Nigg & Breslau, 2007). Such prenatal stressors and exposures seem to be at least a partial proxy for parental lifestyle and genetic risk for externalizing problems. Notably, the association between environmental risk and behavioral outcomes shrinks to at least half when genetic confounds are controlled (Matthys & Lochman, 2017).

Likewise, children with ODD and externalizing problems are typically exposed to harsh parenting practices such as spanking, as well as parental coercion, as described more fully in the next chapter (Burke, Loeber, & Birmaher, 2002; Dishion, Patterson, Cicchetti, & Cohen, 2006; Patterson, Reid, & Dishion, 1992). Low parental warmth is related to increased risk for conduct problems (Matthys & Lochman, 2017). Poor parental monitoring of child activities is associated with conduct problems (Burke et al., 2002; Laird, Pettit, Bates, & Dodge, 2003). Parental domestic violence and discord, including divorce, as well as lack of parents in the household are related to conduct problems (Burt, Krueger, McGue, & Iacono, 2003; Burt, McGue, Krueger, & Iacono, 2005; Kouros, Cummings, & Davies, 2010; Lahey & Waldman, 2017; Matthys & Lochman, 2017). Finally, abuse and chronic stressors such as unemployment and low socioeconomic status (SES) increase risk for childhood externalizing problems (Boden et al., 2010; Dishion, French, & Patterson, 1995; Lahey & Waldman, 2017). Overall, harsh parenting, poor monitoring, and discord and stress in the home seem to increase risk for child conduct problems.

Peer and cultural factors are also important in externalizing disorders. The experience of bullying and/or peer rejection leaves some youth more at risk for conduct problems (Dodge et al., 2003; Lansford, Criss, Pettit, Dodge, & Bates, 2003; Viding, McCrory, Blakemore, & Frederickson, 2011; Wolke, Woods, Bloomfield, & Karstadt, 2000). Affiliation with deviant peers is linked with child and adolescent conduct problems (Boden et al., 2010; Lansford et al., 2003). Finally, it is well established that exposure to violent media increases the likelihood of violent behaviors in youth (Anderson & Bushman, 2001; Bushman & Huesmann, 2006; Ferguson & Kilburn, 2009; Huesmann, Moise-Titus, Podolski, & Eron, 2003; Savage & Yancey, 2008). Therefore, problems with peers, association with deviant peers, and exposure to violent media seem to increase risk for conduct problems in youth.

Living in poor and disadvantaged neighborhoods is associated with conduct problems in children. Likewise, parental unemployment, family poverty/low SES, and neighborhood violence increase a child's likelihood of conduct problems (Boden et al., 2010; Burke et al., 2002). In particular, low social connectedness among neighbors in high-crime neighborhoods seems to increase risk for conduct problems (Lahey & Waldman, 2017). Interactions among all of these risk factors can also be important. Specifically, parental factors can and do interact with more global neighborhood characteristics.

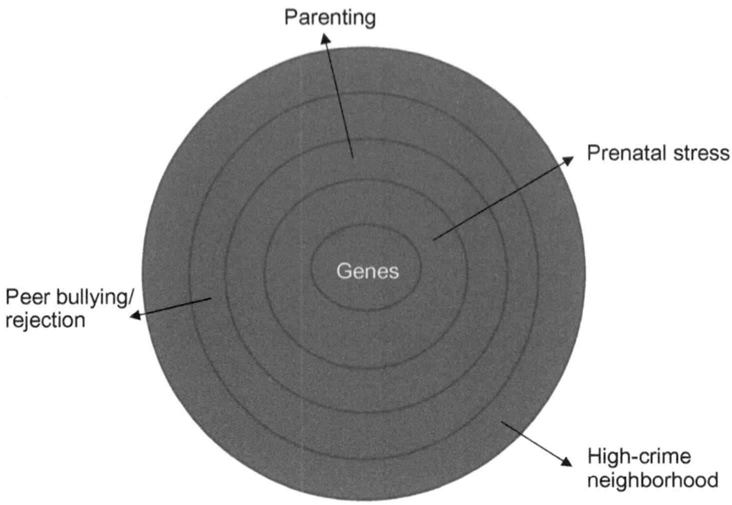

FIGURE 2.3 Nested risk factors in conduct problems.

For example, parental monitoring protects against youth externalizing problems, particularly in neighborhoods characterized by residential instability (Beyers, Bates, Pettit, & Dodge, 2003). Therefore living in a disadvantaged or poor neighborhood seems to increase risk for youth conduct problems.

Therefore, a number of prenatal, parental, peer, and neighborhood environmental influences have been associated with child conduct problems. Fig. 2.3 shows a schematic of environmental risk factors associated with child conduct problems. Specifically, prenatal stress and exposure, harsh parenting and family discord, poor monitoring, bullying and peer rejection, peer delinquency, exposure to violent media, and disadvantaged neighborhoods seem to increase risk for child conduct problems.

***

Illustrations through case examples

We can see elements of these risks in our case examples of Luis, Frederick, and Anna.

Luis

Luis is a 4-year-old Latino male. He was referred by his pediatrician for an evaluation after his parents presented complaining about Luis' aggression. Luis only uses one- to two-word phrases to communicate and is difficult to understand. His parents speak Spanish at home and both work long hours at minimum wage jobs. They have five kids total, ages 1, 4, 8, 10, and 12.

Luis' parents report that he was born 1 month premature, weighing 4 lb and 3 oz. Luis' mother had severe hypertension toward the end of her pregnancy. Although his motor milestones were reported to be on time, Luis did not say his first words until age 3. He is still not potty trained and sleeps in bed with his parents. Luis' parents complain that he becomes angry and aggressive with minimal provocation. Luis will hit, kick, bite, and throw a tantrum if he does not get his way. He frequently does things that he knows his parents find annoying (such as yelling and running away at the supermarket). He does not comply with adult commands, yelling no and running away. He once ran away in a store parking lot and was almost hit by a car. His parents were worried that social services would be called. Luis' parents are concerned about him starting school next year, given they cannot currently leave him at home with even a babysitter due to his severe misbehavior.

Likely causal factors

Luis is one of the youngest children in a large family with limited income, and his parents have to work most of the time. He was born prematurely and at low birth weight because his mother had severe hypertension, leading to a developmental delay in language. In Luis' case, problems with understanding language and with communicating seem to be resulting in reactive aggression, noncompliance, and temper tantrums.

***

Frederick

Frederick is a 10-year-old African American male. His mother presented with him to the emergency room when his school called her to come and pick him up during the middle of the day after he threatened to "gut" another 10-year-old boy in his class. The school reported that the provocation for this incident was that Frederick became angry when the other boy asked him to share his colored pencil. More concerning, Frederick was found to have had a knife hidden in his schoolbag and indicated that he planned to use it on the other boy, so that the other boy would "get what was coming to him." The school has suspended Frederick until his mother obtains treatment for him. Frederick has a history of problems with peers. He has few friends and his peers report being scared of him. Frederick frequently, graphically threatens his peers following minor disagreements, telling them he will "cut them open," he "wants to explore their insides," and he will "show them their hearts." He is known to hold a grudge and will wait for a peer following a disagreement after school, threatening them and saying he will hurt them. Frederick lives with his mother, who is single. His biological father has been in jail for armed robbery since Frederick was born. His mother is a mortician with little family in the area. Frederick often spends his afternoons largely unsupervised at the morgue. Frederick's mother acknowledges that she is sometimes scared of him. He reportedly does not listen to her, often argues with her, and she is at a loss as to how to discipline him. Frederick's mother indicated that he has always been difficult to parent. She is worried because his school is insisting that she seek some kind of treatment for Frederick; otherwise, they have said they will expel him.

Likely causal factors

Frederick appears to have a genetic predisposition to conduct problems given his father was convicted of armed robbery. Further, his mother is single, has little social support, and works long hours, leaving her minimal time to supervise Frederick. Frederick appears to exhibit callous–unemotional traits, graphically threatening his peers and being vindictive. His peers are scared of him and largely avoid or shun him. Further, Frederick and his mother do not enjoy a close relationship; at times, she is scared of him.

***

Anna

Anna is a 15-year-old Caucasian female whose parents present with concerns about possible drug use, sexting, and promiscuous sex. Anna has been diagnosed with depression and has been taking antidepressants since age 13. She was described as irritable and easily annoyed most of the time. She acknowledges frequent marijuana use with friends and being sexually active with several males. She has been grounded for the last 2 weeks after she sent a naked picture to one of these males, and her parents were informed by a friend's mother, who saw the picture on her daughter's Snapchat. Anna acknowledges that her current friend group has not been the best influence. She complains that the girls are all catty and talk about her behind her back. She reports engaging in sexting or sex, as well as impulsivity, without a lot of forethought about the consequences, or while under the influence of alcohol. She indicated that she has no desire to listen to her parents and often argues with them about curfews and rules. She justified her behavior by reporting that she was bullied extensively in grade school and feels the need to fit in with her peers whatever the cost.

Likely causal factors

Anna has a history of being bullied in school. She currently hangs out with a group of deviant peers who smoke marijuana and engage in sexting and promiscuous sex. She has a history of being irritable and depressed and frequently argues with her parents.

***

Pathways

Thus, there is not just one set of causal factors or one pathway to conduct problems. In fact, there appear to be several neurobiological pathways to conduct problems, as shown in Fig. 2.2. In an elaborated version of Frick and Morris' (2004) pathways, which were discussed in the previous chapter, one group of youth with conduct problems—the largest group—are predisposed to conduct problems due to early psychosocial adversity, which leads to low IQ and verbal/language abilities, which predisposes them to reactive aggression and conduct problems. Luis is a good example of this subgroup. This group of reactive children appears to be characterized by high negative emotionality, high serotonin, poor prefrontal control of the amygdala, poor cognitive control, and high cortisol, the prominent stress hormone (Lahey & Waldman, 2017; Matthys, Vanderschuren, & Schutter, 2013; van Goozen, Fairchild, Snoek, & Harold, 2007).

In contrast, there is a smaller subgroup of youth with conduct problems who are at risk due to a more heavily genetically influenced trait profile characterized by low empathy or callous–unemotional traits. Frederick is a good example of this subgroup. This subset of youth appears to be characterized by low punishment sensitivity, low serotonin, amygdala hypofunction, low cortisol, low affective empathy, decreased sensitivity to reward, low anxiety, and high sensation-seeking (Barker, Oliver, Viding, Salekin, & Maughan, 2011; Blair, 2007; Frick, Ray, Thornton, & Kahn, 2014; Marsh et al., 2008; Matthys et al., 2013; Van Goozen et al., 2007). In fact, comprehensive reviews show that there is a stronger association between these biological risk factors and conduct problems for youth in this subgroup who come from more affluent, or lower stress, environments (Frick et al., 2014; Raine, 2002).

Therefore, most children will be at risk for conduct problems due to environmental adversity and a profile of low behavioral control, like Luis, whereas in other, rarer cases, like with Frederick, there will be a genetic predisposition to callous–unemotional traits.

Gene–environment correlations

Of course, much of the genetic risk and prenatal (e.g., maternal substance abuse during pregnancy) and early environmental (parental conflict and violence, abuse, job loss) stressors described previously are likely to be confounded (Dodge & Pettit, 2003). This can be seen in both Luis' and Frederick's cases. In Luis' case, a stressful, low SES environment may have led to difficulties with prenatal care and increased likelihood of prenatal problems that increased risk for ODD. In Frederick's case, having a father with externalizing problems who engaged in criminality is likely to result in an absentee father and a stressed mother working long hours who is unable to provide much supervision. This is what is known as a gene–environment correlation, in which genes are associated with environmental conditions (Rutter, Moffitt, & Caspi, 2006; Rutter & Silberg, 2002).

Such gene–environment correlations can be passive, active, or evocative (Rutter et al., 2006). A passive gene–environment correlation occurs without any action on the child's part. In many cases, such passive gene–environment correlations are due to associations between parents' own inherited behavioral characteristics and the rearing environment they provide. For example, parents with externalizing problems have a tendency to use reactive physical discipline on their children, such as spanking their children when they are angry. An active gene–environment correlation occurs when a child's behavior selects or shapes the environment experienced. For example, a child may have a genetic predisposition that makes school more difficult for them so they choose not to study and are subsequently placed in remedial classes. An evocative gene–environment correlation occurs when a child's behavior evokes a reaction from the environment. For example, a child may have an inherited propensity to engage in annoying behaviors such as impulsivity, and they may subsequently be subject to more reactive discipline (e.g., yelling, spanking) by caregivers.

Therefore, genetic and environmental influences often cooccur and impact one another. The existence of such gene–environment correlations can lead to negative downward spirals between parents and children and facilitate intergenerational transmission of risk.

Epigenetics

As described above, genetic predispositions can also interact with the environment (Moffitt, Caspi, & Rutter, 2006). In relation to conduct problems, this can happen when someone inherits a genetic predisposition that makes them vulnerable to an environmental trigger like our earlier example of individuals with the low functioning MAOA gene being more vulnerable to abuse. Such effects likely operate through a variety of mechanisms, but epigenetics is a key mechanism currently being explored (Meaney, 2010).

Epigenetics refers to environmental effects on the transcription of genes. That is, although the environment cannot change your genetic code after conception, it *can* affect the way that code is expressed, or built into proteins, which changes the way DNA functions. Thus, prenatal or early childhood stress can change the way genetic code is expressed in the building blocks or functions of the brain, and can do so transiently, permanently across the lifespan, or even across generations. For example, research in rodents suggests that the quality of early maternal care influences stress response even much later during the lifespan and can even influence individuals' behavior across generations (Meaney, 2010).

Such epigenetic influences are likely one such mechanisms of gene–environment interplay, and they represent an exciting new direction for work on pathways to child conduct problems.

Summary

Overall, ODD is approximately 50% heritable and 50% environmental. Risk factors span from the individual to the cultural and include genetic alleles affecting dopaminergic and serotonergic neurotransmission, difficult child temperament, parenting practices such as harsh discipline and poor monitoring, peer influences such as bulling and rejection, and social influences such as poverty and exposure to violence. Gene–environment interactions, or interplay, and correlations, or associations, are strongly implicated in the disorder. Epigenetics is a promising mechanism of such effects.

Yet, individual pathways to the disorder are apparent. One group of youth with conduct problems—the largest group—appears to be predisposed to conduct problems due to early environmental adversity, which leads to low IQ and verbal/language abilities, which predisposes to reactive aggression and conduct problems. A second, smaller subgroup of youth with conduct problems seems to be at risk due to a more heavily genetically influenced trait profile characterized by low empathy or callous–unemotional traits.

Of course, aside from vulnerability genes and risky environments, there is also the possibility of protective environments. Therefore by changing the environment, we can hopefully mitigate the way genes are expressed. Such a possibility is explored in more detail in subsequent chapters about treatment.

References

Anderson, C. A., & Bushman, B. J. (2001). Effects of violent video games on aggressive behavior, aggressive cognition, aggressive affect, physiological arousal, and prosocial behavior: A meta-analytic review of the scientific literature. *Psychological Science*, *12*(5), 353–359.

Barker, E. D., Oliver, B. R., Viding, E., Salekin, R. T., & Maughan, B. (2011). The impact of prenatal maternal risk, fearless temperament and early parenting on adolescent callous-unemotional traits: A 14-year longitudinal investigation. *Journal of Child Psychology and Psychiatry*, *52*(8), 878–888.

Beyers, J. M., Bates, J. E., Pettit, G. S., & Dodge, K. A. (2003). Neighborhood structure, parenting processes, and the development of youths' externalizing behaviors: A multilevel analysis. *American Journal of Community Psychology*, *31*(1–2), 35–53.

Bezdjian, S., Raine, A., Baker, L. A., & Lynam, D. R. (2011). Psychopathic personality in children: Genetic and environmental contributions. *Psychological Medicine*, *41*(3), 589–600.

Blair, R. J. R. (2007). The amygdala and ventromedial prefrontal cortex in morality and psychopathy. *Trends in Cognitive Sciences*, *11*(9), 387–392.

Blonigen, D. M., Hicks, B. M., Krueger, R. F., Patrick, C. J., & Iacono, W. G. (2005). Psychopathic personality traits: Heritability and genetic overlap with internalizing and externalizing psychopathology. *Psychological Medicine*, *35*(5), 637–648.

Boden, J. M., Fergusson, D. M., & Horwood, L. J. (2010). Risk factors for conduct disorder and oppositional/defiant disorder: Evidence from a New Zealand birth cohort. *Journal of the American Academy of Child & Adolescent Psychiatry*, *49*(11), 1125–1133.

Burke, J. D., Loeber, R., & Birmaher, B. (2002). Oppositional defiant disorder and conduct disorder: A review of the past 10 years, part II. *Journal of the American Academy of Child & Adolescent Psychiatry*, *41*(11), 1275–1293.

Burt, S. A., Krueger, R. F., McGue, M., & Iacono, W. G. (2001). Sources of covariation among attention-deficit/hyperactivity disorder, oppositional defiant disorder, and conduct disorder: The importance of shared environment. *Journal of Abnormal Psychology*, *110*(4), 516.

Burt, S. A., Krueger, R. F., McGue, M., & Iacono, W. (2003). Parent-child conflict and the comorbidity among childhood externalizing disorders. *Archives of General Psychiatry*, *60*(5), 505–513.

Burt, S. A., McGue, M. A. T. T., Krueger, R. F., & Iacono, W. G. (2005). How are parent–child conflict and childhood externalizing symptoms related over time? Results from a genetically informative cross-lagged study. *Development and Psychopathology*, *17*(1), 145–165.

Bushman, B. J., & Huesmann, L. R. (2006). Short-term and long-term effects of violent media on aggression in children and adults. *Archives of Pediatrics & Adolescent Medicine*, *160*(4), 348–352.

Dick, D. M., Viken, R. J., Kaprio, J., Pulkkinen, L., & Rose, R. J. (2005). Understanding the covariation among childhood externalizing symptoms: Genetic and environmental influences on conduct disorder, attention deficit hyperactivity disorder, and oppositional defiant disorder symptoms. *Journal of Abnormal Child Psychology*, *33*(2), 219–229.

Dishion, T. J., French, D. C., & Patterson, G. R. (1995). *The development and ecology of antisocial behavior*. John Wiley & Sons.

Dishion, T. J., Patterson, G. R., Cicchetti, D., & Cohen, D. J. (2006). *The development and ecology of antisocial behavior in children and adolescents. Developmental psychopathology. Risk, disorder, and adaptation*. New York: Wiley.

Dodge, K. A., Lansford, J. E., Burks, V. S., Bates, J. E., Pettit, G. S., Fontaine, R., & Price, J. M. (2003). Peer rejection and social information-processing factors in the development of aggressive behavior problems in children. *Child Development*, *74*(2), 374–393.

Dodge, K. A., & Pettit, G. S. (2003). A biopsychosocial model of the development of chronic conduct problems in adolescence. *Developmental Psychology*, *39*(2), 349.

D'Onofrio, B. M., Van Hulle, C. A., Waldman, I. D., Rodgers, J. L., Harden, K. P., Rathouz, P. J., & Lahey, B. B. (2008). Smoking during pregnancy and offspring externalizing problems: An exploration of genetic and environmental confounds. *Development and Psychopathology*, *20*(1), 139–164.

Ferguson, C. J., & Kilburn, J. (2009). The public health risks of media violence: A meta-analytic review. *The Journal of Pediatrics*, *154*(5), 759–763.

Frick, P. J., & Morris, A. S. (2004). Temperament and developmental pathways to conduct problems. *Journal of Clinical Child & Adolescent Psychology*, *33*, 54–68.

Frick, P. J., Ray, J. V., Thornton, L. C., & Kahn, R. E. (2014). Can callous-unemotional traits enhance the understanding, diagnosis, and treatment of serious conduct problems in children and adolescents? A comprehensive review. *Psychological Bulletin*, *140*(1), 1–57.

Huesmann, L. R., Moise-Titus, J., Podolski, C. L., & Eron, L. D. (2003). Longitudinal relations between children's exposure to TV violence and their aggressive and violent behavior in young adulthood: 1977-1992. *Developmental Psychology*, *39*(2), 201.

Kim-Cohen, J., Caspi, A., Taylor, A., Williams, B., Newcombe, R., Craig, I. W., & Moffitt, T. E. (2006). MAOA, maltreatment, and gene–environment interaction predicting children's mental health: New evidence and a meta-analysis. *Molecular Psychiatry, 11*(10), 903.

Kirley, A., Lowe, N., Mullins, C., McCarron, M., Daly, G., Waldman, I., ... Hawi, Z. (2004). Phenotype studies of the DRD4 gene polymorphisms in ADHD: Association with oppositional defiant disorder and positive family history. *American Journal of Medical Genetics Part B: Neuropsychiatric Genetics, 131*(1), 38–42.

Kouros, C. D., Cummings, E. M., & Davies, P. T. (2010). Early trajectories of interparental conflict and externalizing problems as predictors of social competence in preadolescence. *Development and Psychopathology, 22*(3), 527–537.

Lahey, B. B., & Waldman, I. W. (2017). Oppositional defiant disorder, conduct disorder, and juvenile delinquency. In T. P. Beauchaine, & S. P. Hinshaw (Eds.), *Child and adolescent psychopathology* (3rd ed., pp. 449–496). Hoboken, NJ: Wiley.

Laird, R. D., Pettit, G. S., Bates, J. E., & Dodge, K. A. (2003). Parents' monitoring-relevant knowledge and adolescents' delinquent behavior: Evidence of correlated developmental changes and reciprocal influences. *Child Development, 74*(3), 752–768.

Lansford, J. E., Criss, M. M., Pettit, G. S., Dodge, K. A., & Bates, J. E. (2003). Friendship quality, peer group affiliation, and peer antisocial behavior as moderators of the link between negative parenting and adolescent externalizing behavior. *Journal of Research on Adolescence, 13*(2), 161–184.

Larsson, H., Viding, E., & Plomin, R. (2008). Callous—Unemotional traits and antisocial behavior: Genetic, environmental, and early parenting characteristics. *Criminal Justice and Behavior, 35*(2), 197–211.

Marsh, A. A., Finger, E. C., Mitchell, D. G., Reid, M. E., Sims, C., Kosson, D. S., ... Blair, R. J. R. (2008). Reduced amygdala response to fearful expressions in children and adolescents with callous-unemotional traits and disruptive behavior disorders. *American Journal of Psychiatry, 165*(6), 712–720.

Martel, M. M., Nikolas, M., Jernigan, K., Friderici, K., & Nigg, J. T. (2012). Diversity in pathways to common childhood disruptive behavior disorders. *Journal of Abnormal Child Psychology, 40*(8), 1223–1236.

Martin, N. C., Levy, F., Pieka, J., & Hay, D. A. (2006). A genetic study of attention deficit hyperactivity disorder, conduct disorder, oppositional defiant disorder and reading disability: Aetiological overlaps and implications. *International Journal of Disability, Development and Education, 53*(1), 21–34.

Matthys, W., & Lochman, J. E. (2017). *Oppositional defiant disorder and conduct disorder in childhood*. John Wiley & Sons.

Matthys, W., Vanderschuren, L. J., & Schutter, D. J. (2013). The neurobiology of oppositional defiant disorder and conduct disorder: Altered functioning in three mental domains. *Development and Psychopathology, 25*(1), 193–207.

Meaney, M. J. (2010). Epigenetics and the biological definition of gene × environment interactions. *Child Development, 81*(1), 41–79.

Moffitt, T. E., Caspi, A., & Rutter, M. (2006). Measured gene-environment interactions in psychopathology: Concepts, research strategies, and implications for research, intervention, and public understanding of genetics. *Perspectives on Psychological Science, 1*(1), 5–27.

Nadder, T. S., Rutter, M., Silberg, J. L., Maes, H. H., & Eaves, L. J. (2002). Genetic effects on the variation and covariation of attention deficit-hyperactivity disorder (ADHD) and oppositional-defiant disorder/conduct disorder (ODD/CD) symptomatologies across informant and occasion of measurement. *Psychological Medicine, 32*(1), 39–53.

Nigg, J. T., & Breslau, N. (2007). Prenatal smoking exposure, low birth weight, and disruptive behavior disorders. *Journal of the American Academy of Child & Adolescent Psychiatry, 46* (3), 362–369.

Patterson, G. R., Reid, J. B., & Dishion, T. J. (1992). *Antisocial boys: A social interactional approach*. Eugene, OR: Castalia.

Raine, A. (2002). Biosocial studies of antisocial and violent behavior in children and adults: A review. *Journal of Abnormal Child Psychology, 30*(4), 311–326.

Rhee, S. H., & Waldman, I. D. (2002). Genetic and environmental influences on antisocial behavior: A meta-analysis of twin and adoption studies. *Psychological Bulletin, 128*(3), 490.

Rutter, M., Moffitt, T. E., & Caspi, A. (2006). Gene–environment interplay and psychopathology: Multiple varieties but real effects. *Journal of Child Psychology and Psychiatry, 47* (3–4), 226–261.

Rutter, M., & Silberg, J. (2002). Gene-environment interplay in relation to emotional and behavioral disturbance. *Annual Review of Psychology, 53*(1), 463–490.

Savage, J., & Yancey, C. (2008). The effects of media violence exposure on criminal aggression: A meta-analysis. *Criminal Justice and Behavior, 35*(6), 772–791.

Tuvblad, C., Zheng, M., Raine, A., & Baker, L. A. (2009). A common genetic factor explains the covariation among ADHD ODD and CD symptoms in 9–10 year old boys and girls. *Journal of Abnormal Child Psychology, 37*(2), 153–167.

van Goozen, S. H., Fairchild, G., Snoek, H., & Harold, G. T. (2007). The evidence for a neurobiological model of childhood antisocial behavior. *Psychological Bulletin, 133*(1), 149.

Viding, E., Blair, R. J. R., Moffitt, T. E., & Plomin, R. (2005). Evidence for substantial genetic risk for psychopathy in 7-year-olds. *Journal of Child Psychology and Psychiatry, 46*(6), 592–597.

Viding, E., Jones, A. P., Paul, J. F., Moffitt, T. E., & Plomin, R. (2008). Heritability of antisocial behaviour at 9: Do callous-unemotional traits matter? *Developmental Science, 11*(1), 17–22.

Viding, E., McCrory, E. J., Blakemore, S. J., & Frederickson, N. (2011). Behavioural problems and bullying at school: Can cognitive neuroscience shed new light on an old problem? *Trends in Cognitive Sciences, 15*(7), 289–291.

Waldman, I. D., & Lahey, B. B. (2013). Oppositional defiant disorder, conduct disorder, and juvenile delinquency. *Child and Adolescent Psychopathology*, 411–452.

Wolke, D., Woods, S., Bloomfield, L., & Karstadt, L. (2000). The association between direct and relational bullying and behaviour problems among primary school children. *The Journal of Child Psychology and Psychiatry and Allied Disciplines, 41*(8), 989–1002.

3

CHAPTER

Theories of oppositional defiant disorder

Based on Chapter 2, Causal factors of oppositional defiant disorder, we know that genetic and environmental factors are about equally involved in child conduct problems. In addition, we know that there are a wide variety of factors implicated in child conduct problems, beginning with genetic risk and including both proximate environmental risk factors such as harsh parenting practices and abuse, as well as more distal environmental risk factors including peer, media, and neighborhood-based exposure to violence. Finally, there is individual variability in the role such factors play in particular pathways to conduct problems. For example, those with callous–unemotional traits may have more genetic risk. Yet, the prominent role of the environment in these disorders gives us optimism for efficacious treatments that focus on changing the environment, from parenting all the way out to community-level factors. There are several different theories that seem to explain child conduct problems by focusing on environmental influence and impact. Such work has implications for the expression of genes across the lifespan, or epigenetics, as well as intergenerational transmission and perpetuation of problems.

The Clinician's Guide to Oppositional Defiant Disorder. DOI: https://doi.org/10.1016/B978-0-12-815682-7.00003-3

Attachment theory

Most theories of conduct problems and resulting treatment models focus on the family and parenting in particular as key points of intervention, particularly early during child development. One prominent theory focuses on child attachment, as shown in Fig. 3.1. As discussed in the previous chapter, children with externalizing problems are more likely to live in stressed households, where they are exposed to early child abuse or aggression, such as domestic violence. Such issues can negatively impact parental responsiveness, or parents' ability to respond sensitively to their child. This can, in turn, lead to disruptions in children's ability to generate a warm bond with parents and other caregivers, called child attachment. In fact, children with externalizing problems are more likely to exhibit insecure attachment, being more avoidant (detached), ambivalent (unstable), or even erratically attached (i.e., disorganized) toward their parents.

Importantly, parents come to the parenting experience with internal working models, or cognitive frameworks comprising mental processes for understanding self and others, based on their own history of family and other important interpersonal relationships. These internal working models influence how parents parent and this, in turn, affects the attachment and emotion regulation strategies of their children (Keiley, 2002). Parents of children with externalizing problems often have insecure attachment themselves given intergenerational risk factors such as poverty. That is, parents of children with externalizing problems are likely to come themselves from chaotic, stressed households with relatively unresponsive parents.

Therefore parents with avoidant (detached) attachment may be controlling, rejecting, conflictual, and/or emotionally unavailable to their children

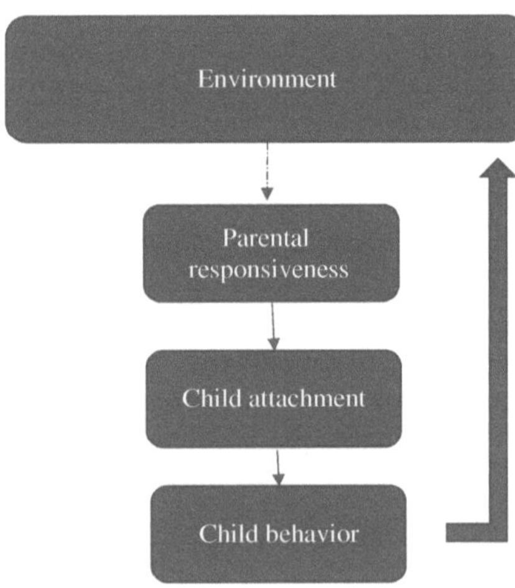

FIGURE 3.1 Attachment theory.

and may discipline their children using poorly controlled anger; the result is anger, aggression, and acting out behavior in their children. Parents with ambivalent (unstable) attachment may be dependent, neglectful, or inconsistent, leading to impulsivity and poor frustration tolerance in children. Finally, parents and children who are not securely attached to one another will not have a warm and predicable relationship.

Therefore, attachment theory of child conduct problems suggests that stressed parents who were raised by stressed, less responsive parents themselves are less likely to have a responsive and warm relationship with their children. Such relationships undermine discipline strategies that are more effective in a warm, responsive environment. Further, such problems often lead to poor monitoring of child behavior, as well as the coercive cycles described below.

Coercive cycles

Using a more microlevel analysis of parenting and child behavior, a second theory focuses on negative child–parent response patterns, or coercive cycles. Based on coercion theory (Patterson, 1982), caregivers can inadvertently reinforce children's negative behaviors, which in turn increases caregiver negativity in a vicious cycle until the child "wins" by becoming excessively negative. As shown in Fig. 3.2, a typical example of this is when the child reacts negatively via disrespect, whining, or tantrums, and the parent responds with anger or hostility, evoking more disrespect, whining, or

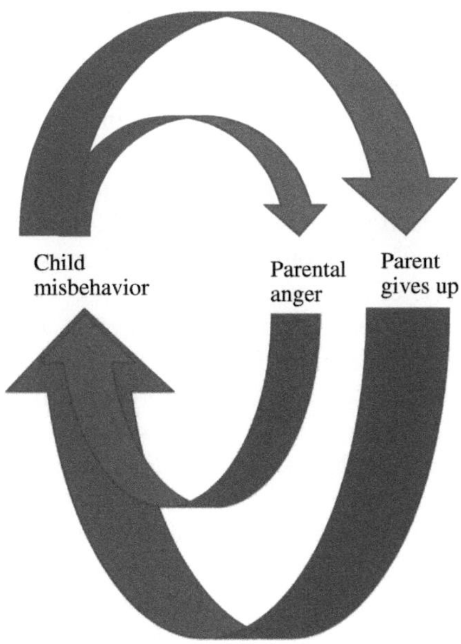

FIGURE 3.2 Coercive cycles theory.

tantrums from the child until the parent finally gives up. This inadvertently negatively reinforces the child's original bad behavior by giving the child a break from the parent's aversive behavior (i.e., the yelling), or occasionally also provides positive reinforcement by letting the child have his/her way.

Knowledge of behavioral modification theory is helpful for understanding coercive cycles. Behavioral modification theory divides strategies for managing behaviors into two different categories: reinforcement and punishment. Reinforcement is anything one does to increase the likelihood of a behavior, while punishment is anything one does to diminish the likelihood of a behavior. Further, one can divide both reinforcement and punishment into positive and negative strategies; *positive* being the term used to describe when one adds a discipline strategy to modify behavior, and *negative* being the term used when one takes something away to modify behavior. So, an example of a positive reinforcement strategy is giving a child a reward (e.g., a small prize or even just a smile or encouragement) to reinforce some good behavior (like picking up their toys or sharing), while an example of negative reinforcement is termination of nagging or repeated commands once the child complies. An example of positive punishment is spanking or extra chores given to decrease a negative behavior such as aggression or lying, while an example of negative punishment would be loss of privileges or toys. Notably, the most effective behavioral modification strategy is positive reinforcement; ironically, it is often the least utilized by parents. Negative reinforcement and positive punishment are usually the least effective, despite their popularity. Notably, coercive cycles largely work through negative reinforcement; the child acts out to terminate the negative behavior (e.g., yelling) of the parent.

Such a pattern of parent–child behavior makes it more likely for children to act out in future instances (Patterson, Reid, & Dishion, 1992). Coercive cycles, observed in the home, predict escalation in conduct problems between middle childhood and adolescence (Dishion, Patterson, Cicchetti, & Cohen, 2006; Smith et al., 2014) and are particularly linked to reactive aggression (Patterson, 2002). Interactions between young children with behavioral difficulties and caregivers who are only marginally competent at responding to children's cues (because of poor attachment, psychosocial stressors, their own psychopathology, or other reasons) are the ones most at risk for the development of coercive cycles (Keenan & Shaw, 1995; Patterson, 2002; Scaramella & Leve, 2004; Shaw & Bell, 1993). Importantly, interventions targeting reduction in these coercive cycles decrease escalations in conduct problems in at-risk youth (Dishion, Patterson, & Kavanagh, 1992).

Therefore, a second, more microlevel theory of parent–child response patterns suggests that caregivers may inadvertently reinforce children's negative behaviors, which in turn increases caregiver negativity in a vicious cycle until the child "wins" by becoming excessively negative and noncompliant. Targeting of such coercive cycles in treatment decreases child conduct problems.

Social information processing

Social information processing theory is a third theory of conduct problems. It focuses on the way children and often particularly teenagers process information in social situations. Social information processing theory suggests that children with disruptive behavior problems perceive, interpret, and make decisions about social information in ways that increase their likelihood to engage in aggressive behaviors (Dodge & Crick, 1990). Such difficulties with social processing could be due to a history of attachment problems or the presence of coercive cycles in the home.

As shown in Fig. 3.3, children with externalizing problems make several key mistakes in their social information processing (Dodge, 2006; Matthys, Vanderschuren, Schutter, & Lochman, 2012). First of all, they are more likely to attribute hostile intentions to their peers. They attend to fewer cues and more hostile cues (Matthys & Lochman, 2017). For example, if a child is pushed by another child in the lunch line, he/she may be more likely to assume the other child did it intentionally to hurt them, rather than assume that it was an accident, particularly if they are likely to turn around and notice other children laughing (vs an apologetic expression on the face of the child who pushed them).

Second, children with externalizing problems generate fewer possible responses in these situations and are more likely to generate responses that are aggressive (vs nonaggressive). For example, in the previous example, such a child may be more likely to push back, rather than asking the other child what is going on or ignoring it. Third, children with externalizing problems often evaluate aggressive behavior more favorably, expect more favorable outcomes from aggressive behaviors, and have more confidence in their ability to enact aggressive (vs more prosocial) behaviors. Likewise, they often evaluate prosocial behavior less favorably, expect less favorable outcomes from submissive or prosocial behaviors, and have less confidence in

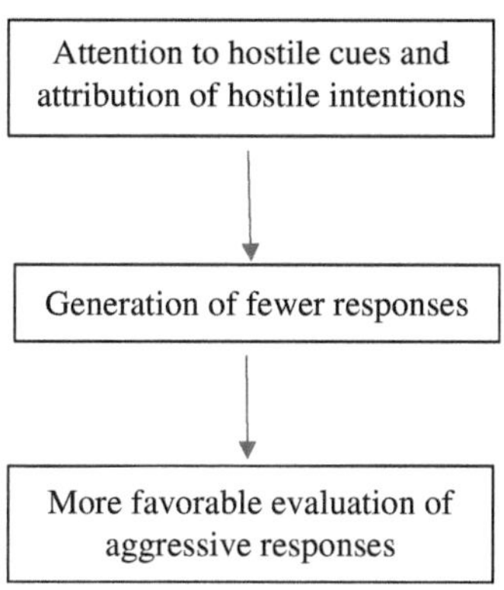

FIGURE 3.3 Social information processing theory.

their ability to withdraw or inhibit an aggressive response. So, in this example, a child who was pushed in the lunch line may decide they need to stand up for themselves by pushing back because they believe that any other response will make them a target in the future. These social information processing deficits seem to arise from early adversity, including family problems at home, including parental modeling and encouragement of aggression (Dodge, 2003).

In sum, children with externalizing problems seem to exhibit several social information processing problems. They are more likely to attribute hostile intentions to their peers, and they attend to fewer and more hostile cues. They generate fewer and more aggressive responses. Finally, they often evaluate aggressive responses more favorably and prosocial responses less favorably—behaviors they may have learned at home.

Linkage between theory and treatment

These three theories are often somewhat differentially applied based on child age. Attachment theories are typically viewed as more important for young children and are often involved in treatments for young children, such as parent–child interaction therapy, which is detailed in subsequent chapters. Coercion theory is often viewed as particularly important during early socialization between early and middle childhood; this parenting interaction pattern is a key target in behavioral treatments. Finally, social learning theory is arguably important throughout the lifespan as it underpins behavior in multiple environments including home, school, and work. Further, social learning theory provides the key theoretical underpinning of cognitive behavioral treatments offered in group and school settings.

Theories of oppositional defiant disorder (ODD) also suggest some general tips for working with parents of children and adolescents with conduct problems. Two are especially important. It is often particularly challenging for parents to present for treatment in the first place due to the stressful nature of their lives. It is very difficult for any parent, even one with minimal stressors, to seek out a professional's help with parenting, which is a very personal and highly judged task. For highly stressed parents, it is almost impossible to seek out this help. Such families often feel defensive before they even arrive at the session. For this reason, it is often helpful to minimize the idea that parenting itself is heavily involved in problem presentation, but rather to state explicitly something like the following:

> *Most discipline strategies work with most children, but strong-willed children require specialized strategies. This is where the therapist and research on large groups of people can be helpful. We know which strategies are going to provide you with the most bang for your buck. You, the parent, are the expert on your child, and this is why I am working with you individually instead of*

sending you home with a book, video, or one-size-fits-all approach. You, the parent, need to work with me so we can tweak strategies we know work to fit your child's individual temperament and your busy life. In addition, together, we can find ways to help your child continue to grow and develop using modifications of these strategies even when your child is going through difficult periods such as adolescence.

Secondly, parents of children with conduct problems will often model poor ways of handling their anger that their children will mimic, for example, screaming. Parents may not realize it, but when they curse and yell when they get angry, they are in effect modeling tantrum-like behaviors that their child will then emulate. It is often not easy for a parent to own such behaviors, but it is important for parents to try to work on modeling behaviors they want to see in their children. So, parents should model taking deep breaths and pausing for a moment to cool off whenever possible. It is also important for parents to monitor their child's or teenager's activities. Of course, this is easier said than done in highly stressed and very busy families with little social support. However, for this reason, adjunct individual therapy, for families with time and resources, or occasional family therapy sessions, for those without, are often useful as a time to work on personal factors and stressors that negatively impact parenting.

In applied settings, it is often helpful to conceptualize each clinical case individually to tailor therapy to an individual child and family's risk factors (Greene & Doyle, 1999).

Illustration through case examples

Luis

Luis is a 4-year-old Latino male. He was referred by his pediatrician for an evaluation after his parents presented complaining about Luis' aggression. Luis only uses one- to two-word phrases to communicate and is difficult to understand. His parents speak Spanish at home and both work long hours at minimum wage jobs. They have five kids in total, ages 1, 4, 8, 10, and 12. Luis' parents report that he was born 1 month premature, weighing 4 lb and 3 oz. Luis' mother had severe hypertension toward the end of her pregnancy. Although his motor milestones were reported to be on time, Luis did not say his first words until age 3. He is still not potty trained and sleeps in bed with his parents. Luis' parents complain that he becomes angry and aggressive with minimal provocation. Luis will hit, kick, bite, and throw a tantrum if he does not get his way. He frequently does things that he knows his parents find annoying (such as yelling and running away at the supermarket). He does not comply with adult commands, yelling no and running away. He once ran away in a store parking lot and was almost hit by a car. His parents were worried that social services would be called. Luis' parents are

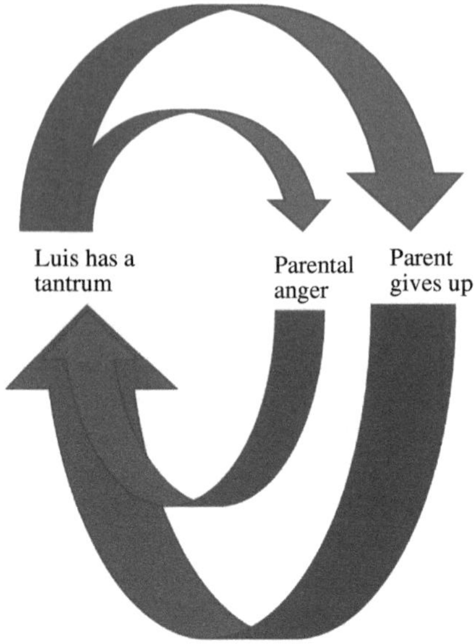

FIGURE 3.4 Luis' conceptualization.

concerned about him starting school next year, given they cannot currently leave him at home with even a babysitter due to his severe misbehavior.

Conceptualization: Luis is exhibiting ODD in the context of speech and language problems and other delays with independent sleep and elimination problems. Luis is the youngest child in a large family. His parents are under economic and personal stress, working long hours to provide for the family. Luis was also exposed to a number of prenatal risk factors, including stress during pregnancy, hypertension, prematurity, and low birth weight. He also experienced developmental delays, particularly with language. The high stress at home, large number of siblings, his parents' limited time, and Luis' language delays have led to coercive cycles between Luis and his parents, as shown in Fig. 3.4. He may have difficulty communicating his needs and understanding parental requests. He may also have difficulty obtaining parental attention using appropriate strategies. Therefore he often resorts to aggression, tantrums, and noncompliance. He has been delayed with potty training and refuses to sleep independently.

***

Frederick

Frederick is a 10-year-old African American male. His mother presented with him to the emergency room when his school called her to come and pick him up during the middle of the day after he threatened to "gut" another

10-year-old boy in his class. The school reported that the provocation for this incident was that Frederick became angry when the other boy asked him to share his colored pencil. More concerning, Frederick was found to have had a knife hidden in his schoolbag and indicated that he planned to use it on the other boy, so that the other boy would "get what was coming to him." The school has suspended Frederick until his mother obtains treatment for him. Frederick has a history of problems with peers. He has few friends and his peers report being scared of him. Frederick frequently, graphically threatens his peers following minor disagreements, telling them he will "cut them open," he "wants to explore their insides," and he will "show them their hearts." He is known to hold a grudge and will wait for a peer following a disagreement after school, threatening them and saying he will hurt them. Frederick lives with his mother, who is single. His biological father has been in jail for armed robbery since Frederick was born. His mother is a mortician with little family in the area. Frederick often spends his afternoons largely unsupervised at the morgue. Frederick's mother acknowledges that she is sometimes scared of him. He reportedly does not listen to her, often argues with her, and she is at a loss as to how to discipline him. Frederick's mother indicated that he has always been difficult to parent. She is worried because his school is insisting that she seek some kind of treatment for Frederick; otherwise, they have said they will expel him.

Conceptualization: Frederick is exhibiting ODD with high callous–unemotional traits. Frederick may have a genetic predisposition toward conduct problems and callous–unemotional traits in particular given the fact that his father is currently serving time in jail for armed robbery, and Frederick is described as vindictive and engaging in proactive or instrumental forms of aggression that are premeditated. This genetic predisposition may particularly increase his risk for conduct problems given family stressors such as an absent father and little social support. In addition, the fact that Frederick's mother spends long hours at work means she has little time to supervise him. His exposure to dead bodies seems to be increasing his callousness and detachment toward others. Finally, Frederick does not get along with his peers and is isolated at school. Perhaps most critically, Frederick and his mother do not have a warm and loving relationship, and he is likely insecurely attached, as shown in Fig. 3.5. She acknowledges that she is sometimes scared of him and is at a loss as to how to discipline him.

***

Anna

Anna is a 15-year-old Caucasian female whose parents present with concerns about possible drug use, sexting, and promiscuous sex. Anna has been

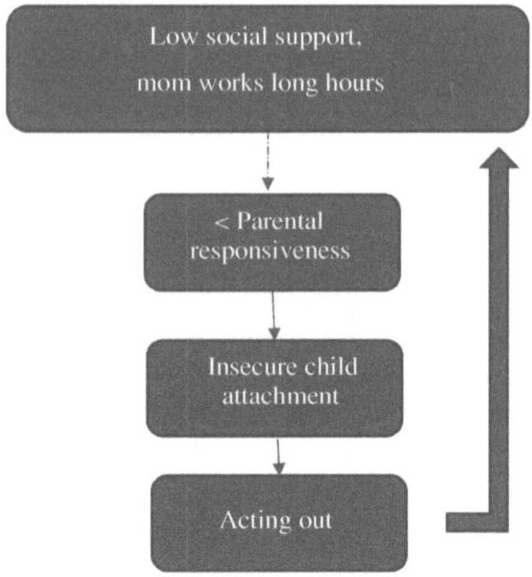

FIGURE 3.5 Frederick's conceptualization.

diagnosed with depression and has been taking antidepressants since age 13. She was described as irritable and easily annoyed most of the time. She acknowledges frequent marijuana use with friends and being sexually active with several males. She has been grounded for the last 2 weeks after she sent a naked picture to one of these males, and her parents were informed by a friend's mother, who saw the picture on her daughter's Snapchat. Anna acknowledges that her current friend group has not been the best influence. She complains that the girls are all catty and talk about her behind her back. She reports engaging in sexting or sex, as well as impulsivity, without a lot of forethought about the consequences, or while under the influence of alcohol. She indicated that she has no desire to listen to her parents and often argues with them about curfews and rules. She justified her behavior by reporting that she was bullied extensively in grade school and feels the need to fit in with her peers whatever the cost.

Conceptualization: Anna exhibits ODD in the context of a preexisting depression diagnosis. She is also at risk for emerging substance use problems with marijuana and alcohol. She has a history of peer problems including bullying through covert aggression (e.g., rumors). Through these experiences, she seems to have developed faulty social information processing in that she almost always attributes hostile intentions to her peers, and she impulsively engages in inappropriate reactions such as substance use and sexting. As shown in Fig. 3.6, she furthermore does not seem to have learned to evaluate the negative consequences of her actions. Her parents, to date, have been largely ineffective at monitoring or disciplining her to obtain desired behaviors.

***

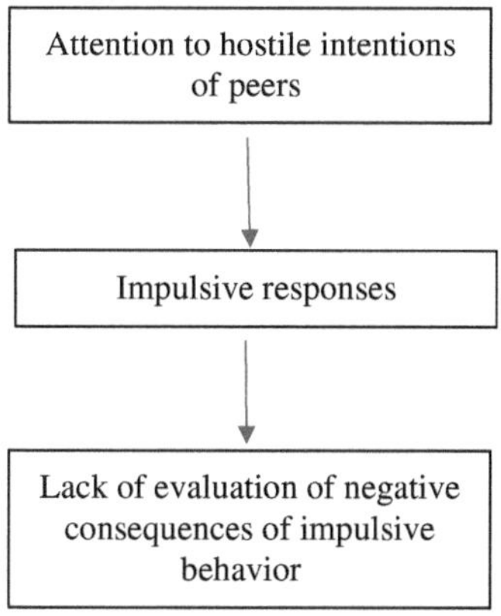

FIGURE 3.6 Anna's conceptualization.

Conclusion

In conclusion, there are three major theories of conduct problems. Attachment theory suggests that environmental stressors negatively impact parental responsiveness, or parents' ability to respond sensitively to their child. This can, in turn, lead to disruptions in children's ability to generate a warm bond with parents and other caregivers, called child attachment. The theory of coercive cycles focuses on more microlevel interactions by which caregivers can inadvertently reinforce children's negative behaviors, which in turn increases caregiver negativity in a vicious cycle until the child "wins" by becoming excessively negative. Social information processing theory suggests that children with disruptive behavior problems perceive, interpret, and make decisions about social information in ways that increase their likelihood to engage in aggressive behaviors. Treatment in younger children typically focuses more on attachment theories, while work in adolescents typically focuses on social information processing. Yet, such theories suggest that environmental stressors encountered by parents and adolescents will negatively impact their ability to engage in treatment and also lead to poor handling of negative emotions—issues that are important to address in treatment.

References

Dishion, T. J., Patterson, G. R., Cicchetti, D., & Cohen, D. J. (2006). *The development and ecology of antisocial behavior in children and adolescents. Developmental psychopathology. Risk, disorder, and adaptation.* New York: Wiley.

Dishion, T. J., Patterson, G. R., & Kavanagh, K. A. (1992). An experimental test of the coercion model: Linking theory, measurement, and intervention. In J. McCord, & R. E. Tremblay (Eds.), *Preventing antisocial behavior: Interventions from birth through adolescence* (pp. 253–282). New York, NY, US: Guilford Press.

Dodge, K. A. (2003). Do social information-processing patterns mediate aggressive behavior? In B. B. Lahey, T. E. Moffitt, & A. Caspi (Eds.), *Causes of conduct disorder and juvenile delinquency*. New York: Wiley.

Dodge, K. A. (2006). Translational science in action: Hostile attributional style and the development of aggressive behavior problems. *Development and Psychopathology, 18*(3), 791–814.

Dodge, K. A., & Crick, N. R. (1990). Social information-processing bases of aggressive behavior in children. *Personality and Social Psychology Bulletin, 16*(1), 8–22.

Greene, R. W., & Doyle, A. E. (1999). Toward a transactional conceptualization of oppositional defiant disorder: Implications for assessment and treatment. *Clinical Child and Family Psychology Review, 2*(3), 129–148.

Keenan, K., & Shaw, D. S. (1995). *The development of coercive family processes: The interaction between aversive toddler behavior and parenting factors. Coercion and punishment in long-term perspectives* (pp. 165–180). Cambridge University Press.

Keiley, M. K. (2002). Attachment and affect regulation: A framework for family treatment of conduct disorder. *Family Process, 41*(3), 477–493.

Matthys, W., & Lochman, J. E. (2017). *Oppositional defiant disorder and conduct disorder in childhood.* John Wiley & Sons.

Matthys, W., Vanderschuren, L. J., Schutter, D. J., & Lochman, J. E. (2012). Impaired neurocognitive functions affect social learning processes in oppositional defiant disorder and conduct disorder: Implications for interventions. *Clinical Child and Family Psychology Review, 15* (3), 234–246.

Patterson, G. R. (1982). *Coercive family interactions.* Eugene, OR: Castalia.

Patterson, G. R. (2002). The early development of coercive family process. In J. B. Reid, G. R. Patterson, & J. Snyder (Eds.), *Antisocial behavior in children and adolescents: A developmental analysis and model for intervention* (pp. 25–44). Washington, DC, US: American Psychological Association.

Patterson, G. R., Reid, J. B., & Dishion, T. J. (1992). *Antisocial boys: A social interactional approach.* Eugene, OR: Castalia.

Scaramella, L. V., & Leve, L. D. (2004). Clarifying parent–child reciprocities during early childhood: The early childhood coercion model. *Clinical Child and Family Psychology Review, 7*(2), 89–107.

Shaw, D. S., & Bell, R. Q. (1993). Developmental theories of parental contributors to antisocial behavior. *Journal of Abnormal Child Psychology, 21*(5), 493–518.

Smith, J. D., Dishion, T. J., Shaw, D. S., Wilson, M. N., Winter, C. C., & Patterson, G. R. (2014). Coercive family process and early-onset conduct problems from age 2 to school entry. *Development and Psychopathology, 26*(4pt1), 917–932.

4

CHAPTER

The importance and ease of assessment of oppositional-defiant disorder

Assessment of oppositional-defiant disorder (ODD) is fairly straightforward. However, choice of assessment tool will depend on setting, context, presenting concerns, time, and—in some cases—cost. The biggest issues to consider when assessing ODD are the presence of cooccurring conditions and how important it is to rule them in or out. Another major concern is how much time one has to conduct the assessment.

When short on time, money, or in settings where mental health is not the only or most pressing concern, a screener may be useful. For example, screeners can be used at pediatrician appointments or as an initial assessment step preceding a more comprehensive evaluation. However, if families request a more comprehensive assessment, then longer questionnaires and/or testing may be useful following or instead of screeners (McMahon & Frick, 2005; Steiner & Remsing, 2007). In addition, the nature of the family's presenting problem is important to consider. If a family only wants to rule in or

The Clinician's Guide to Oppositional Defiant Disorder. DOI: https://doi.org/10.1016/B978-0-12-815682-7.00004-5

TABLE 4.1 List of assessment tools.
Screening
Strengths and Difficulties Questionnaire
Narrowband
Disruptive Behavior Rating Scale
Inventory of Callous–Unemotional Traits
Comprehensive
Child and Adolescent Symptom Inventory
Supplemental
Language
Academics

out disruptive behavior problems, then a shorter, more focused assessment may be most efficient and economical. In contrast, if there are numerous concerns (e.g., conduct, emotional, and learning problems), then it may make the most sense to do a comprehensive evaluation.

Table 4.1 provides a list of assessment tools for screening and more comprehensive evaluation scenarios. Instruments are listed by category in the order described below. It is generally agreed that multiple informants (e.g., parents and teachers) can provide important information about child misbehavior. Although young children may not be able to provide accurate information about their misbehavior, particularly during the preschool period, adolescents are often important sources of information about more private, or covert, forms of misbehavior.

Screening

A key screening tool is the Strengths and Difficulties Questionnaire (SDQ). This is a brief, 25-item behavioral screening questionnaire that assesses emotional, conduct, hyperactivity/inattention, and peer relationship problems in 2–17 years old. It uses a 0–2 rating format where 0 is not true, 1 is somewhat true, and 2 is certainly true. The SDQ can be used with children as young as preschool age (i.e., ages 2–3; Goodman, 1997) through adolescence (i.e., up to age 17; Goodman, Meltzer, & Bailey, 1998). Further, it includes parent and teacher rating forms for all ages, and self-report for adolescents only. The SDQ has been validated for screening the general population (Goodman, Lamping, & Ploubidis, 2010) and is appropriate for use cross-culturally. It has online scoring, as well as hand scoring key options. Finally, the SDQ has clinical cutoffs, meaning one can easily compare a given child's score with normative ratings to empirically assess severity of problems. Importantly, it is free and available online at http://www.sdqinfo.org/py/sdqinfo/b3.py?language = Englishqz(USA).

Importantly, the SDQ is a broadband screener that assesses a variety of different problems, but does so in only 25 questions. This makes it an ideal screener for mental health issues and disruptive behavior problems that can be used in a variety of settings, including pediatricians' offices.

Narrowband assessment of oppositional-defiant disorder and other disruptive behavior problems

If a family only wants to rule in or out disruptive behavior problems, then a shorter, more focused assessment may be most efficient and economical. A targeted, or narrowband, diagnostic measure assessing for ODD and other disruptive behavior problems, including conduct disorder (CD) and attention-deficit/hyperactivity disorder (ADHD), is the Disruptive Behavior Rating Scale (DBRS; Barkley & Murphy, 1998, 2006). The DBRS is a 45-item questionnaire that assesses symptoms of ODD, CD, and ADHD using a 0–3 scale, where 0 signifies not at all, 1 signifies just a little, 2 signifies pretty much, and 3 signifies very much. Ratings of 2 or 3 count as endorsed symptoms. Endorsed symptoms are summed within each diagnostic subdomain (i.e., ODD symptoms, CD symptoms, ADHD symptoms of inattention and hyperactivity–impulsivity) to determine symptom counts within these categories. To meet criteria for ODD requires four endorsed symptoms. To meet criteria for CD requires three endorsed symptoms, and to meet criteria for ADHD in children up to age 17 requires six endorsed symptoms within either the inattentive or hyperactive–impulsive symptom domain. The DBRS has both a parent and teacher report form. The DBRS has high internal consistency ranging from 0.78 to 0.96, down to the preschool age range (Pelletier, Collett, Gimple, & Cowley, 2006), and both the parent and teacher report have high internal reliability. One can either count symptoms or compare averaged ratings to norms. It is available online at https://ccf.fiu.edu/_assets/pdfs/dbd%20rating%20scale.pdf, as shown in Table 4.2.

The Inventory of Callous–Unemotional Traits (ICU; Frick, 2004) allows for specific assessment of callous–unemotional traits. This 24-item parent report questionnaire is designed to assess callous and unemotional traits in youth from preschool through adolescence. It includes positively worded (e.g., "Easily admits to being wrong") and negatively worded (e.g., "Shows no remorse when he/she has done something wrong") items and uses a 4-point Likert scale ranging from 0 (not at all true) to 3 (definitely true). Twelve positively worded items require reverse-scoring before calculation of the total scores. The measure has three scales: callousness, uncaring, and unemotional. For most ages, there are three forms: parent, teacher, and youth self-report. In preschoolers, there are two forms: parent and teacher. The ICU exhibits high internal consistency, even in the preschool age range. Use

TABLE 4.2 Disruptive Behavior Rating Scale.

Parent / Teacher DBD Rating Scale

Child's Name: ______________________________ Form Completed by: _________________

Grade: _______________ Date of Birth: ____________Sex: __________Date Completed________

Check the column that best describes your/this child. **Please write DK next to any items for which you don't know the answer.**

	Not at All	Just a Little	Pretty Much	Very Much
1. often interrupts or intrudes on others (e.g., butts into conversations or games)				
2. has run away from home overnight at least twice while living in parental or parental surrogate home (or once without returning for a lengthy period)				
3. often argues with adults				
4. often lies to obtain goods or favors or to avoid obligations (i.e., "cons" others)				
5. often initiates physical fights with other members of his or her household				
6. has been physically cruel to people				
7. often talks excessively				
8. has stolen items of nontrivial value without confronting a victim (e.g., shoplifting, but without breaking and entering; forgery)				
9. is often easily distracted by extraneous stimuli				
10. often engages in physically dangerous activities without considering possible consequences (not for the purpose of thrill-seeking), e.g., runs into street without looking				
11. often truant from school, beginning before age 13 years				
12. often fidgets with hands or feet or squirms in seat				
13. is often spiteful or vindictive				
14. often swears or uses obscene language				
15. often blames others for his or her mistakes or misbehavior				
16. has deliberately destroyed others' property (other than by fire setting)				
17. often actively defies or refuses to comply with adults' requests or rules				
18. often does not seem to listen when spoken to directly				
19. often blurts out answers before questions have been completed				
20. often initiates physical fights with others who do not live in his or her household (e.g., peers at school or in the neighborhood)				
21. often shifts from one uncompleted activity to another				
22. often has difficulty playing or engaging in leisure activities quietly				
23. often fails to give close attention to details or makes careless mistakes in schoolwork, work, or other activities				
24. is often angry and resentful				
25. often leaves seat in classroom or in other situations in which remaining seated is expected				
26. is often touchy or easily annoyed by others				
27. often does not follow through on instructions and fails to finish schoolwork, chores, or duties in the workplace (not due to oppositional behavior or failure to understand instructions)				
28. often loses temper				
29. often has difficulty sustaining attention in tasks or play activities				
30. often has difficulty awaiting turn				
31. has forced someone into sexual activity				
32. often bullies, threatens, or intimidates others				
33. is often "on the go" or often acts as if "driven by a motor"				
34. often loses things necessary for tasks or activities (e.g., toys, school assignments, pencils, books, or tools)				
35. often runs about or climbs excessively in situations in which it is inappropriate (in adolescents or adults, may be limited to subjective feelings of restlessness)				
36. has been physically cruel to animals				
37. often avoids, dislikes, or is reluctant to engage in tasks that require sustained mental effort (such as schoolwork or homework)				
38. often stays out at night despite parental prohibitions, beginning before age 13 years				
39. often deliberately annoys people				
40. has stolen while confronting a victim (e.g., mugging, purse snatching, extortion, armed robbery)				
41. has deliberately engaged in fire setting with the intention of causing serious damage				
42. often has difficulty organizing tasks and activities				
43. has broken into someone else's house, building, or car				
44. is often forgetful in daily activities				
45. has used a weapon that can cause serious physical harm to others (e.g., a bat, brick, broken bottle, knife, gun)				

parent/teacher dbdv. 1

(Continued)

TABLE 4.2 (Continued)

SCORING INSTRUCTIONS FOR THE DISRUPTIVE BEHAVIOR DISORDER RATING SCALE

There are two ways to determine if a child meets the criteria for DSM IV diagnoses of Attention-Deficit/Hyperactivity Disorder, Oppositional Defiant Disorder, or Conduct Disorder. The first method involves counting symptoms for each disorder using the Disruptive Behavior Disorders (DBD) rating scale. The second method involves comparing the target child's factor scores on the DBD Rating Scale to established norms. The factor scores method is preferable for diagnosis of females (e.g., using a 2 SD cutoff), as the symptom counting method often results in underdiagnosis of female children. Please note that Items 10, 14, and 21 are from DSM-III-R and are not included in the scoring for a DSM-IV diagnosis.

Method 1: Counting Symptoms
To determine if a child meets the symptom criteria for DSM IV diagnoses of Attention-Deficit/Hyperactivity Disorder, Oppositional Defiant Disorder, or Conduct Disorder as measured by the DBD Parent / Teacher Rating Scale, count the number of symptoms that are endorsed "pretty much" or "very much" by either parent or teacher in each of the following categories: Note that impairment and other criteria must be evaluated in addition to symptom counts.

Attention-Deficit/Hyperactivity Disorder

_______Attention-Deficit/Hyperactivity Disorder - Inattention Symptoms
(items 9, 18, 23, 27, 29, 34, 37, 42, 44)

6 or more items must be endorsed as "pretty much" or "very much" to meet criteria for **Attention-Deficit/Hyperactivity Disorder, Predominantly Inattentive Type.** The six items may be endorsed on the teacher DBD, the parent DBD, or can be a combination of items from both rating scales (e.g., 4 symptoms endorsed on the teacher DBD and 2 separate symptoms endorsed on the parent DBD). The same symptom should **not** be counted twice if it appears on both versions (parent and teacher) of the rating scale.

_______Attention-Deficit/Hyperactivity Disorder - Hyperactivity/impulsivity Symptoms
(items 1, 7, 12, 19, 22, 25, 30, 33, 35)

6 or more items must be endorsed as "pretty much" or "very much" on the parent and/or the teacher DBD to meet criteria for **Attention-Deficit/Hyperactivity Disorder, Predominantly Hyperactive-Impulsive Type.**
If 6 or more items are endorsed for Attention-Deficit/Hyperactivity Disorder - inattention **and** 6 or more items are endorsed for Attention-Deficit/Hyperactivity Disorder - hyperactivity/impulsivity, then criteria is met for **Attention-Deficit/Hyperactivity Disorder, Combined Type.**

Some impairment from the symptoms must be present in two or more settings (e.g., school, home)

Oppositional Defiant Disorder
________Oppositional Defiant Disorder (items 3, 13, 15, 17, 24, 26, 28, 39)

A total of 4 or more items must be endorsed as "pretty much" or "very much" on either the parent or the teacher DBD to meet criteria for **Oppositional Defiant Disorder**

Conduct Disorder
_________Conduct Disorder - aggression to people and animals (items 6, 20, 31, 32, 36, 40, 45)
_________Conduct Disorder - destruction of property (items 16, 41)
_________Conduct Disorder - deceitfulness or theft (items 4, 8, 43)
_________Conduct Disorder - serious violation of rules (items 2, 11, 38)

A total of 3 or more items in any category or any combination of categories must be endorsed as "pretty much" or "very much" on either the parent or the teacher DBD to meet criteria for **Conduct Disorder**

Method 2: Using Factor Scores
Factor scores for the two ADHD and ODD dimensions for teacher ratings on the DBD are reported in Pelham, et al (1992), Teacher ratings of DSMIII-R symptoms for the disruptive behavior disorders: Journal of the American Academy of Child and Adolescent Psychiatry, 31, 210-218. The factor scores for DSM IV factors are the same as for the DSM III-R factors reported in that paper. To determine how a child's scores compare to normative data, compute the average rating for the items from each factor (listed below) using the following scoring: Not at all = 0, Just a little = 1, Pretty Much= 2, Very much = 3. Then, using the information from the attached table of norms, determine where the child falls in relation to other children. A variety of cutoff scores can be used (e.g., 2 standard deviations above the mean).

Factors
________Oppositional / Defiant (items 3, 13, 15, 17, 24, 26, 28, 39)
________Inattention (items 9, 18, 23, 27, 29, 34, 37, 42, 44)
________Impulsivity / Overactivity (items 1, 7, 12, 19, 22, 25, 30, 33, 35)

parent/teacher dbdv. 1 © CTADD

Source: Reproduced with permission from https://ccf.fiu.edu/_assets/pdfs/dbd%20rating%20scale.pdf. © Dr. William Pelham Jr.

of the ICU has been previously validated in preschool-age children (Expeleta, Osa, Granero, Penelo, & Domenech, 2013). Recommended clinical cutoffs are 24 for mother report and 27 for father report (Kimonis, Fanti, & Singh, 2014). Importantly, it is free and available online at https://sites01.lsu.edu/faculty/pfricklab/icu/, as shown in Table 4.3.

Therefore for narrowband or specific assessment of disruptive behavior disorders including ODD, CD, and ADHD, the DBRS can be helpful. For assessment of callous–unemotional traits, the ICU is ideal.

Broadband assessment of comorbid psychopathology

If there are numerous concerns (e.g., conduct, emotional, and learning problems), then it may make the most sense to perform a more comprehensive assessment. To assess more comprehensively for comorbid psychopathology, the Child and Adolescent Symptom Inventory-5 (CASI-5; Gadow, 2015) is probably the most helpful tool given its breadth of coverage even compared with other broadband measures such as Achenbach's Child Behavior Checklist and the Reynolds and Kamphaus' Behavior Assessment System for Children. The CASI-5 is a broadband measure that can be completed by parents for children ages 5–18. It has 173 items and assesses ADHD, ODD, CD, generalized anxiety disorder, social anxiety disorder, separation anxiety disorder, disruptive mood dysregulation disorder, major depressive episode, manic episode, dysthymic disorder, schizophrenia, autistic/Asperger's disorder, anorexia, and bulimia. One or two key symptoms of each of the following disorders are also included: posttraumatic stress disorder, obsessive–compulsive disorder, specific phobia, panic disorder, selective mutism, trichotillomania, motor tics, vocal tics, and substance use. Symptom cutoff scores, dimensional severity scores, impairment cutoffs, and clinical cutoffs (a combination of symptom count and impairment cutoffs) are available. The cutoffs show high correspondence with psychiatric diagnoses and correlate well with dimensional scales. Further, an older version, the Early Childhood Inventory-4R, can be used with children as young as age 3. However, the measure is not free and costs about $150. More information is available at http://www.checkmateplus.com/product/casi5.htm.

Therefore, the CASI-5 can be useful for ruling in or out other commonly comorbid conditions, given its breadth of coverage and wide age range.

Formal testing: speech and academics

Finally, formal testing can sometimes be helpful, particularly if the family presents with a variety of concerns that include speech and language problems and/or academic concerns. All such testing can be completed by a clinical or school psychologist. Alternately, one can refer to a speech and language therapist for speech and language testing. Given that any necessary interventions will be provided or overseen by speech and language therapists and school psychologists, it may be most efficient to refer families who

TABLE 4.3 Inventory of Callous and Unemotional Traits.

1

ICU
(Parent Version)

Name of Child: ______________ Date of Birth: ______________

Completed by: Mother Father Other: ______________

Date completed: ______________

Instructions: *Please complete the background information above. Then read each statement and decide how well it describes your child. Mark your answer by circling the appropriate number (0-3) for each statement. Do not leave any statement unrated.*

	Not at all true	Somewhat true	Very true	Definitely True
1. Expresses his/her feelings openly.	0	1	2	3
2. Does not seem to know "right" from "wrong".	0	1	2	3
3. Is concerned about schoolwork.	0	1	2	3
4. Does not care who he/she hurts to get what he/she wants.	0	1	2	3
5. Feels bad or guilty when he/she has done something wrong.	0	1	2	3
6. Does not show emotions.	0	1	2	3
7. Does not care about being on time.	0	1	2	3
8. Is concerned about the feelings of others.	0	1	2	3
9. Does not care if he/she is in trouble.	0	1	2	3
10. Does not let feelings control him/her.	0	1	2	3
11. Does not care about doing things well.	0	1	2	3
12. Seems very cold and uncaring.	0	1	2	3
13. Easily admits to being wrong.	0	1	2	3
14. It is easy to tell how he/she is feeling.	0	1	2	3
15. Always tries his/her best.	0	1	2	3
16. Apologizes ("says he/she is sorry") to persons he/she has hurt.	0	1	2	3
17. Tries not to hurt others' feelings.	0	1	2	3

2

18. Shows no remorse when he/she has done something wrong.	0	1	2	3
19. Is very expressive and emotional.	0	1	2	3
20. Does not like to put the time into doing things well.	0	1	2	3
21. The feelings of others are unimportant to him/her.	0	1	2	3
22. Hides his/her feelings from others.	0	1	2	3
23. Works hard on everything.	0	1	2	3
24. Does things to make others feel good.	0	1	2	3

Unpublished rating scale by Paul J. Frick, Department of Psychology, University of New Orleans (pfrick@uno.edu)

(*Continued*)

TABLE 4.3 (Continued)

1

ICU
(Teacher Version)

Name of child: ______________ Date completed: ______________

Teacher's name: ______________ Length of time you have known the student: __________

Subjects you teach the child: ____

Instructions: *Please complete the background information above. Then read each statement and decide how well it describes the student. Mark your answer by circling the appropriate number (0-3) for each statement. Do not leave any statement unrated.*

	Not at all true	Somewhat true	Very true	Definitely True
1. Expresses his/her feelings openly.	0	1	2	3
2. Does not seem to know "right" from "wrong".	0	1	2	3
3. Is concerned about schoolwork.	0	1	2	3
4. Does not care who he/she hurts to get what he/she wants.	0	1	2	3
5. Feels bad or guilty when he/she has done something wrong.	0	1	2	3
6. Does not show emotions.	0	1	2	3
7. Does not care about being on time.	0	1	2	3
8. Is concerned about the feelings of others.	0	1	2	3
9. Does not care if he/she is in trouble.	0	1	2	3
10. Does not let feelings control him/her.	0	1	2	3
11. Does not care about doing things well.	0	1	2	3
12. Seems very cold and uncaring.	0	1	2	3
13. Easily admits to being wrong.	0	1	2	3
14. It is easy to tell how he/she is feeling.	0	1	2	3
15. Always tries his/her best.	0	1	2	3
16. Apologizes ("says he/she is sorry") to persons he/she has hurt.	0	1	2	3
17. Tries not to hurt others' feelings.	0	1	2	3

2

18. Shows no remorse when he/she has done something wrong.	0	1	2	3
19. Is very expressive and emotional.	0	1	2	3
20. Does not like to put the time into doing things well.	0	1	2	3
21. The feelings of others are unimportant to him/her.	0	1	2	3
22. Hides his/her feelings from others.	0	1	2	3
23. Works hard on everything.	0	1	2	3
24. Does things to make others feel good.	0	1	2	3

Unpublished rating scale by Paul J. Frick, Department of Psychology, University of New Orleans (pfrick@uno.edu) .

(*Continued*)

TABLE 4.3 (Continued)

1

ICU
(Youth Version)

Name: ____________________

Date Completed: ____________________

Instructions: *Please read each statement and decide how well it describes you. Mark your answer by circling the appropriate number (0-3) for each statement. Do not leave any statement unrated.*

	Not at all true	Somewhat true	Very true	Definitely True
1. I express my feelings openly.	0	1	2	3
2. What I think is "right" and "wrong" is different from what other people think.	0	1	2	3
3. I care about how well I do at school or work.	0	1	2	3
4. I do not care who I hurt to get what I want.	0	1	2	3
5. I feel bad or guilty when I do something wrong.	0	1	2	3
6. I do not show my emotions to others.	0	1	2	3
7. I do not care about being on time.	0	1	2	3
8. I am concerned about the feelings of others.	0	1	2	3
9. I do not care if I get into trouble.	0	1	2	3
10. I do not let my feelings control me.	0	1	2	3
11. I do not care about doing things well.	0	1	2	3
12. I seem very cold and uncaring to others.	0	1	2	3
13. I easily admit to being wrong.	0	1	2	3
14. It is easy for others to tell how I am feeling.	0	1	2	3
15. I always try my best.	0	1	2	3
16. I apologize ("say I am sorry") to persons I hurt.	0	1	2	3
17. I try not to hurt others' feelings.	0	1	2	3
18. I do not feel remorseful when I do something wrong.	0	1	2	3
19. I am very expressive and emotional.	0	1	2	3
20. I do not like to put the time into doing things well.	0	1	2	3

2

21. The feelings of others are unimportant to me.	0	1	2	3
22. I hide my feelings from others.	0	1	2	3
23. I work hard on everything I do.	0	1	2	3
24. I do things to make others feel good.	0	1	2	3

Unpublished rating scale by Paul J. Frick, Department of Psychology, University of New Orleans (pfrick@uno.edu) .

seem to need more immediate services back to their school. If the child attends public school, the school likely offers both assessment and intervention services. Yet, additional, outside assessment and intervention services can also be sought and provided by psychologists or speech and language therapists. For speech and language assessment, numerous tests are available including Dunn and Dunn's Peabody Picture Vocabulary Test for receptive (or understood) language, Williams' Expressive Vocabulary Test for expressive (or spoken) language, and Carrow-Woolfolk's Comprehensive Assessment of Spoken Language for pragmatic, or everyday use of, language. For academic concerns, prominent academic achievement batteries include the Weschler Individual Achievement Test, Woodcock–Johnson Tests of Achievement, and the Kaufman Test of Educational Achievement.

Therefore, more formal and comprehensive assessments of speech and language and academic concerns are available by psychologists or other trained professionals through the school or outside agencies (e.g., through speech and language therapists).

Functional assessment: Antecedent–Behavior–Consequence charts

For all cases of disruptive behavior problems, Antecedent–Behavior–Consequence (ABC) charts can be helpful in providing functional information for treatment. For this reason, clinician will often want to send parents home with individualized assessment tools called ABC charts. As shown in Table 4.4, an ABC chart has three columns. Parents should first complete the middle column (B). This is where they log their child's problem behavior (e.g., tantrums, aggression, disrespect, etc.). Then, they should complete the rest of the chart left to right by writing down what happened before their child's misbehavior (A; Antecedent) and what did they did, or tried to do, after the misbehavior (C; Consequence; e.g., yell, punish, give in, etc.).

Completion of an ABC chart provides important information about parenting skills that should be covered in treatment and provides great examples for the clinician to draw upon when going over these skills in treatment. ABC charts also help facilitate problem-solving about new skill implementation and provide the therapist with good information about which skills the parent is having particular difficulty implementing. Importantly, this measure is free. More tech-savvy parents can also use smartphone apps to record these issues at minimal charge. Two examples are the Tantrum Tracker app for $2.99 and the Behavioral Tracker Pro for $29.99, which also includes a frequency record for logging specific behaviors (e.g., tantrums).

Therefore functional assessment of child misbehavior using ABC charts is highly desirable, particularly at the beginning of and during treatment. Overall, assessment of ODD is fairly straightforward, but choice of assessment tool will depend on setting, context, presenting concerns, time, and—in some cases—cost.

TABLE 4.4 Antecedent–Behavior–Consequence chart.

Day/time	*A*ntecedent: what happened before?	*B*ehavior: child's misbehavior	*C*onsequence: what happened after?

Illustration through case examples

Going back to our case examples, let's think about what assessment tools we need.

***

Luis

Luis is a 4-year-old Latino male. He was referred by his pediatrician for an evaluation after his parents presented complaining about Luis' aggression. Luis only uses one- to two-word phrases to communicate and is difficult to understand. His parents speak Spanish at home and both work long hours at minimum wage jobs. They have five kids total, ages 1, 4, 8, 10, and 12. Luis' parents report that he was born 1 month premature, weighing four pounds and three ounces. Luis' mother had severe hypertension toward the end of her pregnancy. Although his motor milestones were reported to be on time, Luis did not say his first words until age 3. He is still not potty trained and sleeps in bed with his parents. Luis' parents complain that he becomes angry and aggressive with minimal provocation. Luis will hit, kick, bite, and throw a tantrum if he does not get his way. He frequently does things that he knows his parents find annoying (such as yelling and running away at the supermarket). He does not comply with adult commands, yelling no and running away. He once ran away in a store parking lot and was almost hit by a car. His parents were worried that social services would be called. Luis' parents are concerned about him starting school next year, given they cannot currently leave him at home with even a babysitter due to his severe misbehavior.

Recommended Assessment Tools: Parent report on SDQ and DBRS; outside testing of speech and language

***

Frederick

Frederick is a 10-year-old African American male. His mother presented with him to the emergency room when his school called her to come and pick him up during the middle of the day after he threatened to "gut" another 10-year-old boy in his class. The school reported that the provocation for this incident was that Frederick became angry when the other boy asked him to share his colored pencil. More concerning, Frederick was found to have had a knife hidden in his schoolbag and indicated that he planned to use it on the other boy, so that the other boy would "get what was coming to him." The school has suspended Frederick until his mother obtains treatment for him. Frederick has a history of problems with peers. He has few friends and his peers report being scared of him. Frederick frequently, graphically threatens his peers following minor disagreements, telling them he will "cut them open," he "wants to explore their insides," and he will "show them their hearts." He is known to hold a grudge and will wait for a peer following a disagreement after school, threatening them and saying he will hurt them. Frederick lives with his mother, who is single. His biological father has been in jail for armed robbery since Frederick was born. His mother is a mortician with little family in the area. Frederick often spends his afternoons largely unsupervised at the morgue. Frederick's mother acknowledges that she is sometimes scared of him. He reportedly does not listen to her, often argues with her, and she is at a loss as to how to discipline him. Frederick's mother indicated that he has always been difficult to parent. She is worried because his school is insisting that she seek some kind of treatment for Frederick; otherwise, they have said they will expel him.

Recommended Assessment Tools: Parent and teacher report on DBRS and ICU

***

Anna

Anna is a 15-year-old Caucasian female whose parents present with concerns about possible drug use, sexting, and promiscuous sex. Anna has been diagnosed with depression and has been taking antidepressants since age 13. She was described as irritable and easily annoyed most of the time. She acknowledges frequent marijuana use with friends and being sexually active with several males. She has been grounded for the last 2 weeks after she sent a naked picture to one of these males, and her parents were informed by a friend's mother, who saw the picture on her daughter's Snapchat. Anna acknowledges that her current friend group has not been the best influence. She complains that the girls are all catty and talk about her behind her back. She reports engaging in sexting or sex and impulsivity, without a lot of forethought about the consequences, or while under the influence of alcohol. She indicated that she has no desire to listen to her parents and often argues with them about curfews and rules. She justified her behavior by reporting that she was bullied extensively in grade school and feels the need to fit in with her peers whatever the cost.

Recommended Assessment Tools: Parent, teacher, and self-report on DBRS and CASI-5

***

Conclusion

In sum, ODD can be fairly straightforward to assess and diagnose, but it is often important to consider cooccurring problems. For screening, the SDQ is recommended. If the focus of assessment is on ODD and other disruptive behavior problems, the DBRS is recommended, and the ICU is helpful for assessing a particularly severe type of ODD. Broadband questionnaires such as the CASI-5 or formal testing of speech and academics can be helpful for assessing broadband psychopathology. Finally, for treatment, functional assessment of behaviors in context can be achieved using ABC charts. Once one has assessed and diagnosed ODD, there are multiple effective options for treatment, detailed in the remaining chapters.

References

Barkley, R. A., & Murphy, K. R. (1998). *Attention-deficit hyperactivity disorder: A clinical workbook*. Guilford Press.

Barkley, R. A., & Murphy, K. R. (2006). *Attention-Deficit Hyperactivity Disorder: A clinical workbook* (3rd ed.). New York: The Guilford Press.

Expeleta, L., Osa, N. D. L., Granero, R., Penelo, E., & Domenech, J. M. (2013). Inventory of Callous-Unemotional Traits in a community sample of preschoolers. *Journal of Clinical Child & Adolescent Psychology*, *42*, 91–105.

Frick, P. J. (2004). *The Inventory of Callous-Unemotional Traits. Unpublished rating scale.*

Gadow, K. D. (2015). *The Symptom Inventories: An annotated bibliography*. Stony Brook, NY: Checkmate Plus.

Goodman, A., Lamping, D. L., & Ploubidis, G. B. (2010). When to use broader internalising and externalising subscales instead of the hypothesised five subscales on the Strengths and Difficulties Questionnaire (SDQ): Data from British parents, teachers and children. *Journal of Abnormal Child Psychology*, *38*, 1179–1191.

Goodman, R. (1997). The Strengths and Difficulties Questionnaire: A research note. *Journal of Child Psychology and Psychiatry*, *38*, 581–586.

Goodman, R., Meltzer, H., & Bailey, V. (1998). The Strengths and Difficulties Questionnaire: A pilot study on the validity of the self-report version. *European Child and Adolescent Psychiatry*, *7*, 125–130.

Kimonis, E. R., Fanti, K. A., & Singh, J. P. (2014). Establishing cut-off scores for the parent-reported Inventory of Callous-Unemotional Traits. *Archives of Forensic Psychology*, *1*(1), 27–48.

McMahon, R. J., & Frick, P. J. (2005). Evidence-based assessment of conduct problems in children and adolescents. *Journal of Clinical Child and Adolescent Psychology*, *34*(3), 477–505.

Pelletier, J., Collett, B., Gimple, G., & Cowley, S. (2006). Assessment of disruptive behaviors in preschoolers: Psychometric properties of the Disruptive Behavior Disorders Rating Scale and School Situations Questionnaire. *Journal of Psychoeducational Assessment*, *24*(1), 3–18.

Steiner, H., & Remsing, L. (2007). Practice parameter for the assessment and treatment of children and adolescents with oppositional defiant disorder. *Journal of the American Academy of Child & Adolescent Psychiatry*, *46*(1), 126–141.

Further reading

There are additional, comprehensive tables of measures available at:

https://www.aap.org/en-us/advocacy-and-policy/aap-health-initiatives/Mental-Health/Documents/MH_ScreeningChart.pdf

https://humanservices.ucdavis.edu/sites/default/files/104056-MentalHealthLR.pdf

https://www.chadis.com/site/clinicians

5

CHAPTER

Overview of evidence-based treatments of oppositional defiant disorder

Once oppositional defiant disorder (ODD) has been assessed and diagnosed, there are a number of evidence-based treatments available. These treatments fall roughly into three categories: behavioral management training programs, behavioral management training programs with a family component, and cognitive treatments. For a list of efficacious treatments, see Table 5.1. Each category of treatment will be described below. Several prominent examples of each type of treatment will be described. Additional, common examples will be listed. Finally, links to relevant materials (where relevant) will be provided.

Efficacy of treatments

How do we know what is effective, or—more technically—efficacious? Researchers require that evidence-based treatments meet a number of different criteria. Such treatments must have been tested using well-conducted treatment

The Clinician's Guide to Oppositional Defiant Disorder. DOI: https://doi.org/10.1016/B978-0-12-815682-7.00005-7

TABLE 5.1 List of efficacious treatments.

Behavioral management training programs
Parent management training—Oregon model
Helping the noncompliant child
Behavioral management training programs with a family component
Parent–child interaction therapy
Positive Parenting Program
Multisystemic therapy
Parent management training + problem-solving
Multidimensional treatment foster care
Cognitive treatments
Anger control
Problem-solving skills training
Incredible Years
Rational-emotive mental health program
Cognitive-behavioral therapy

studies, as shown in Table 5.2. Well-conducted treatment studies must (1) use a prospective study design, (2) have clear inclusion/exclusion criteria for the sample, (3) have appropriate control or comparison conditions, (4) randomly assign participants to conditions, (5) use reliable measures of disruptive behavior, (6) have clearly specified sample characteristics, and (7) utilize clearly described statistical procedures. There must also be a clearly defined treatment proposal or manual and some assurance of treatment fidelity.

For a treatment to be classified as well established (which in the treatment literature is described as level 1, or best support, as compared with possibly efficacious), it must be (8) validated by two good between-group experiments demonstrating superiority to pill, placebo, or another treatment; (9) demonstrate equivalency to an already established treatment in two between-group experiments with adequate sample sizes; or (10) show effects using a large series of nine or more single-case studies that used good experimental design and compared the treatment with another treatment. Finally, the treatment must (11) utilize treatment manuals and (12) demonstrate effects in studies by at least two different investigators or teams (Brestan & Eyberg, 1998; Chorpita & Daleiden, 2009; Eyberg, Nelson, & Boggs, 2008; Kaminski & Claussen, 2017; McCart & Sheidow, 2016; see Chambless & Hollon, 1998). All the of following types of treatment are well established, as shown in Table 5.3.

TABLE 5.2 Studies compromising evidence base for treatment of disruptive behavior.

Target treatment	Study authors	Nathan and Gorman level	Sample type	Child race	Child sex (% male)	Child age	Number of target treatment completers	Therapists	Comparison conditions	Types of disruptive behavior measures	Significant group differences favoring target treatment[a]	Effect sizes greater than 0.20 favoring target treatment[b]
Anger control training	Lochman, Coie, Underwood, and Terry (1993)	2	Children with disruptive behavior who are socially rejected	100% AA	52	4th grade (age NA)	9	Graduate students in psychology; doctoral-level psychologist	No treatment control	PE, T	1/2	NA
Anger control training	Robinson, Smith, and Miller (2002)	2	Children with disruptive behavior	41% C 54% AA 5% H	100	11–15 years (mean NA)	22	Teachers	No treatment control	S, T	4/5	4/5
Group assertive training (counselor led)	Huey and Rank (1984)	2	Youth with aggressive behavior	100% AA	100	8th and 9th grade (age NA)	12	Professional counselors	Discussion group (counselor led)	T	1/1	NA
									Discussion group (peer led)	T	1/1	NA
									No treatment control	T	1/1	NA
Group assertive training (peer led)	Huey and Rank (1984)	2	Youth with aggressive behavior	100% AA	100	8th and 9th grade (age NA)	12	Peer counselors	Discussion group (counselor led)	T	1/1	NA
									Discussion group (peer led)	T	0/1	NA
									No treatment control	T	1/1	NA

(Continued)

TABLE 5.2 (Continued)

Target treatment	Study authors	Nathan and Gorman level	Sample type	Child race	Child sex (% male)	Child age	Number of target treatment completers	Therapists	Comparison conditions	Types of disruptive behavior measures	Significant group differences favoring target treatment[a]	Effect sizes greater than 0.20 favoring target treatment[b]
Helping the noncompliant child	Peed, Roberts, and Forehand (1977)	2	Children with disruptive behavior	NA	75	3–7 years (mean = 5)	6	Graduate students	Waitlist control	P, O	2/5	NA
Helping the noncompliant child	Wells and Egan (1988)	2	Children with disruptive behavior	NA	NA	3–8 years (mean NA)	9	Clinical psychology interns	Systems family therapy	O	1/1	1/1
Incredible Years parent training	Webster-Stratton and Hammond (1997)	1	Children with disruptive behavior disorders	85% C	81	4–8 years (mean = 5.3)	26	MA or PhD in mental health field	Waitlist control	O, P, T	8/11	10/11
Incredible Years parent training	Webster-Stratton, Reid, and Hammond (2004)	1	Children with disruptive behavior disorders	79% C	90	4–8 years (mean = 5.8)	31	MA or PhD in mental health field	Waitlist control	O, P, T	3/3	3/3
Incredible Years child training	Webster-Stratton and Hammond (1997)	1	Children with disruptive behavior disorders	85% C	74	4–8 years (Mean = 6.0)	27	MA or PhD in mental health field	Waitlist control	O, P, T	7/11	9/11

Incredible Years child training	Webster-Stratton, Reid, and Hammond (2001)	1	Children with disruptive behavior disorders	88% C	82	4–8 years (mean = 6.0)	49	MA or PhD in mental health field; BA in psychology or education	Waitlist control	O + P + T composite	1/1	1/1
Incredible Years child training	Webster-Stratton, Reid, and Hammond (2004)	1	Children with disruptive behavior disorders	79%	93	4–8 years (Mean = 6.1)	30	MA or PhD in mental health field	Waitlist control	O, P, T	2/3	3/3
Multidimensional treatment foster care	Chamberlain and Reid (1998)	1	Youth with histories of chronic delinquency	85% C 6% AA 6% H 3% Nat A	100	12–17 years (mean = 14.9)	27	Trained foster parents and professional case managers	Usual group home care	R, S	4/4	4/4
Multidimensional treatment foster care	Leve, Chamberlain, and Reid (2005)	1	Youth with histories of chronic delinquency	74% C 2% AA 9% H 1% Asian 2% Mixed heritage 12% Nat A	0	13–17 years (mean NA)	37	Trained foster parents and professional case managers	Usual group home care	P, R, S	2/4	3/4
Multisystemic therapy	Henggeler, Melton, and Smith (1992)	1	Youth at risk for incarceration due to criminal offenses	42% C 56% AA 2% H	77	*M* = 15.2 years	33	MA-level mental health professionals	Usual community services	P, R, S	4/5	4/5
Multisystemic therapy	Scherer, Brondino, Henggeler, Melton, and Hanley (1994)	2	Youth with disruptive behavior who committed criminal offenses	22% C 78% AA	82	11–17 years (mean = 15.1)	23	MA-level mental health professionals	Usual community services	P, S	1/3	2/2 1-NA

(*Continued*)

TABLE 5.2 (Continued)

Target treatment	Study authors	Nathan and Gorman level	Sample type	Child race	Child sex (% male)	Child age	Number of target treatment completers	Therapists	Comparison conditions	Types of disruptive behavior measures	Significant group differences favoring target treatment[a]	Effect sizes greater than 0.20 favoring target treatment[b]
Multisystemic therapy	Borduin et al. (1995)	1	Youth with disruptive behavior who committed criminal offenses	70% C 30% AA	68	12–17 years (M = 14.8)	70	Graduate students in clinical	Alternative community treatments	P, R, T	3/4	4/4
Multisystemic therapy	Henggeler, Melton, Brondino, Scherer, and Hanley (1997)	1	Youth with disruptive behavior who committed criminal offenses	19% C 81% AA	82	11–17 years (M = 15.2)	75	MA-level mental health professionals in social work or pastoral counseling	Usual community services	P, R, S	1/7	1/7
Multisystemic therapy	Henggeler, Pickrel, and Brondino (1999)	1	Youth with disruptive behavior on probation	47% C 50% AA 1% H 1% Asian 1% NA	79	12–17 years (M = 15.8)	57	MA-and BA-level mental health counselors	Usual community services	R, S	0/2	0/2
Parent–child interaction therapy	Schuhmann, Foote, Eyberg, Boggs, and Algina (1998)	1	Children with disruptive behavior	77% C 14% AA 9% Other	81	3–6 years (M = 4.9)	22	Graduate students in clinical psychology	Waitlist control	O, P	5/6	4/4 2-NA

Parent–child interaction therapy	Nixon, Sweeney, Erickson, and Touyz (2003)	1	Children with disruptive behavior	94% C 2% Australian Koori 2% Australian Chinese 2% Australian Indian	70	3–5 years ($M = 3.9$)	17	MA-level clinical psychologist; graduate student in clinical psychology	Waitlist control	O, P	4/7	7/7
Parent Management Training Oregon	Bernal, Klinnert, and Schultz (1980)	1	Children with disruptive behavior	NA	86	5–12 years ($M = 8.4$)	12	Graduate students in clinical or counseling psychology	Waitlist control	O, P	3/4	NA
									Client-centered treatment	O, P	3/4	NA
Parent Management Training Oregon	Christensen, Johnson, Phillips, and Glasgow (1980)	1	Children with disruptive behavior	NA	78	4–12 years ($M = 6.8$)	17	Graduate students in clinical or counseling psychology; one PhD in clinical psychology	Bibliotherapy	O, P	1/4	NA
Parent Management Training Oregon	Patterson, Chamberlain, and Reid (1982)	2	Children with disruptive behavior	NA	60	3–10 years ($M = 6.8$)	10	MA-level therapists	Alternative community treatments	O, P	1/2	1/1 1-NA
Parent Management Training Oregon	Hughes and Wilson (1988)	2	Youth with disruptive behavior	NA	81	6–15 years ($M = 12.1$)	8	Psychologists, social workers	Communication skills training	P	0/3	2/3
									Waitlist control	P	1/3	3/3
Problem-solving skills training	Kazdin, Esveldt-Dawson, French, and Unis (1987b)	2	Children hospitalized for treatment of antisocial behavior	77% C 23% AA	80	7–13 years ($M = 10.9$)	17	Clinicians with postgraduate coursework and 1–2 years direct care experience	Relationship therapy	P, T	2/2	2/2
									Contact control	P, T	2/2	2/2

(*Continued*)

TABLE 5.2 (Continued)

Target treatment	Study authors	Nathan and Gorman level	Sample type	Child race	Child sex (% male)	Child age	Number of target treatment completers	Therapists	Comparison conditions	Types of disruptive behavior measures	Significant group differences favoring target treatment[a]	Effect sizes greater than 0.20 favoring target treatment[b]
Problem-solving skills training	Kazdin, Bass, Siegel, and Thomas (1989)	2	Children referred for treatment of antisocial behavior	54% C 46% AA	78	7–13 years ($M = 11.0$)	34	Master's degree in mental health field	Relationship therapy	P, S, T	3/6	4/6
Problem-solving skills training	Kazdin, Siegel, and Bass (1992)	2	Children with aggressive and antisocial behavior	69% C 31% AA	77	7–13 years ($M = 10.3$)	25	Master's degree in mental health field	Parent management training	P, S, T	2/7	5/7
Problem-solving skills training + practice	Kazdin, Bass, Siegel, and Thomas (1989)	2	Children referred for antisocial behavior	56% C 46% AA	78	7–13 years ($M = 11.0$)	32	Master's degree in mental health field	Relationship therapy	P, S, T	6/6	6/6
Problem-solving skills training + parent management training	Kazdin, Esveldt-Dawson, French, and Unis (1987a)	2	Children hospitalized for treatment of antisocial behavior	75% C 25% AA	77	7–12 years ($M = 10.1$)	20	Clinicians who had completed postgraduate coursework and 1–2 years direct care experience	Contact placebo control	P, T	2/2	2/2

Rational emotive mental health program	Block (1978)	1	Youth with disruptive behavior	All AA and H (% NA)	48	10th and 11th grade (age NA)	16	Master's-level therapists	Human relations training	T, R	2/2	2/2
									No treatment control	T, R	2/2	2/2
Triple P (enhanced)	Sanders, Markie-Dadds, Tully, and Bor (2000)	1	Children with disruptive behavior	Predominantly Caucasian	67	3–4 years ($M = 3.4$)	58	Graduate students, psychologists, psychiatrists	Waitlist control	O, P	5/5	5/5
Triple P (enhanced)	Bor, Sanders, and Markie-Dadds (2002)	1	Children with disruptive behavior	Mostly Caucasian	73	3–4 years ($M = 3.3$)	15	Graduate students and psychologists	Waitlist control	O, P	3/4	4/4
Triple P (standard)	Sanders, Markie-Dadds, Tully, and Bor (2000)	1	Children with disruptive behavior	Predominantly Caucasian	68	3–4 years ($M = 3.5$)	65	Graduate students, psychologists, psychiatrists	Waitlist control	O, P	5/5	5/5
Triple P (standard)	Bor, Sanders, and Markie-Dadds (2002)	1	Children with disruptive behavior	Mostly Caucasian	57	3–4 years ($M = 3.3$)	21	Graduate students and psychologists	Waitlist control	O, P	3/4	3/4

Note: Treatment studies that included comparisons of one treatment to a component of itself were not included in this table. *AA*, African American; *C*, Caucasian; *H*, Hispanic; *Nat A*, Native American; *O*, direct observation; *P*, parent or caregiver report; *PE*, peer report; *R*, official records; *S*, self-report; *T*, teacher report.

[a]*This column indicates the number of disruptive behavior measures in the study that showed a statistically significant ($P < .05$) between-group difference favoring the target treatment. For example, an entry of 2/3 would indicate that the study included 3 measures of disruptive behavior and that the EBT showed significantly better outcomes on 2 of these measures than the control condition.*

[b]*This column refers to the effect sizes of between-group differences favoring the EBT obtained on the measures of disruptive behavior examined in the study. Effect sizes were those reported by the investigator in the published study or were calculated from data presented in the study by subtracting the posttreatment mean of the EBT condition from the posttreatment mean of the control/comparison condition and dividing that number by the pooled standard deviation of the posttreatment scores; an entry of 3/4 in this column would indicate that there were 4 measures of disruptive behavior in the study and that the effect sizes for differences was 0.20 or greater in favor of the EBT on 3 of the measures.*

Source: Table 1 and all citations in Table 1 from Eyberg, S. M., Nelson, M. M., & Boggs, S. R. (2008). Evidence-based psychosocial treatments for children and adolescents with disruptive behavior. *Journal of Clinical Child & Adolescent Psychology, 37*(1), 215–237.

TABLE 5.3 Criteria met by evidence-based treatments for disruptive behavior.

Treatment	WE Ia	WE Ib	WE II	WE III	WE IV	WE V	PE I	PE II	PE III
	Two good between-group experiments demonstrating superiority to pill or placebo or another treatment	Two good between-group design experiments demonstrating equivalency to an already established treatment in experiments with adequate sample sizes	Large series of single-case design studies (≥ 9) that used good experimental design and compare treatment with another treatment	Experiments conducted with treatment manuals	Sample characteristics clearly specified	Effects demonstrated by at least 2 different investigators or investigating teams	Two good between-group experiments showing the treatment is superior to a waiting-list control group	One or more experiments meeting well-established treatment criteria IA or IB, III, and IV but not V	Small series of single-case design experiments (≥ 3) otherwise meeting well-established treatment criteria II, III, and IV
Anger control training (PE)	No	No	No	Yes	Yes	Yes	Yes (2 studies) Lochman, Coie, Underwood, and Terry (1993); Robinson, Smith, and Miller (2002)	No	No
Group assertiveness training (counselor led) (PE)	No	No	No	Yes	Yes	No	No	Yes (1 study) Huey and Rank (1984)	No
Group assertiveness training (peer led) (PE)	No	No	No	Yes	Yes	No	No	Yes (1 study) Huey and Rank (1984)	No

Helping the noncompliant child (PE)	No	No	No	Yes	Yes	No	No	Yes (1 study) Wells and Egan (1988)	No
Incredible Years parent training (PE)	No	No	No	Yes	Yes	No	Yes (2 studies) Webster-Stratton and Hammond (1997); Webster-Stratton, Reid, and Hammond (2004)	No	No
Incredible Years child training (PE)	No	No	No	Yes	Yes	No	Yes (3 studies) Webster-Stratton and Hammond (1997); Webster-Stratton, Reid, and Hammond (2001, 2004)	No	No
Multidimensional treatment foster care (PE)	No	No	No	Yes	Yes	No	No	Yes (2 studies) Chamberlain and Reid (1998); Leve, Chamberlain, and Reid (2005)	No
Multisystemic therapy (PE)	No	No	No	Yes	Yes	No	No	Yes (2 studies) Borduin et al. (1995), Henggeler, Melton, and Smith (1992)	No

(*Continued*)

TABLE 5.3 (Continued)

Treatment	WE Ia	WE Ib	WE II	WE III	WE IV	WE V	PE I	PE II	PE III
	Two good between-group experiments demonstrating superiority to pill or placebo or another treatment	Two good between-group design experiments demonstrating equivalency to an already established treatment in experiments with adequate sample sizes	Large series of single-case design studies (≥ 9) that used good experimental design and compare treatment with another treatment	Experiments conducted with treatment manuals	Sample characteristics clearly specified	Effects demonstrated by at least 2 different investigators or investigating teams	Two good between-group experiments showing the treatment is superior to a waiting-list control group	One or more experiments meeting well-established treatment criteria IA or IB, III, and IV but not V	Small series of single-case design experiments (≥ 3) otherwise meeting well-established treatment criteria II, III, and IV
Parent–child interaction therapy (PE)	No	No	No	Yes	Yes	Yes	Yes (2 studies) Nixon, Sweeney, Erickson, and Touyz (2003); Schuhmann, Foote, Eyberg Boggs, and Algina (1998)	No	No
Parent management training—Oregon Model (WE)	Yes (2 studies) Bernal, Klinnert, and Schultz, (1980); Patterson, Chamberlain, and Reid (1982)	No	No	Yes	Yes	Yes	No	No	No

Problem-solving skills training (PE)	Yes	No	No	Yes	Yes	No	No	Yes (2 studies) Kazdin, Esveldt-Dawson, French, and Unis (1987b); Kazdin, Bass, Siegel, and Thomas, (1989)	No
Problem-solving skills training + practice (PE)	No	No	No	Yes	Yes	No	No	Yes (1 study) Kazdin, Bass, Siegel, and Thomas (1989)	No
Problem-solving skills training + parent management training (PE)	Yes	No	No	Yes	Yes	No	No	Yes (1 study) Kazdin, Esveldt-Dawson, French, and Unis (1987a)	No
Rational emotive mental health program (PE)	No	No	No	Yes	Yes	No	No	Yes (1 study) Block (1978)	No
Triple P (Positive Parenting Program) enhanced (PE)	No	No	No	Yes	Yes	No	Yes (2 studies) Bor, Sanders, and Markie-Dadds (2002); Sanders, Markie-Dadds, Tully, and Bor (2000)	No	No

(Continued)

TABLE 5.3 (Continued)

Treatment	WE Ia	WE Ib	WE II	WE III	WE IV	WE V	PE I	PE II	PE III
	Two good between-group experiments demonstrating superiority to pill or placebo or another treatment	**Two good between-group design experiments demonstrating equivalency to an already established treatment in experiments with adequate sample sizes**	**Large series of single-case design studies (≥9) that used good experimental design and compare treatment with another treatment**	**Experiments conducted with treatment manuals**	**Sample characteristics clearly specified**	**Effects demonstrated by at least 2 different investigators or investigating teams**	**Two good between-group experiments showing the treatment is superior to a waiting-list control group**	**One or more experiments meeting well-established treatment criteria IA or IB, III, and IV but not V**	**Small series of single-case design experiments (≥3) otherwise meeting well-established treatment criteria II, III, and IV**
Triple P standard individual treatment (PE)	No	No	No	Yes	Yes	No	Yes (2 studies) Bor, Sanders, and Markie-Dadds (2002); Sanders, Markie-Dadds, Tully, and Bor (2000)	No	No

Note: *PE*, Probably efficacious treatment; *WE*, well-established treatment.
Source: Table 2 from Eyberg, S. M., Nelson, M. M., & Boggs, S. R. (2008). Evidence-based psychosocial treatments for children and adolescents with disruptive behavior. *Journal of Clinical Child & Adolescent Psychology, 37*(1), 215–237.

Behavioral management training programs

Behavioral management training programs focus on teaching parents behavioral strategies for modifying child behavior, monitoring child behavior, and developing token economies for addressing child misbehavior. These behavioral management programs are largely based on behavioral theory of behavioral modification. These programs stress the importance of increasing positive reinforcement parenting strategies and diminishing use of negative reinforcement and positive punishment strategies. In this way, these programs attempt to interrupt coercive cycles between parent and child, which often work through negative reinforcement.

Example

Parent management training Oregon model (PMTO; Patterson, Reid, Jones, & Conger, 1975; Reid, Webster-Stratton, & Hammond, 2003): PMTO is a behavioral parent training program for parents of children ages 3–12. Therapists meet with parents individually for weekly therapy sessions, and make telephone contacts for a length of time that depends on the family's needs. This treatment seeks to change family interactions and avoid coercion by teaching behavioral modification principles such increased monitoring, use of rewards, and consistent use of consequences. Specifically, the treatment seeks to increase positive parenting skills; increase positive child behaviors; provide systematic, mild consequences for negative child behavior; increase parental monitoring; and facilitate interpersonal problem-solving.

Additional examples

Helping the noncompliant child (HNC)

Relevant materials

Forehand, R., & Long, N. (2002). *Parenting the strong-willed child: The clinically proven five-week program for parents of two- to six-year-olds* (revised and updated). New York: McGraw-Hill.

Behavioral management training programs with family component

Some behavioral management training programs also add a component for addressing family and broader community stressors/issues, including teaching more responsive parenting and increased monitoring. These programs differ from the aforementioned behavioral management training programs without a family component due to their emphasis on family and community components. Therefore, these programs often add a treatment component that seeks to enhance parenting responsiveness and facilitate social support and increased monitoring of child behavior, as well as community engagement and activities. In this way, these treatments generally address both coercive cycles and family attachment issues.

Example

Parent–child interaction therapy (PCIT; Brinkmeyer & Eyberg, 2003; Hembree-Kigin & McNeil, 2013): PCIT is a parenting skills program for parents of young children (ages 2–7). It targets change in parent–child interaction patterns. Parents meet for 1 hour a week for 12–16 sessions. In the first child-directed interaction phase of treatment, families learn positive attention skills and active ignoring skills, or differential attention, to increase positive parenting and warmth in parent–child interactions. In the second, parent-directed interaction phase, parents learn and practice giving clear instructions when needed and following through with praise, consequences, or time-out, as needed. Therapists coach parents during the sessions and homework is given.

Relevant materials

Basic information about PCIT for parents: http://www.pcit.org/pcit-certification.html.

PCIT International is an organization for parents who want to learn about PCIT or find a provider, and professionals who want to be trained in PCIT: http://www.pcit.org/pcit-certification.html.

Example

Positive Parenting Program (Triple P; Sanders, 1999): Triple P is a multilevel treatment system with the level of intensity matched to child problem severity. Levels 4 (standard) and 5 (enhanced) are efficacious. Standard Triple P teaches parents 17 core parenting skills (e.g., talking to children, physical affection, attention, setting limits, planned ignoring) to increase positive behaviors and decrease negative ones with use of planned practice activities. *Enhanced* Triple P adds home visits to enhance parenting skills, partner support, and mood management/stress coping.

Relevant materials

Online Triple P: https://www.triplep-parenting.com/us/triple-p/.

Example

Multisystemic therapy (MST; Henggler & Lee, 2003): MST provides intensive family- and community-based intervention with the goal of promoting responsible behavior and preventing out-of-the-home placement. It includes cognitive behavioral and behavioral treatment, parenting training, pragmatic family therapies, and pharmacological interventions. The intervention is delivered in the family's natural environment and lasts 3–5 months. Therapists usually contact the family more than once a week and are always available to assist. The treatment focuses on assessing how problems are maintained by the social context; emphasizing positive family dynamics; trying to increase responsible behaviors and decrease irresponsible ones; developing interventions to specific problems that are easily tracked; fostering competencies of youth in the different environments; and promoting generalizations across different contexts.

Additional examples

Parent management training + problem-solving

Multidimensional treatment foster care

Cognitive therapies

Cognitive therapies are generally targeted to changing maladaptive social cognition related to aggression and disruptive behavior. These treatments target children's poor social–cognitive and decision-making skills, poor self-regulation, peer context, and ability to resist peer pressure. In addition, the treatment also addresses parental involvement with and discipline of children. These treatments typically teach children and adolescents to recognize their anger and develop behavioral and cognitive strategies for managing such anger. Some treatments additionally focus on disrupting negative interactions in the home by teaching problem-solving strategies that can be utilized by parents and adolescents/children. In this way, these treatments target social information processing problems in children and adolescents.

Examples

Anger control training (Lochman, Barry, & Pardini, 2003): Anger control training is a cognitive behavioral intervention for elementary school age children. Children meet once a week at school in groups of about six children. In group sessions, children discuss vignettes of social encounters with peers and social cues and possible motives of individuals in the vignettes. Children learn to use problem-solving for dealing with anger-provoking situations and practice appropriate social responses and self-statements in response to different situations, with behavioral rehearsal and feedback. Later, children practice in situations designed to arouse their anger with support provided. Children also learn strategies to increase their awareness of feelings.

Problem-solving skills training (PSST; Kazdin, 2003; Kazdin, 2010): PSST is a behavioral treatment for children ages 7–13. Treatment is conducted with the child, with occasional parental contact for 20–25 sessions. Children are taught problem-solving strategies such as identifying the problem, generating solutions, weighing pros and cons, making a decision, and evaluating the outcome. They are also taught to generalize to real-life problems. Therapists use in-session practice, modeling, role playing, corrective feedback, social reinforcement, and token response cost beginning with games and progressing to more complex interpersonal situations through role play.

Relevant materials

Webinars for parents: https://yaleparentingcenter.yale.edu/kazdin-method-sessions

Additional examples

Assertiveness training

Incredible Years (IY)
Rational emotive mental health program (REMH)
Cognitive behavioral therapy (CBT)

Relevant materials

http://www.incredibleyears.com/parents-teachers/articles-for-parents/

Summary

Efficacious treatments for disruptive behavior problems can be grouped into behavioral management training programs, behavioral management training programs with a family component, and cognitive therapies. Behavioral management training programs focus on teaching parents' behavioral strategies for modifying child behavior, monitoring child behavior, and developing token economies for addressing child misbehavior to interrupt coercive cycles. A prominent example is PMTO. Behavioral management programs with a family component add a family or community component to facilitate attachment and/or monitoring, and prominent examples include PCIT, Triple P, and MST. Cognitive therapies address faulty social information processing by teaching problem-solving for dealing with anger-provoking situations and training appropriate social responses and self-statements in response to different situations, with behavioral rehearsal and feedback. Prominent examples include anger control training and PSST. Behavioral management training programs both with and without a family component are more geared toward younger children and families, and cognitive treatments are more geared toward older children and adolescents, generally speaking.

Illustration through case examples

Let's return to our case examples and determine what treatments might be best for these families based on our conceptualizations.

***

Luis

Luis is a 4-year-old Latino male. He was referred by his pediatrician for an evaluation after his parents presented complaining about Luis' aggression. Luis only uses one- to two-word phrases to communicate and is difficult to understand. His parents speak Spanish at home and both work long hours at minimum wage jobs. They have five kids total, ages 1, 4, 8, 10, and 12. Luis' parents report that he was born 1 month premature, weighing 4 lb and 3 oz. Luis' mother had severe hypertension toward the end of her pregnancy. Although his motor milestones were reported to be on time, Luis did not say his first words until age 3. He is still not potty trained and sleeps in bed with his parents. Luis' parents complain that he becomes angry and aggressive with minimal provocation. Luis will hit, kick, bite, and throw a tantrum if he does not get his way. He frequently does things that he knows his parents find annoying (such as yelling and running away at the supermarket). He does not comply with adult commands, yelling no and running away. He once ran away in a store parking lot and was almost hit by a car. His parents were worried that social services would be called. Luis' parents are concerned about him starting school next year, given they cannot currently leave him at home with even a babysitter due to his severe misbehavior.

Conceptualization: Luis is exhibiting ODD in the context of speech and language problems and other delays with independent sleep and elimination problems. Luis is the youngest in a large family. His parents are under economic and personal stress, working long hours to provide for the family. Luis was also exposed to a number of prenatal risk factors, including stress during pregnancy, hypertension, prematurity, and low birth weight. He also experienced developmental delays, particularly with language. The high stress at home, large number of siblings, his parent's limited time, and Luis' language delays have led to coercive cycles between Luis and his parents. He may have difficulty communicating his needs and understanding parental requests. He may also have difficulty obtaining parental attention using appropriate strategies. Therefore he often resorts to aggression, tantrums, and noncompliance. He has been delayed with potty training and refuses to sleep independently.

Personalization of treatment tips: Given the number of family stressors, a family level intervention with a focus on behavioral skills and addressing sleep and elimination issues would probably be best. Speech and language evaluation and treatment with consideration of the family's bilingualism will also be critical. A consultation with a pediatrician regarding elimination issues will be important. Attention-deficit/Hyperactivity disorder (ADHD) will also need to be considered for impulsive behaviors.

Ideal treatment

PCIT or enhanced Triple P

Back-up treatment possibilities

PMTO

Standard Triple P
HNC

How to find providers

For PCIT: http://www.pcit.org/pcit-certification.html

APA Division 53 (Society for Clinical Child and Adolescent Psychology): https://sccap53.org/find-a-therapist/

Reading and online resources

https://www.triplep-parenting.com/us/triple-p/

https://www.cdc.gov/parents/essentials/index.html
Forehand, R., & Long, N. (2002). *Parenting the strong-willed child: the clinically proven five-week program for parents of two- to six-year-olds* (revised and updated). New York: McGraw-Hill.

***

Frederick

Frederick is a 10-year-old African American male. His mother presented with him to the emergency room when his school called her to come and pick him up during the middle of the day after he threatened to "gut" another 10-year-old boy in his class. The school reported that the provocation for this incident was that Frederick became angry when the other boy asked him to share his colored pencil. More concerning, Frederick was found to have had a knife hidden in his schoolbag and indicated that he planned to use it on the other boy, so that the other boy would "get what was coming to him." The school has suspended Frederick until his mother obtains treatment for him. Frederick has a history of problems with peers. He has few friends and his peers report being scared of him. Frederick frequently, graphically threatens his peers following minor disagreements, telling them he will "cut them open," he "wants to explore their insides," and he will "show them their hearts." He is known to hold a grudge and will wait for a peer following a disagreement after school, threatening them and saying he will hurt them. Frederick lives with his mother, who is single. His biological father has been in jail for armed robbery since Frederick was born. His mother is a mortician with little family in the area. Frederick often spends his afternoons largely unsupervised at the morgue. Frederick's mother acknowledges that she is sometimes scared of him. He reportedly does not listen to her, often argues with her, and she is at a loss as to how to discipline him. Frederick's mother indicated that he has always been difficult to parent. She is worried because his school is insisting that she seek some kind of treatment for Frederick; otherwise, they have said they will expel him.

Conceptualization: Frederick is exhibiting ODD with high callous–unemotional traits. Frederick may have a genetic predisposition toward conduct problems and callous–unemotional traits in particular given that his father is currently serving time in jail for armed robbery, and Frederick is described as vindictive and engaging in proactive or instrumental forms of aggression that are premeditated. This genetic predisposition may particularly increase his risk for conduct problems given family stressors such as an absent father and little social support. In addition, Frederick's mother spends long hours at work, which means she has little time to supervise him. His exposure to dead bodies seems to be increasing his callousness and detachment toward others. Finally, Frederick does not get along with his peers and is isolated at school. Perhaps most critically, Frederick and his mother do not have a warm and loving relationship, and he is likely insecurely attached. She acknowledges that she is sometimes scared of him and is at a loss as to how to discipline him.

Personalization of treatment tips: Given the severity of Frederick's current behaviors and the family's lack of social support, an intensive, community-level intervention is likely to be best. It will be critical to involve the school and neighborhood to provide increased monitoring of Frederick's behavior while his mother is working and to facilitate peer friendships. Frederick's mother will also need consultation about how to build more warmth and affection into their relationship. The use of a reward system to reinforce appropriate behaviors will be critical, given the presence of callous–unemotional traits. Frederick will need to be assessed for conduct disorder.

Ideal treatment

MST

Back-up treatment possibilities

Enhanced Triple P

How to find providers

APA Division 53: https://effectivechildtherapy.org/tips-tools/locate-a-psychologist-near-you/

Insurance company

Reading and online resources

https://www.triplep-parenting.com/us/triple-p/

http://parentsanonymous.org/
Privilege Points application

***

Anna

Anna is a 15-year-old Caucasian female whose parents present with concerns about possible drug use, sexting, and promiscuous sex. Anna has been diagnosed with depression and has been taking antidepressants since age 13. She was described as irritable and easily annoyed most of the time. She acknowledges frequent marijuana use with friends and being sexually active with several males. She has been grounded for the last 2 weeks after she sent a naked picture to one of these males, and her parents were informed by a friend's mother, who saw the picture on her daughter's Snapchat. Anna acknowledges that her current friend group has not been the best influence. She complains that the girls are all catty and talk about her behind her back. She reports engaging in sexting or sex, as well as impulsivity, without a lot of forethought about the consequences, or while under the influence of alcohol. She indicated that she has no desire to listen to her parents and often argues with them about curfews and rules. She justified her behavior by reporting that she was bullied extensively in grade school and feels the need to fit in with her peers whatever the cost.

Conceptualization: Anna exhibits ODD in the context of a preexisting depression diagnosis. She is also at risk for emerging substance use problems with marijuana and alcohol. She has a history of peer problems including bullying through covert aggression (e.g., rumors). Through these experiences, she seems to have developed faulty social information processing in that she almost always attributes hostile intentions to her peers, and she impulsively engages in inappropriate reactions such as substance use and sexting. She furthermore does not seem to have learned to evaluate the negative consequences of her actions. Her parents, to date, have been largely ineffective at monitoring or disciplining her to obtain desired behaviors.

Personalization of treatment tips: Given Anna's depression and the prominent role peers are playing in her problems, a social learning approach would probably be most effective. It will also be important to involve Anna's parents in the treatment to facilitate a more effective problem-solving approach to setting rules and consequences for her. Better monitoring of Anna's behavior, including use of substances, will be critical. Assessment for ADHD for Anna's impulsive behaviors may also be helpful. A psychiatric consultation regarding the effectiveness of Anna's antidepressant at its current dosage for managing depressive symptomatology will also be important.

Ideal treatment

PSST

Back-up treatment possibilities

CBT
Assertiveness training
REMH

How to find providers

Association for Behavioral and Cognitive Therapies (ABCT): http://www.findcbt.org/xFAT/

Reading and online resources

Faber, A., & Mazlish, E. (2012). *How to talk so kids will listen & listen so kids will talk*. Simon and Schuster.

Future directions

Obviously, there is a real need for additional online materials, including online applications for skills training (McGoron & Ondersma, 2015). This is a rapidly changing, up-and-coming area. Importantly, however, each of these efficacious treatments consists of a number of efficacious treatment components that can be used as a package, as described in this chapter. Alternatively, to personalize and make treatment more efficient, treatment components can be utilized individually, as described in the next chapter and subsequent chapters.

References

Brestan, E. V., & Eyberg, S. M. (1998). Effective psychosocial treatments of conduct-disordered children and adolescents: 29 years, 82 studies, and 5,272 kids. *Journal of Clinical Child Psychology*, *27*(2), 180–189.

Brinkmeyer, M. Y., & Eyberg, S. M. (2003). Parent-child interaction therapy for oppositional children. In A. E. Kazdin, & J. R. Weisz (Eds.), *Evidence-based psychotherapies for children and adolescents* (pp. 204–223). New York, NY, US: The Guilford Press.

Chambless, D. L., & Hollon, S. D. (1998). Defining empirically supported therapies. *Journal of Consulting and Clinical Psychology*, *66*(1), 7.

Chorpita, B. F., & Daleiden, E. L. (2009). *CAMHD biennial report: Effective psychosocial interventions for youth with behavioral and emotional needs*. Honolulu, HI: Hawaii Department of Health, Child and Mental Health Division.

Eyberg, S. M., Nelson, M. M., & Boggs, S. R. (2008). Evidence-based psychosocial treatments for children and adolescents with disruptive behavior. *Journal of Clinical Child & Adolescent Psychology*, *37*(1), 215–237.

Faber, A., & Mazlish, E. (2012). *How to talk so kids will listen & listen so kids will talk*. New York: Simon and Schuster.

Forehand, R., & Long, N. (2002). *Parenting the strong-willed child: The clinically proven five-week program for parents of two- to six-year-olds*. New York: McGraw-Hill. (revised and updated).

Hembree-Kigin, T. L., & McNeil, C. B. (2013). *Parent–child interaction therapy*. Springer Science & Business Media.

Henggeler, S. W., & Lee, T. (2003). Multisystemic treatment of serious clinical problems. In A. E. Kazdin, & J. R. Weisz (Eds.), *Evidence-based psychotherapies for children and adolescents* (pp. 301–322). New York, NY, US: The Guilford Press.

Kaminski, J., & Claussen, A. (2017). Evidence base update for psychosocial treatments for disruptive behaviors in children. *Journal of Clinical Child & Adolescent Psychology*, 1–23. Available from https://doi.org/10.1080/15374416.2017.1310044.

Kazdin, A. E. (2003). Problem-solving skills training and parent management training for conduct disorder. In A. E. Kazdin, & J. R. Weisz (Eds.), *Evidence-based psychotherapies for children and adolescents* (pp. 241–262). New York, NY, US: The Guilford Press.

Kazdin, A. E. (2010). *Problem-solving skills training and parent management training for oppositional defiant disorder and conduct disorder. Evidence-based psychotherapies for children and adolescents* (pp. 211–226). Guilford Press.

Lochman, J. E., Barry, T. D., & Pardini, D. A. (2003). *Anger control training for aggressive youth. Evidence-based psychotherapies for children and adolescents* (2nd ed., pp. 227–242).

McCart, M. R., & Sheidow, A. J. (2016). Evidence-based psychosocial treatments for adolescents with disruptive behavior. *Journal of Clinical Child & Adolescent Psychology*, *45*, 529–563. Available from https://doi.org/10.1080/15374416.2016.1146990.

McGoron, L., & Ondersma, S. J. (2015). Reviewing the need for technological and other expansions of evidence-based parent training for young children. *Children and Youth Services Review*, *59*, 71–83.

Patterson, G. R., Reid, J. B., Jones, R. R., & Conger, R. E. (1975). *A social learning approach to family intervention: Families with aggressive children* (Vol. 1). Eugene, OR: Castalia.

Reid, M. J., Webster-Stratton, C., & Hammond, M. (2003). Follow-up of children who received the Incredible Years intervention for oppositional-defiant disorder: Maintenance and prediction of 2-year outcome. *Behavior Therapy*, *34*(4), 471–491.

Sanders, M. R. (1999). Triple P-Positive Parenting Program: Towards an empirically validated multilevel parenting and family support strategy for the prevention of behavior and emotional problems in children. *Clinical Child and Family Psychology Review*, *2*(2), 71–90.

Further reading

Online consumer resources:

Division 53 website: http://effectivechildtherapy.org/tips-tools/what-is-evidence-based-treatment/

ABCT website: http://www.abct.org/Information/?m = mInformation&fa = FactSheets

Online therapist resources:

REACH Institute: For providers who want training in evidence-based mental health care for children: http://www.thereachinstitute.org/

6

CHAPTER

Overview of evidence-based treatment components for oppositional defiant disorder

Another approach to identifying effective treatments of childhood disruptive behaviors is to focus on evidence-based practice elements, or individual components of treatment (e.g., praise, time-out). Because many interventions are related to one another and share common practice elements, it is often useful to provide information on the best supported "clinical ingredients" from interventions so clinicians can have some means to decide among various interventions and/or personalize or tailor interventions to particular children and families. In the fairly common case where a family has limited financial resources and may not be able to afford to participate in the full course of treatment, knowledge of the efficacy of individual treatment components allows a clinician to provide treatment components in the order of their likely positive impact on the family. That way, when a family

The Clinician's Guide to Oppositional Defiant Disorder. DOI: https://doi.org/10.1016/B978-0-12-815682-7.00006-9

discontinues treatment, one can be sure that they have received the most powerful components of treatment possible.

The current chapter will review criteria for establishing efficacy of treatment components. Then, the chapter will review groups of efficacious treatment components, including differential attention, effective commands and consistent consequences including rewards, time-out, cognitive skills, problem-solving, and treatment for other related problems. Then, examples of treatment components, links to treatments, and relevant resources will be provided. Finally, how to personalize treatment using a component approach will be illustrated using case examples.

Efficacy of treatment components

To determine the relative efficacy of individual components of treatment, a committee sought to identify therapeutic strategies using a clinical coding system (Chorpita & Daleiden, 2009). Two independent judges evaluated the presence or absence of each strategy in each protocol, and a third judge provided a final review. Then, graphs were developed to show the relative frequency with which each element was included in a successful treatment protocol. For example, as shown in Fig. 6.1, a value of 50% for differential reinforcement means that 50% of the coded successful treatment protocols included differential reinforcement as a treatment strategy in their protocol. For disruptive behavior problems, these evidence-based treatment components can be divided into those that work best for children ages 12 and under (shown in Fig. 6.1) versus those that work best for ages 13 and over (shown in Fig. 6.2).

The current chapter will provide an overview of the top 20 treatment strategies, or evidence-based treatment components, from each list, organized into overarching categories for simplicity. As one can see in Figs. 6.1 and 6.2, there are many treatment components that work well in both young children and older adolescents. In the lists below, components in plain font are rated highly on both the child *and* adolescent lists. Those components in italics are typically rated much more highly on the child (vs adolescent) list. Although this chapter provides an introduction, these evidence-based treatment components will be explained in much greater detail in subsequent chapters. Online and text resources are also provided for each evidence-based treatment component.

Differential attention

The first evidence-based treatment component is differential attention. Differential attention consists of praise, differential reinforcement, attending, therapist praise/rewards, and relationship/rapport building. Overall, these components can be summarized as consisting of positive attention and active ignoring. This component is heavily involved in behavioral management

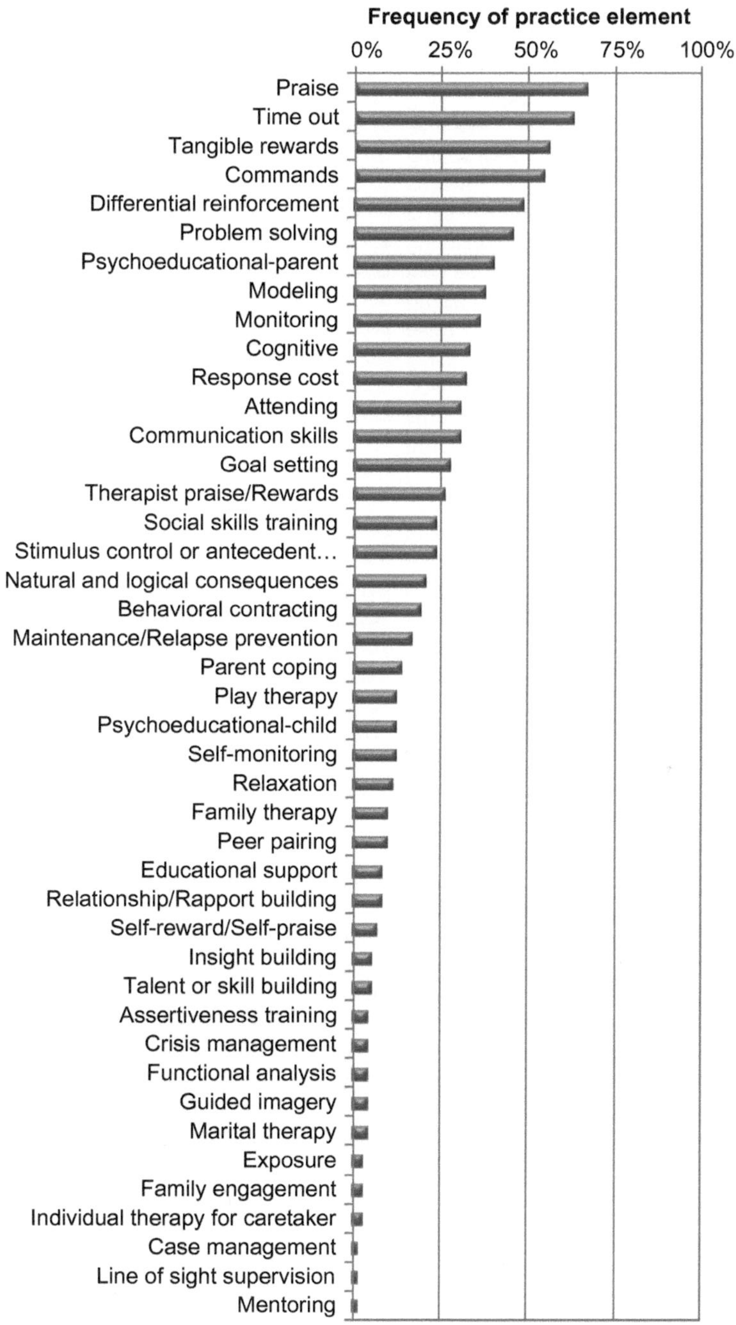

FIGURE 6.1 Evidence-based treatment components for disruptive behavior disorder ages 12 and under (Chorpita & Daleiden, 2009: p. 32).

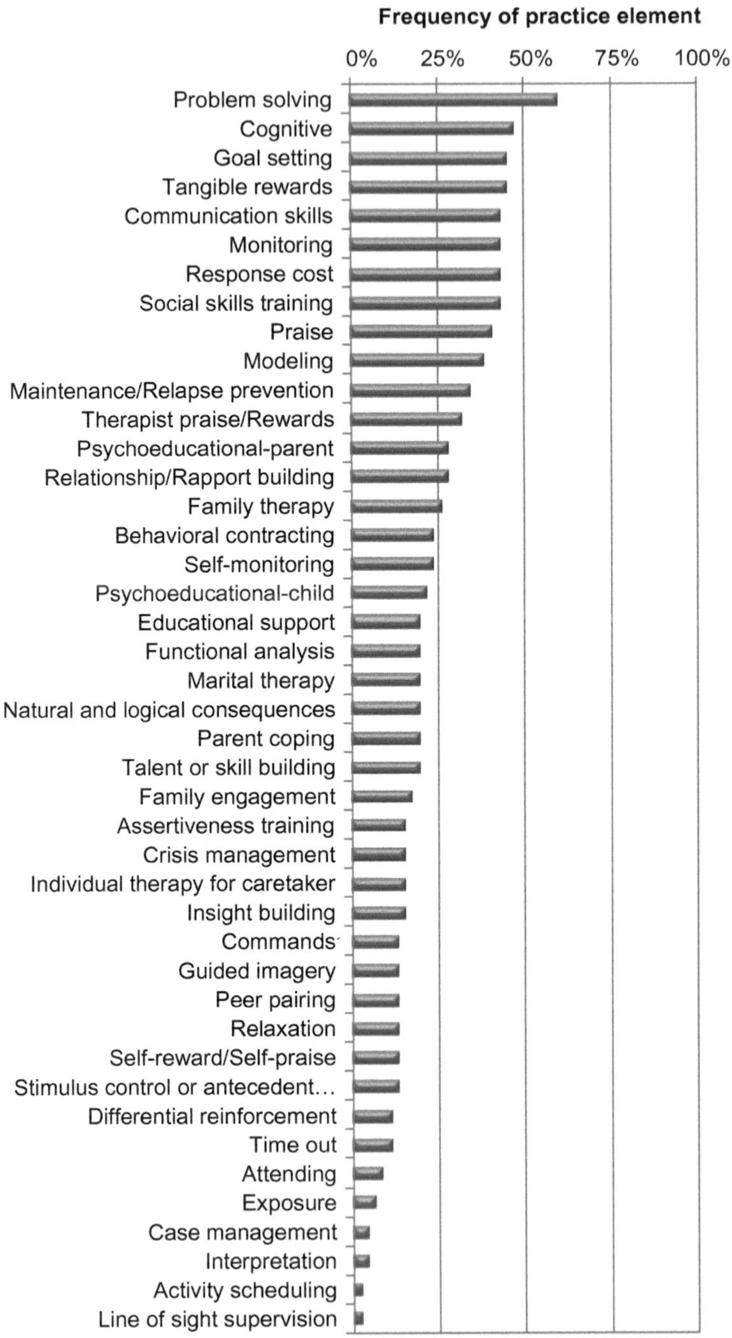

FIGURE 6.2 Evidence-based treatment components for disruptive behavior disorder ages 13 and over (Chorpita & Daleiden, 2009: p. 33).

training programs with and without a family component [e.g., parent management training—Oregon model (PMTO); parent–child interaction therapy (PCIT); Positive Parenting Program (Triple P)].

Differential attention remedies both attachment problems and coercive cycles. Positive attention should improve parent–child attachment and generate a warm parent–child relationship. Active ignoring cuts short coercive cycles, and positive attention should decrease the likelihood that they start in the first place. It is particularly important for young children. Individual treatment components related to differential attention are detailed in Chapter 7, Treatment component #1: Differential attention.

Chapter 7: Treatment component #1: Differential attention

Praise

Differential reinforcement

Attending

Therapist praise/rewards

Relationship/rapport building

Online resources

Parenting check up: https://www.parentingcheckup.org/
Brief behavioral intervention materials: https://www.mededportal.org/publication/10376/

Further reading

Barkley, R. A., & Benton, C. M. (2013). *Your defiant child: Eight steps to better behavior.* Guilford Press.

Forehand, R., & Long, N. (2002). *Parenting the strong-willed child: The clinically proven five-week program for parents of two- to six-year-olds* (revised and updated). New York: McGraw-Hill.

Kazdin, A. E. (2009). *The Kazdin method for parenting the defiant child.* Houghton Mifflin Harcourt.

Kazdin, A. E. (2013). *The everyday parenting toolkit: The Kazdin method for easy, step-by-step lasting change for you and your child.* Boston, MA: Mariner.

Webster-Stratton, C., Mostyn, D., & Marie, J. S. (2005). *The Incredible Years: A trouble-shooting guide for parents of children aged 2-8 years.* Seattle, WA: Incredible Years.

***

Effective commands and consistent consequences including rewards

The second evidence-based treatment component comprises logical consequences and reward systems. Logical consequences and reward systems include tangible rewards, commands, monitoring, response cost, goal setting, stimulus control, natural or logical consequences, behavioral contracting, and functional analysis. This evidence-based treatment component can be summed up as giving effective commands and providing consistent consequences for them. This component is also heavily involved in behavioral management training programs with and without a family component (e.g., PMTO, PCIT, Triple P).

Effective commands and consistent consequences can reverse coercive cycles by eliminating the need for repeated requests and threats, as well as decreasing reliance on punishment. Such strategies will increase parental consistency and follow-through. Further, increased use of rewards, to the extent possible, should facilitate a warmer relationship at home and help improve caregiver–child attachment. Research demonstrates that rewards work particularly well for children with callous–unemotional traits. This overarching treatment component is described more thoroughly in Chapter 8, Treatment component #2: Effective commands and consistent consequences including rewards.

Chapter 8: Treatment component #2: Effective commands and consistent consequences including rewards

Tangible rewards

Commands

Monitoring

Response cost

Goal setting

Stimulus control

Natural or logical consequences

Behavioral contracting

Functional analysis

Online resources

Privilege Points application
Parenting check up: https://www.parentingcheckup.org/
Brief behavioral intervention materials: https://www.mededportal.org/publication/10376/

Further reading

Barkley, R. A., & Benton, C. M. (2013). *Your defiant child: Eight steps to better behavior.* Guilford Press.

Forehand, R., & Long, N. (2002). *Parenting the strong-willed child: The clinically proven five-week program for parents of two- to six-year-olds* (revised and updated). New York: McGraw-Hill.

Greene, R. W. (1999). *The explosive child*. HarperCollins World.

Kazdin, A. E. (2009). *The Kazdin method for parenting the defiant child*. Houghton Mifflin Harcourt.

Kazdin, A. E. (2013). *The everyday parenting toolkit: The Kazdin method for easy, step-by-step lasting change for you and your child*. Boston, MA: Mariner.

Webster-Stratton, C., Mostyn, D., & Marie, J. S. (2005). *The Incredible Years: A trouble-shooting guide for parents of children aged 2-8 years*. Seattle, WA: Incredible Years.

***

Time-out

The third evidence-based treatment component is time-out. It only includes one evidence-based treatment component: time-out. Time-out consists of removing the child from a warm, positive environment and in that way serves as a negative punishment strategy. Time-out is typically utilized for highly problematic behaviors such as aggression or rule-breaking and can help disrupt coercive cycles between caregivers and children. This component is also heavily involved in behavioral management training programs with and without a family component (e.g., PMTO, PCIT, Triple P).

Time-out can be used for a few misbehaviors at a time, such as noncompliance or breaking of house rules, including serious misbehavior such as aggression, repeated offenses, and noncompletion of longer tasks. Critically, it should be used sparingly, administered in a calm fashion, and connected with positive attention to those behaviors one wants to see. It this way, it can help short-circuit coercive cycles. Like the previous two chapters, this chapter is particularly important for working with young children. It is described more thoroughly in Chapter 9, Treatment component #3: Time-out.

Chapter 9: Treatment component #3: Time-out

Time-out

Online resources

Parenting check up: https://www.parentingcheckup.org/
Brief behavioral intervention materials: https://www.mededportal.org/publication/10376/

Further reading

Barkley, R. A., & Benton, C. M. (2013). *Your defiant child: Eight steps to better behavior*. Guilford Press.

Forehand, R., & Long, N. (2002). *Parenting the strong-willed child: The clinically proven five-week program for parents of two- to six-year-olds* (revised and updated). New York: McGraw-Hill.

Kazdin, A. E. (2009). *The Kazdin method for parenting the defiant child*. Houghton Mifflin Harcourt.

Kazdin, A. E. (2013). *The everyday parenting toolkit: The Kazdin method for easy, step-by-step lasting change for you and your child.* Boston, MA: Mariner.

Webster-Stratton, C., Mostyn, D., & Marie, J. S. (2005). *The Incredible Years: A trouble-shooting guide for parents of children aged 2-8 years.* Seattle, WA: Incredible Years.

***

Cognitive skills

The fourth evidence-based treatment component is cognitive skills. Cognitive skills include self-monitoring and positively impact social learning. This component consists of anger identification, perspective taking, and problem-solving around strategies to manage anger. This component is heavily involved in cognitive treatments such as anger control training and problem-solving skills training (PSST).

Cognitive skills teach children and adolescents how to cope with anger, accurately appraise and generate alternate appraisals of problem situations through perspective taking, generate more and different possible solutions to the problem, and evaluate the likely and actual consequences of their behavior. These skills facilitate social information processing across numerous situations and can improve child and adolescent relationships with parents, peers, and teachers. Cognitive skills training is often particularly useful for working with adolescents. It is described more thoroughly in Chapter 10, Treatment component #4: Cognitive skills.

Chapter 10: Treatment component #4: Cognitive skills

Cognitive

Self-monitoring

Further reading

Lochman, J. E., Wells, K., & Lenhart, L. A. (2008). *Coping power: Child group facilitator's guide* (Vol. 2). Oxford University Press.

Wells, K., Lochman, J. E., & Lenhart, L. (2008). *Coping power: Parent group facilitator's guide.* Oxford University Press.

***

Problem-solving

The fifth evidence-based treatment component is problem-solving. Problem-solving includes communication skills, family therapy, and modeling. This component consists of teaching parents and children or adolescents problem-solving and communication skills. This component is heavily involved with cognitive treatments such as anger control training and PSST.

Problem-solving teaches parents and adolescents how to utilize perspective taking, generate more and different possible solutions to the problem, agree on a compromise, and evaluate the outcome. It is also important for improving social information processing, both inside and outside the home environment. These skills are particularly important for use with adolescents. These skills are thoroughly covered in Chapter 11, Treatment component #5. problem-solving.

Chapter 11: Treatment component #5: Problem-solving

Problem-solving

Communication skills

Family therapy

Modeling

Further reading

Barkley, R. A., & Robin, A. L. (2014). *Defiant teens: A clinician's manual for assessment and family intervention*. Guilford Publications.

Faber, A., & Mazlish, E. (2012). *How to talk so kids will listen & listen so kids will talk*. Simon and Schuster.

Lochman, J. E., Wells, K., & Lenhart, L. A. (2008). *Coping Power: Child group facilitator's guide* (Vol. 2). Oxford University Press.

Webster-Stratton, C., Mostyn, D., & Marie, J. S. (2005). *The Incredible Years: A trouble-shooting guide for parents of children aged 2-8 years*. Seattle, WA: Incredible Years.

Wells, K., Lochman, J. E., & Lenhart, L. (2008). *Coping power: Parent group facilitator's guide*. Oxford University Press.

***

Other related problem treatment

Chapter 12, Related treatment issues: how to address sleep, toilet training, social skills, and learning problems and when to consider medication for comorbid disorders, addresses cooccurring problems commonly experienced by children with oppositional defiant disorder (ODD), such as developmental, academic, and peer problems with comorbid psychopathology, initially described in Chapter 1, Oppositional defiant disorder dimensions and prediction of later problems. Treatment components covered in this chapter include social skills training and educational support, as well as behavioral skills helpful for treating problems with independent sleep and toilet training. Medication options for comorbid psychopathology are also reviewed in this chapter.

Chapter 12: Related treatment issues: how to address sleep, toilet training, social skills, and learning problems and when to consider medication for comorbid disorders

Social skills training

Educational support

Further reading

Barkley, R. A., & Robin, A. L. (2014). *Defiant teens: A clinician's manual for assessment and family intervention*. Guilford Publications.

Bloomquist, M.L. *Skills training for struggling kids: Promoting your child's behavioral, emotional, academic, and social development*. New York: Guilford.

Webster-Stratton, C., Mostyn, D., & Marie, J. S. (2005). *The Incredible Years: A trouble-shooting guide for parents of children aged 2-8 years*. Seattle, WA: Incredible Years.

***

Interim summary

Evidence-based treatment components can be grouped into the categories of differential attention, effective commands and consistent consequences including rewards, time-out, cognitive skills, problem-solving, and treatment for other related problems, which will each be detailed in subsequent chapters. The next three chapters (Chapters 7–9: differential attention, effective commands and consistent consequences including rewards, and time-out) are most important for young children. The later chapters (Chapter 10: Treatment component #4: Cognitive skills, and Chapter 11: Treatment component #5: Problem-solving: cognitive and problem-solving treatment components) tend to become more important as children move into adolescence. Chapter 12, Related treatment issues: how to address sleep, toilet training, social skills, and learning problems and when to consider medication for comorbid disorders, is particularly relevant for children and adolescents with ODD who have cooccurring problems. These evidence-based components allow therapists to personalize treatment based on an individual child's or adolescent's presenting problems.

Illustration through case examples

One can apply evidence-based treatment components in clinical practice, either in addition to or instead of the packaged treatments reviewed in the last chapter. Our case examples will allow us to examine how this is possible.

***

Luis

Luis is a 4-year-old Latino male. He was referred by his pediatrician for an evaluation after his parents presented complaining about Luis' aggression. Luis only uses one- to two-word phrases to communicate and is difficult to understand. His parents speak Spanish at home and both work long hours at minimum wage jobs. They have five kids total, ages 1, 4, 8, 10, and 12. Luis' parents report that he was born 1 month premature, weighing 4 lb and 3 oz. Luis' mother had severe hypertension toward the end of her pregnancy. Although his motor milestones were reported to be on time, Luis did not say his first words until age 3. He is still not potty trained and sleeps in bed with his parents. Luis' parents complain that he becomes angry and aggressive with minimal provocation. Luis will hit, kick, bite, and throw a tantrum if he does not get his way. He frequently does things that he knows his parents find annoying (such as yelling and running away at the supermarket). He does not comply with adult commands, yelling no and running away. He once ran away in a store parking lot and was almost hit by a car. His parents were worried that social services would be called. Luis' parents are concerned about him starting school next year, given they cannot currently leave him at home with even a babysitter due to his severe misbehavior.

Conceptualization: Luis is exhibiting ODD in the context of speech and language problems and other delays with independent sleep and elimination problems. Luis is the youngest in a large family. His parents are under economic and personal stress, working long hours to provide for the family. Luis was also exposed to a number of prenatal risk factors, including stress during pregnancy, hypertension, prematurity, and low birth weight. He also experienced developmental delays, particularly with language. The high stress at home, large number of siblings, his parent's limited time, and Luis' language delays have led to coercive cycles between Luis and his parents. He may have difficulty communicating his needs and understanding parental requests. He may also have difficulty obtaining parental attention using appropriate strategies. Therefore he often resorts to aggression, tantrums, and noncompliance. He has been delayed with potty training and refuses to sleep independently.

Personalization of treatment tips: Given the number of family stressors, a family level intervention with a focus on behavioral skills and addressing sleep and elimination issues would probably be best. Speech and language evaluation and treatment with consideration of the family's bilingualism will also be critical. A consultation with a pediatrician regarding elimination issues will be important. Attention-deficit/Hyperactivity disorder (ADHD) will also need to be considered for impulsive behaviors.

Ideal treatment

PCIT or Enhanced Triple P

Back-up treatment possibilities

PMTO

Standard Triple P

Helping the noncompliant child

Useful treatment components

Praise

Differential reinforcement

Relationship/rapport building

Tangible rewards

Commands

Monitoring

Response cost

Goal setting

Stimulus control

Natural or logical consequences

Behavioral contracting

Functional analysis

Time-out

Online resources

Parenting check up: https://www.parentingcheckup.org/
Brief behavioral intervention materials: https://www.mededportal.org/publication/10376/
Privilege Points application

Further reading

Barkley, R. A., & Robin, A. L. (2014). *Defiant teens: A clinician's manual for assessment and family intervention*. Guilford Publications.

Forehand, R., & Long, N. (2002). *Parenting the Strong-Willed Child: The Clinically Proven Five-Week Program for Parents of Two- to Six-Year-Olds* (revised and updated). New York: McGraw-Hill.

Greene, R. W. (1999). *The explosive child*. HarperCollins World.

Kazdin, A. E. (2009). *The Kazdin method for parenting the defiant child*. Houghton Mifflin Harcourt.

Kazdin, A. E. (2013). *The everyday parenting toolkit: The Kazdin method for easy, step-by-step lasting change for you and your child*. Boston, MA: Mariner.

Webster-Stratton, C., Mostyn, D., & Marie, J. S. (2005). *The Incredible Years: A trouble-shooting guide for parents of children aged 2-8 years*. Seattle, WA: Incredible Years.

***

Frederick

Frederick is a 10-year-old African American male. His mother presented with him to the emergency room when his school called her to come and pick him up during the middle of the day after he threatened to "gut" another 10-year-old boy in his class. The school reported that the provocation for this incident was that Frederick became angry when the other boy asked him to share his colored pencil. More concerning, Frederick was found to have had a knife hidden in his schoolbag and indicated that he planned to use it on the other boy, so that the other boy would "get what was coming to him." The school has suspended Frederick until his mother obtains treatment for him. Frederick has a history of problems with peers. He has few friends and his peers report being scared of him. Frederick frequently, graphically threatens his peers following minor disagreements, telling them he will "cut them open," he "wants to explore their insides," and he will "show them their hearts." He is known to hold a grudge and will wait for a peer following a disagreement after school, threatening them and saying he will hurt them. Frederick lives with his mother, who is single. His biological father has been in jail for armed robbery since Frederick was born. His mother is a mortician with little family in the area. Frederick often spends his afternoons largely unsupervised at the morgue. Frederick's mother acknowledges that she is sometimes scared of him. He reportedly does not listen to her, often argues with her, and she is at a loss as to how to discipline him. Frederick's mother indicated that he has always been difficult to parent. She is worried because his school is insisting that she seek some kind of treatment for Frederick; otherwise, they have said they will expel him.

Conceptualization: Frederick is exhibiting ODD with high callous–unemotional traits. Frederick may have a genetic predisposition toward conduct problems and callous–unemotional traits in particular given that his father is currently serving time in jail for armed robbery, and Frederick is described as vindictive and engaging in proactive or instrumental forms of aggression that are premeditated. This genetic predisposition may particularly increase his risk for conduct problems given family stressors such as an absent father and little social support. In addition, Frederick's mother spends long hours at work, which means she has little time to supervise him. His exposure to dead bodies seems to be increasing his callousness and detachment toward others. Finally, Frederick does not get along with his peers and is isolated at school. Perhaps most critically, Frederick and his mother do not have a warm and loving relationship, and he is likely insecurely attached. She acknowledges that she is sometimes scared of him and is at a loss as to how to discipline him.

Personalization of treatment tips: Given the severity of Frederick's current behaviors and the family's lack of social support, an intensive, community-level intervention is likely to be best. It will be critical to involve the school and neighborhood to provide increased monitoring of Frederick's behavior while his mother is working and to facilitate peer friendships. Frederick's mother will also need consultation about how to build more warmth and affection into their relationship. The use of a reward system to reinforce appropriate behaviors will be critical, given the presence of callous—unemotional traits. Frederick will need to be assessed for CD.

Ideal treatment

Multisystemic therapy

Back-up treatment possibilities

Enhanced Triple P

Useful treatment components

Praise

Differential reinforcement

Relationship/rapport building

Tangible rewards!!!

Online resources

Parenting check up: https://www.parentingcheckup.org/
Brief behavioral intervention materials: https://www.mededportal.org/publication/10376/
Privilege Points application

Further reading

Barkley, R. A., & Robin, A. L. (2014). *Defiant teens: A clinician's manual for assessment and family intervention*. Guilford Publications.

Forehand, R., & Long, N. (2002). *Parenting the strong-willed child: The clinically proven five-week program for parents of two- to six-year-olds* (revised and updated). New York: McGraw-Hill.

Kazdin, A. E. (2009). *The Kazdin method for parenting the defiant child*. Houghton Mifflin Harcourt.

Kazdin, A. E. (2013). *The Everyday Parenting Toolkit: The Kazdin method for easy, step-by-step lasting change for you and your child*. Boston, MA: Mariner.

Webster-Stratton, C., Mostyn, D., & Marie, J. S. (2005). *The Incredible Years: A trouble-shooting guide for parents of children aged 2-8 years*. Seattle, WA: Incredible Years.

***

Anna

Anna is a 15-year-old Caucasian female whose parents present with concerns about possible drug use, sexting, and promiscuous sex. Anna has been diagnosed with depression and has been taking antidepressants since age 13. She was described as irritable and easily annoyed most of the time. She acknowledges frequent marijuana use with friends and being sexually active with several males. She has been grounded for the last 2 weeks after she sent a naked picture to one of these males, and her parents were informed by a friend's mother, who saw the picture on her daughter's Snapchat. Anna acknowledges that her current friend group has not been the best influence. She complains that the girls are all catty and talk about her behind her back. She reports engaging in sexting or sex, as well as impulsivity, without a lot of forethought about the consequences, or while under the influence of alcohol. She indicated that she has no desire to listen to her parents and often argues with them about curfews and rules. She justified her behavior by reporting that she was bullied extensively in grade school and feels the need to fit in with her peers whatever the cost.

Conceptualization: Anna exhibits ODD in the context of a preexisting depression diagnosis. She is also at risk for emerging substance use problems with marijuana and alcohol. She has a history of peer problems including bullying through covert aggression (e.g., rumors). Through these experiences, she seems to have developed faulty social information processing in that she almost always attributes hostile intentions to her peers, and she impulsively engages in inappropriate reactions such as substance use and sexting. She furthermore does not seem to have learned to evaluate the negative consequences of her actions. Her parents, to date, have been largely ineffective at monitoring or disciplining her to obtain desired behaviors.

Personalization of treatment tips: Given Anna's depression and the prominent role peers are playing in her problems, a social learning approach would probably be most effective. It will also be important to involve Anna's parents in the treatment to facilitate a more effective problem-solving approach to setting rules and consequences for her. Better monitoring of Anna's behavior, including use of substances, will be critical. Assessment for ADHD for Anna's impulsive behaviors may also be helpful. A psychiatric consultation regarding the effectiveness of Anna's antidepressant at its current dosage for managing depressive symptomatology will also be important.

Ideal treatment

PSST

Back-up treatment possibilities

Cognitive-behavioral therapy

Assertiveness training

Rational–emotive mental health program

Useful treatment components

Cognitive

Self-monitoring

Problem-solving

Communication skills

Family therapy

Modeling

Further reading

Faber, A., & Mazlish, E. (2012). *How to talk so kids will listen & listen so kids will talk.* Simon and Schuster.

Lochman, J. E., Wells, K., & Lenhart, L. A. (2008). *Coping Power: Child group facilitator's guide* (Vol. 2). Oxford University Press.

Webster-Stratton, C., Mostyn, D., & Marie, J. S. (2005). *The Incredible Years: A trouble-shooting guide for parents of children aged 2-8 years.* Seattle, WA: Incredible Years.

Wells, K., Lochman, J. E., & Lenhart, L. (2008). *Coping Power: Parent group facilitator's guide.* Oxford University Press.

***

Conclusion

Evidence-based treatment components include differential attention, effective commands and consistent consequences including rewards, time-out, cognitive skills, problem-solving, and other related problem treatment. Differential attention, effective commands and consistent consequences including rewards, and time-out are most important for young children, while cognitive skills and problem-solving are more important for adolescents. Treatment for other related problems can be important for children with cooccurring problems. A component-based approach can be useful for tailoring treatment to individual child and family needs.

Future directions

There are a number of new, short treatments being developed based on evidence-based treatment components. One is Brief Behavioral Intervention (Axelrad, Butler, Dempsey, & Chapman, 2013; Axelrad, Garland, & Love, 2009). Another is the Parenting Check Up (McGoron, Hvizdos, Bocknek, Montgomery, & Ondersma, 2018; McGoron & Ondersma, 2015). These are both referenced above as online resources and described further in subsequent chapters. Unfortunately, the development of online resources continues to lag behind in-person and text resources, and it is hoped that this area will rapidly expand in the near future. Each evidence-based treatment component introduced above will now be detailed individually in the subsequent chapters and links to online resources provided. Read on for the short clinician's guide to each evidence-based treatment component.

References

Axelrad, M. E., Butler, A. M., Dempsey, J., & Chapman, S. G. (2013). Treatment effectiveness of a brief behavioral intervention for preschool disruptive behavior. *Journal of Clinical Psychology in Medical Settings*, *20*(3), 323–332.

Axelrad, M. E., Garland, B. H., & Love, K. B. (2009). Brief behavioral intervention for young children with disruptive behaviors. *Journal of Clinical Psychology in Medical Settings*, *16* (3), 263–269.

Barkley, R. A., & Benton, C. M. (2013). *Your defiant child: Eight steps to better behavior*. Guilford Press.

Barkley, R. A., & Robin, A. L. (2014). *Defiant teens: A clinician's manual for assessment and family intervention*. Guilford Publications.

Bloomquist, M.L. (2012). *Skills training for struggling kids: Promoting your child's behavioral, emotional, academic, and social development*. New York: Guilford.

Chorpita, B. F., & Daleiden, E. L. (2009). *CAMHD biennial report: Effective psychosocial interventions for youth with behavioral and emotional needs*. Honolulu, HI: Hawaii Department of Health, Child and Mental Health Division.

Faber, A., & Mazlish, E. (2012). *How to talk so kids will listen & listen so kids will talk*. New York: Simon and Schuster.

Forehand, R., & Long, N. (2002). *Parenting the strong-willed child: The clinically proven five-week program for parents of two- to six-year-olds*. New York: McGraw-Hill. (revised and updated).

Greene, R. W. (1999). *The explosive child*. HarperCollins World.

Kazdin, A. E. (2009). *The Kazdin method for parenting the defiant child*. Houghton Mifflin Harcourt.

Kazdin, A. E. (2013). *The everyday parenting toolkit: The Kazdin method for easy, step-by-step lasting change for you and your child*. Boston, MA: Mariner.

Lochman, J. E., Wells, K., & Lenhart, L. A. (2008). *Coping power: Child group facilitator's guide* (Vol. 2). Oxford University Press.

McGoron, L., Hvizdos, E., Bocknek, E. L., Montgomery, E., & Ondersma, S. J. (2018). Feasibility of Internet-based parent training for low-income parents of young children. *Children and Youth Services Review*, *84*, 198–205.

McGoron, L., & Ondersma, S. J. (2015). Reviewing the need for technological and other expansions of evidence-based parent training for young children. *Children and Youth Services Review*, *59*, 71–83.

Webster-Stratton, C., Mostyn, D., & Marie, J. S. (2005). *The Incredible Years: A troubleshooting guide for parents of children aged 2-8 years*. Seattle, WA: Incredible Years.

Wells, K., Lochman, J. E., & Lenhart, L. (2008). *Coping power: Parent group facilitator's guide*. Oxford University Press.

7

CHAPTER

Treatment component #1: Differential attention

The first main treatment component is differential attention. In a nutshell, differential attention consists of the use of positive attention and active ignoring. In regard to our last chapter's evidence-based treatment components, it includes:

- praise
- *differential reinforcement*
- *attending*
- therapist praise/rewards
- relationship/rapport building

It is heavily involved in all behavioral management training programs. Differential attention remedies both attachment problems and coercive cycles. Positive attention should improve parent–child attachment and generate a warm parent–child relationship. Active ignoring cuts short coercive cycles, and positive attention should decrease the likelihood that they start in the first place. It is particularly important for young children. It should be noted that information in this chapter comes from the online and text resources cited at the end of this chapter.

The Clinician's Guide to Oppositional Defiant Disorder. DOI: https://doi.org/10.1016/B978-0-12-815682-7.00007-0

TABLE 7.1 Differential attention overview.

1. Institute a practice playtime
2. Increase use of labeled praise
3. Institute active ignoring of attention-seeking behaviors

Differential attention overview

Table 7.1 lists an overview of differential attention skills. Differential attention should help parents maximize use of their attention to make all other discipline strategies more effective. Use of positive attention is a critical foundation for showing children what they *should* be doing (e.g., compliance). It also serves as a warm foundation that makes all other discipline strategies, including punishment, more effective. Use of strategic ignoring, on top of this warm foundation, provides a very clear message about what behaviors parents do not want to see (e.g., tantrums) and what does *not* generate warm, positive attention from parents.

Practice playtime

First, clinicians should encourage parents to begin to practice their differential attention skills using a practice playtime, as described in Table 7.2. Such a playtime allows parents to practice being a play therapist and increase positive time with their child, enhancing their relationship. This playtime also provides a structured practice time for parents to work on their attending skills. Improvement in use of positive attention will greatly enhance the power of their other discipline strategies.

To engage in practice playtime, parents first need to try to set aside some one-on-one time with their child. About 10 minutes a day is ideal. This time should not be contingent on good behavior, and it should not be taken away as a punishment for bad behavior. Second, parents or the child should choose a task that allows both of them to interact freely without following rules. For example, ideal tasks are usually any type of free play activity such as playing with blocks, LEGOs, dolls, or doing art projects. Parents should stay away from screens, games with rules, or complicated design tasks such as LEGO structures where the parent might be tempted to instruct or give commands. Instead, parents or children should pick something in which the child can lead the play with no problem.

TABLE 7.2 Guidelines for practice playtime.

Special time play

1. *Set aside 15–20 min each day to have special time with your child.* It is helpful to have a consistent time each day so they know when to expect special time.
2. *No other children are to be involved in special time.* If you are the only caregiver available and you have other children, do special time during the other child's nap or when they are involved in other play.
3. *Relax!* Casually watch what your child is doing for a few minutes and then join in when it feels appropriate. Do not do special time when you are upset, very busy, or preoccupied and you cannot pay undivided attention to your child. Do not watch TV at the same time, answer the phone, or read the newspaper.
4. *After watching your child play for a short time, begin to describe out loud what your child is doing.* This is done to show that you find your child's play interesting. Your words should be descriptive and action oriented. You are the sportscaster.
5. *Ask no questions and give no commands.* This is very difficult but extremely important during special time. Special time is not a time for teaching; it is *child-directed* play
6. *Occasionally praise your child and give positive feedback about behavior.* Be accurate and honest. For instance, "I like how you rebuilt that tall tower after it fell."
7. *If your child starts to misbehave, tell them that special time will not continue unless they keep the blocks on the ground, etc.* If the child continues to misbehave after you have removed your attention from them for about 1 min, tell them that if they continue misbehaving, special time is over. If the behavior continues, end special time for the day.
8. *Never take special time away as a punishment for earlier behavior or use special time as a reward.*

Suggested toys for special time

- Construction toys
  - Building blocks
  - LEGOs (age appropriate size)
  - Duplos
  - Tinkertoys
  - Lincoln Logs
- Dollhouse with people
- Transportation toys (cars and trucks)
- Art supplies
  - Play-Doh
  - Crayons and paper

Toys to avoid

- Toys that encourage rough or aggressive play like bats, balls, guns
- Toys that have preset rules like board games and card games
- Activities that require limit-setting like paints or scissors
- Any activity in front of a computer or television screen

During these 10 minutes a day, clinicians encourage the parent to try out some new ways of interacting with the child that will help them improve their positive attending skills. Clinicians should encourage parents to:

- reflect
- imitate
- describe
- be enthusiastic
- use labeled praise

Parents should rephrase and reflect things the child says or imitate what they are doing physically. For example, if the child picks up a block, then the parent picks up a block. It will sound like:

- You are stacking the red block on the blue block.
- You are cuddling your doll.
- You are coloring with the purple crayon.

When the parent sees something they like—such as persistence, quiet play, or neatness—they should feel free to verbally note it and praise it. If there are certain problem behaviors (e.g., being loud, throwing objects) that the parent wants to eliminate, they should try praising the opposite (e.g., playing quietly, keeping objects on the ground).

Importantly, during this time, the parent should stay away from:

- commands/teaching
- questions
- negative comments like criticism

These 10 minutes a day give children some free time away from commands/teaching, questions, and negative comments, as well as help children's self-esteem and language development.

So, a parent should *not* make statements like this during this time:

- Let's build a tower. (command/teaching)
- What should we do with our dolls? (question)
- You're coloring outside the lines. (criticism)

The reason that parents should use this seemingly contrived style of interaction with children is because it will increase positivity in their relationship with their child. Research indicates that, for every one negative comment a parent makes about their child's behavior, there should be at least three positive or neutral comments made toward the child. Even if the parent feels like they cannot make many more positive comments given their child's negative behavior, neutral narration comments can help. Furthermore, making the home environment more positive will make all the other strategies discussed more effective.

Increasing positive attention

This practice time is also key to increasing parental use of positive attention. As shown in Table 7.3, the key aspects of positive attention that make it effective at increasing positive child behaviors are:

- specific
- immediate
- frequent

It is important to communicate what exactly the child is doing right by using labeled praise. If a parent does a good job regularly providing positive attention to their child, the child will work for that praise. But only if the child knows what exactly he/she should do. Further, praising what he/she is doing specifically will communicate exactly what the child can do to earn praise.

Finally, the parent should praise as frequently as possible and try to avoid criticism. Differential attention consists of increasing positive attention, including labeled praise, as described above. Increasing positive attention will make the home environment warmer and more positive and communicate to the child exactly what behaviors parents want to see more. In this way, it is a positive reinforcement strategy. Just as importantly, however, increasing positive attention makes the other part of differential attention—active ignoring—more effective and noticeable. This is because ignoring is negative punishment strategy, and it works only when parents remove their typically warm and positive attention to decrease misbehavior.

Use of strategic ignoring

In tandem with increased use of positive attention, parents should work to ignore behaviors they want to decrease. Nondangerous attention-seeking behaviors are most quickly extinguished by ignoring. Behaviors that are extremely annoying are usually attention-seeking. Some common examples include:

- tantrums
- whining
- yelling
- disrespect

A few important points about ignoring are listed in Table 7.4. Ignoring needs to be:

- immediate
- obvious
- consistent
- powerful

TABLE 7.3 Positive attention.

Increasing positive attention
Children behave in ways to get attention from others. Providing lots of positive attention is a powerful way to teach children how to behave and to let your child know that you enjoy when he/she behaves well. Praising children when they behave is also an important way to help them feel good about themselves.
Steps to giving positive attention
1. *Make positive attention specific.* Tell your child exactly what he/she did that you liked. Example: Billy, you picked up your toys right away when I asked you. It makes me proud when you follow the rules. 2. *Give positive attention right away.* Give your child positive attention while the good behavior is happening and/or right after a good behavior occurs. 3. *Avoid criticism.* When your child learns something new, he/she needs lots of positive attention. First, tell them what they did right. Then, help them with the part they had trouble with. 4. *Catch your child being good.* Watch for times when your child is "being good" and praise them immediately. 5. *Praise frequently.* This allows your children to get used to what you sound like when you are proud of them, and how to work for it.

TABLE 7.4 Active ignoring.

Ignoring misbehavior
Rationale
When children do not get enough positive attention for behaving in an obedient, pleasing way, they learn that a sure way to get attention is to behave in a disobedient, displeasing way.
When parents replace their attention to displeasing behavior with a brief period of ignoring, they signal to children that they must behave appropriately to get attention.
Ignoring is appropriate for minor, annoying behaviors.
Steps to effective ignoring
1. *Ignore immediately.* As soon as your child starts to behave in a displeasing way, immediately stop giving attention. 2. *Ignore consistently.* To teach your child that your attention is only available when his/her behavior is pleasing, ignore the displeasing behavior whenever it occurs. Practice using only one behavior at a time. 3. *Make ignoring obvious.* Make sure your child gets the message that you are ignoring due to a displeasing behavior. Walk away, start a conversation with another person, refuse to answer questions, get engrossed in your phone. Also, remove all competing activities. If a child is watching TV, playing ball, etc., they will not notice ignoring. 4. *Make ignoring powerful.* Taking away your attention is effective only if the major portion of the attention you give your child is positive. 5. *Attend* the moment the behavior you are ignoring ceases and is replaced by a positive or neutral behavior.

The child should immediately and unambiguously know that their parent is ignoring their behavior. To do this, ignoring may need to be overexaggerated. Parents may need to turn completely away, for example. Parents may also need to make sure they always respond to the behavior like that. They also *must* be ready to stay strong and follow through.

Ignored attention-seeking behaviors usually get worse before they get better. This is called an extinction burst. For this reason, ignoring should start at home or in another environment where parents feel comfortable dealing with extreme behaviors such as yelling and all-out tantrums. Also, parents should only start ignoring if they are certain they can follow through. The worst thing one can do is start ignoring and then stop when behaviors get really bad (e.g., screaming). That only teaches a child to escalate behaviors more quickly next time. If the parent does not feel like they are in a good spot (physical, mental, or otherwise) to be able to ignore all the way through the worst of the behavior, it is better not to ignore at all. Instead, the parent should give a consequence. If the child becomes aggressive or begins to engage in a dangerous behavior while the parent is ignoring, the parent should handle that in the manner they usually do (e.g., give a consequence). How to handle aggression will be covered more comprehensively in the next two chapters.

Summary

Overall, the evidence-based component of differential attention consists of practice playtime, increased positive attention, and use of strategic ignoring. Practice playtime allows parents to practice their use of positive attention, which will communicate to their child the behaviors they want to see and create a warmer family environment. Strategic ignoring should be used for attention-seeking (but nondangerous) behaviors that parents want to diminish. Differential attention will magnify the power of all other discipline strategies.

Case example

Luis

Luis is a 4-year-old Latino male. He was referred by his pediatrician for an evaluation after his parents presented complaining about Luis' aggression. Luis only uses one- to two-word phrases to communicate and is difficult to understand. His parents speak Spanish at home and both work long hours at minimum wage jobs. They have five kids total, ages 1, 4, 8, 10, and 12. Luis' parents report that he was born 1 month premature, weighing 4 lb and 3 oz. Luis' mother had severe hypertension toward the end of her pregnancy. Although his motor milestones were reported to be on time, Luis did not say his first words until age 3. He is still not potty trained and sleeps in bed with his parents. Luis' parents complain that he becomes angry and aggressive with minimal provocation. Luis will hit, kick, bite, and throw a tantrum if he does not get his way. He frequently does things that he knows his parents find annoying (such as yelling and running away at the supermarket). He does not comply with adult commands, yelling no and running away. He once ran away in a store parking lot and was almost hit by a car. His parents were worried that social services would be called. Luis' parents are concerned about him starting school next year, given they cannot currently leave him at home with even a babysitter due to his severe misbehavior.

Conceptualization: Luis is exhibiting oppositional-defiant disorder in the context of speech and language problems and other delays with independent sleep and elimination problems. Luis is the youngest in a large family. His parents are under economic and personal stress, working long hours to provide for the family. Luis was also exposed to a number of prenatal risk factors, including stress during pregnancy, hypertension, prematurity, and low birth weight. He also experienced developmental delays, particularly with language. The high stress at home, large number of siblings, his parent's limited time, and Luis' language delays have led to coercive cycles between Luis and his parents. He may have difficulty communicating his needs and understanding parental requests. He may also have difficulty obtaining parental attention using appropriate strategies. Therefore he often resorts to aggression, tantrums, and noncompliance. He has been delayed with potty training and refuses to sleep independently.

Personalization of treatment tips: Given the number of family stressors, a family level intervention with a focus on behavioral skills and addressing sleep and elimination issues would probably be best. Speech and language evaluation and treatment with consideration of the family's bilingualism will also be critical. A consultation with a pediatrician regarding elimination issues will be important. Attention-deficit/Hyperactivity disorder will also need to be considered for impulsive behaviors.

Ideal treatment

Parent–child interaction therapy or enhanced Positive Parenting Program (Triple P)

Back-up treatment possibilities

Parent management training Oregon model

Standard Triple P

Helping the noncompliant child

Useful treatment components

Praise

Differential reinforcement

Relationship/Rapport building

Tangible rewards

Commands

Monitoring

Response cost

Goal setting

Stimulus control

Natural or logical consequences

Behavioral contracting

Functional analysis

Time-out

Practice playtime

Differential attention would be a particularly good strategy to use in Luis' case. When introducing differential attention to Luis' parents, I would say something like the following:

> *I know you came here hoping for discipline strategies, and that is definitely part of this treatment. However, what most people do not realize is that discipline is most effective in the context of a warm relationship. This warm relationship will make all your discipline techniques more effective, which means you will not have to use discipline as often. Further, it will be easier to follow through consistently if you are not always having to discipline. So, this first part of treatment is actually the foundation for the rest of treatment, which includes effective discipline.*
>
> *But today, essentially, I am going to teach you how to be a play therapist. You could come in weekly and pay me a lot of money to do this with your child, but instead I am going to teach you how to do this with your child so you can go home and be your child's own play therapist a little bit each day, every day, all week long.*

But because most parents cannot relate to being a play therapist, I also like to explain that these skills are the same skills used by good bosses:

> *We've all had bad bosses, right? The boss who is always nagging, complaining, and making you stay late to fix your mistakes without ever giving you praise or something positive, like a raise, to work toward. In here, we are going to teach you skills so that your child views you as a good boss: a boss*

who is overall positive, who generally thinks they are doing a good job, and who is also always encouraging them to improve and learn to do better, while noticing and rewarding such improvements.

Now, to do this—especially with a child who has been acting out, just like with a challenging employee—will take some time and practice. So, to allow you time to practice these skills, I am going to ask you to try to set aside about 10 minutes a day to practice with your child one-on-one the differential attention skills I am about to teach you. These are the skills that will make you a more effective and positive "boss" to your child.

A clinician should provide parents with several guidelines for how to best practice these skills. First of all, I suggest parents try to set aside some time one-on-one with their child. About 10 minutes a day is ideal. This time should not be contingent on good behavior, and it should not be taken away as a punishment for bad behavior. Second, parents or the child should choose a task that allows both of them to interact freely without following rules. For example, ideal tasks are usually any type of free play activity such as blocks, LEGOs, playing with dolls, or art. I encourage parents to stay away from screens, games with rules, or complicated design tasks such as LEGO structures where the parent might be tempted to instruct or give commands. Instead, parents or children should pick something in which the child can lead the play with no problem.

Clinicians should encourage the parent to try out some new ways of interacting with the child during these 10 minutes a day that will help them improve their positive attending skills. Clinicians should tell the parents what we want them to do:

- reflect
- imitate
- describe
- be enthusiastic
- use labeled praise

Parents should rephrase and reflect things the child says or imitate what they are doing physically. For example, if the child picks up a block, then the parent should pick up a block. The parent should say, for example:

- You are stacking the red block on the blue block.
- You are cuddling your doll.
- You are coloring with the purple crayon.

I always tell parents that if it feels a little funny, then it is probably right! It is also an acquired skill. It takes practice until it becomes comfortable. I like to tell parents to channel their inner "sportscaster." If they feel like they are giving a play-by-play of their children's activities, then that is exactly it!

This is also an excellent time to work on giving labeled praise, which we cover in detail below. But, in this context, when the parent sees something they like—such as persistence, quiet play, or neatness—they should feel free to verbally note it and praise it. If there are certain problem behaviors (e.g., being loud, throwing objects) that the parent wants to eliminate, they should try praising the opposite (e.g., playing quietly, keeping objects on the ground).

Importantly, during this time, we tell parents to totally refrain from:

- commands/teaching
- questions
- negative comments like criticism

Now, I often tell parents that there is a time and a place for those things, but what we often do not realize as adults is how often we spend teaching and questioning our children. Unfortunately, each of these undoubtedly valuable activities takes its toll on children. It is tiring to always be responding to questions, learning new things, or being corrected. These 10 minutes a day give children some free time away from this, as well as help children's self-esteem and language development. Further, I find that refraining from teaching, questioning, and criticizing helps me, as a parent, realize how often I am otherwise engaged in these activities, which helps me reduce them (just like recording what we eat helps reduce food intake).

So, during this time, a parent should *not* make statements such as these:

- Let's build a tower. (command/teaching)
- What should we do with our dolls? (question)
- You're coloring outside the lines. (criticism)

I tell parents that the reason to use this seemingly contrived style of interaction with children is because it will increase positivity in their relationship with their child. Research indicates that, for every one negative comment a parent makes about their child's behavior, there should be at least three positive or neutral comments made toward the child. Even if the parent feels like they cannot make many more positive comments given their child's negative behavior, neutral narration comments can help. Furthermore, making the home environment more positive will make all the other strategies we discuss later more effective.

Increasing positive attention

I tell parents that this practice time is also key to increasing their use of positive attention. I tell parents that, to be effective, positive attention should be:

- specific
- immediate
- frequent

If the parent can "catch their child being good" (e.g., sharing with a sibling, playing quietly while the parent is on the phone), they should try to notice it right away. In fact, most kids usually start off being good, but if this goes unnoticed (and it often does because—let's face it—adults are often too busy for their own good), children will often switch over to misbehavior. Many parents do not understand why that is, and so I often use an example from adult life.

If you were having an argument with your partner, which would you choose:

- being ignored completely as if you do not exist
- being firmly talked to or even yelled at

Most people would say they would prefer the argument to being totally ignored. Kids are like that too, but even more so. A child will choose positive attention over negative attention, but they will always, always, *always* choose negative attention over no attention at all. So try to make it a habit to catch the child being good whenever possible. Given that most children will be good initially, I try to make it a habit to wait a few minutes to start any activity I am doing (e.g., cooking, a phone call) after I set my child up with an activity to allow for time to praise her for playing quietly. This minimizes the likelihood that I will get distracted before communicating to her the behavior I want to see. However, even in this case, it is still important to periodically praise good behavior, especially with young children. If too much time goes by with absolutely no attention, the child will switch over to their old standby, negative attention-seeking behavior such as whining, yelling, tantrums, or destruction/aggression.

In the scenario above, as well as during the parent–child practice playtime described above, it is important to communicate what exactly the child is doing right by using labeled praise. We call this special form of praise labeled praise to distinguish from the types of praise we usually provide, which is often more generic. For example, parents often say things like "Good job!" or "You are so smart." But what is the child doing particularly well? If the child is coloring, is it coloring skills that you are praising? Or are you praising the fact that he/she is playing quietly while the parent is on the phone? If it is the latter, make sure that is clear.

I explain that if a parent does a good job regularly providing positive attention to their child, the child will work for that praise. But only if the child knows what exactly he/she should do. Further, praising what he/she is doing specifically will communicate exactly what the child can do to earn your praise. This also trains persistence and diligence, qualities that are more important than innate abilities like intelligence. Do you want your child to believe he/she is just smart, or a hard worker who can continue to do better and better? If the latter, then labeled praise is particularly important.

Finally, praise as frequently as possible and try to avoid criticism. For example, do not tell a child that they are doing an excellent job sitting still and that you do not understand why they cannot always be like that. That final criticism sours all the prior praise.

So, differential attention consists of increasing positive attention, including labeled praise. Increasing positive attention should make the home environment warmer and more positive and communicate to the child exactly what behaviors parents want to see more often. In this way, it is a positive reinforcement strategy. Just as importantly, however, I stress that increasing positive attention makes the other part of differential attention—active ignoring—more effective and noticeable. This is because ignoring is a negative punishment strategy, and it works only when parents are removing their typically warm and positive attention to decrease a misbehavior.

Active ignoring

When introducing active ignoring to parents, I usually say something like the following:

> *Based on the same principle of praising behaviors you want to increase, you should ignore behaviors you want to decrease. Ignoring works best if most of your attention toward your child is positive, which is why we spent so much time talking about praise. Now, obviously, there are some behaviors you cannot ignore, such as serious misbehaviors that are a threat to safety or harmful to others (e.g., aggression). However, nondangerous attention-seeking behaviors are most quickly extinguished by ignoring.*
>
> *How can you tell if a behavior is attention-seeking? Usually by how much it gets on your nerves. And your child is the expert at knowing what is most frustrating to you. Behaviors that make you want to rip your hair out are usually attention-seeking. Some common examples include:*
>
> - *tantrums*
> - *whining*
> - *yelling*
> - *disrespect*
>
> *It may make you cringe to think of your child getting no consequence for these misbehaviors, but think about this as part of the entire parenting package. You, as a parent, have limited time and resources for discipline. Save your discipline for serious, or targeted, goals. The more frequently you try to dish it out, the less likely you are to be consistent. And as soon as you start being inconsistent by not following through, the more quickly your child learns that you are not serious and can be safely ignored.*

There are a few important points about ignoring that I stress to parents. Ignoring needs to be:

- immediate
- obvious
- consistent
- powerful

The child should immediately and unambiguously know that their parent is ignoring their behavior. To do this, ignoring may need to be overexaggerated. Parents may need to turn completely away, for example. Parents may also need to make sure that they always respond to the behavior in this way. They also *must* be ready to stay strong and follow through.

A note here, however: ignored attention-seeking behaviors usually get worse before they get better. This is called an extinction burst. To explain this to parents, I usually use the following example:

> *Think about when you go to the dry cleaner. Typically, if no one is at the counter when you arrive, you ring the bell and someone comes out. What happens if, one day, you ring the bell, and no one comes out? Your first thought is to ring the bell again, right? Perhaps more than once? However, what if you rang the bell several times over the course of 5 minutes or so? You would eventually give up, right? This is exactly what your child will do, although they may not learn their lesson as quickly as you, unfortunately.*

For this reason, I always tell parents that they should start ignoring at home or in another environment where they feel comfortable dealing with extreme behaviors such as yelling and all-out tantrums. Also, they should only start ignoring if they are certain they can follow through. The worst thing one can do is start ignoring and then stop when behaviors get really bad (e.g., screaming). That only teaches a child to escalate behaviors more quickly next time. If the parent does not feel like they are in a good spot (physical, mental, or otherwise) to be able to ignore all the way through the worst of it, it is better not to ignore at all. Instead, the parent should give a consequence. Finally, what if the child becomes aggressive during ignoring? For now, I tell parents to just handle this behavior the way they usually would. How to best handle aggression will be covered more comprehensively in the next two chapters.

How to handle common problems

There are several common problems that arise when teaching differential attention to parents. One is that parents sometimes have problems identifying specific positive behaviors to look for that are the opposite of the problematic, negative behaviors. For example, parents will complain about tantrums, but have difficulty figuring out what behavior they would prefer to see instead (often, keeping quiet). Or parents will complain about aggression, but have a difficult time instructing their child on what they would like to see instead (and are also sometimes modeling bad coping skills themselves, such as yelling or throwing things). For example, when a child is being aggressive, it is far more effective to tell them to keep their hands to themselves, or use their words, instead of the instinctive "stop hitting!" It often helps if parents take a few minutes to write down or discuss problem behaviors and what they want to see in place of those behaviors so they can instruct more clearly in the moment when these problem behaviors are actually occurring, rather than just reacting to the problem behavior.

Another very common difficulty faced by parents is prioritizing negative behaviors. Parents often come in with a two-page laundry list of problem behaviors. It is impossible to tackle all of these behaviors at the same time no matter how undesirable each and every misbehavior is. Parents must prioritize this list of misbehaviors. I often recommend prioritizing those behaviors that can be harmful to their child or others (e.g., running off or aggression) or those behaviors that are most frustrating to the parents (e.g., tantrums). Parents should identify, at most, three to four problem behaviors to actively work on and leave the remainder on their list to prioritize once the most problematic behaviors are greatly diminished and do not need a great deal of attention anymore. I always stress to parents that we will eventually make it to all the behaviors on their list, but behaviors will decrease most quickly if they are able to focus on providing very consistent discipline for a small number of particular problems. Not focusing on most of the child's behavior at once also allows the parent to maintain a more positive environment at home so the child is not feeling constantly criticized.

Some parents have a difficult time ignoring without explaining to their child why they are ignoring. I tell such parents that it is okay to give a very brief (one sentence maximum) explanation of why they are ignoring at the very beginning. For example, they can say "I am ignoring until you can speak to me in a quiet voice." However, explanations are usually less effective than actions, and it is important not to engage after that first very short explanation.

And finally—remember that with ignoring, attention-seeking behaviors will escalate before they improve. Wait it out and give it a chance. If parents spend a week giving this strategy a good effort at home and do not see a difference, it might need to be revisited and fine-tuned. Parents are often really concerned about what others will think of them if they ignore their child disrespecting them. I tell parents that most other parents are just glad that it is not them having to deal with such behavior. I also encourage parents to try ignoring at home first and only bring it out in public once they are comfortable with it and confident it will work. Children can tell if parents are not feeling confident and in control, and some children will exploit that at any given opportunity. Finally, if parents have to explain to others what they are doing, it is fine to tell others that this works to address whining. "My child just wants my attention, which is why I am ignoring them. It is the fastest way to get them to stop, although it is unpleasant in the short run."

Finally, when I am working with parents on differential attention skills, I tell them that it is called "good enough parenting" for a reason. The parent will not and cannot be perfect. The parent should just try to practice these strategies as much as they can. It will definitely get easier once they have established them as a habit, but everyone has bad days. Establishing new habits is definitely easier said than done, but practice makes perfect!

Conclusion

In summary, using parental attention to its optimal capacity is key to making all subsequent discipline strategies more effective. Use practice playtime to practice the skills. Increasing positive attention through use of labeled praise should increase the child's positive behaviors, while use of active ignoring of the child's unwanted attention-seeking behaviors should diminish them.

Further reading

Online resources:

Parenting check up: https://www.parentingcheckup.org/

Brief behavioral intervention materials: https://www.mededportal.org/publication/10376/

Text resources:

Barkley, R. A., & Benton, C. M. (2013). *Your defiant child: Eight steps to better behavior.* Guilford Press.

Forehand, R., & Long, N. (2002). *Parenting the strong-willed child: The clinically proven five-week program for parents of two- to six-year-olds* (revised and updated). New York: McGraw-Hill.

Kazdin, A. E. (2009). *The Kazdin method for parenting the defiant child.* Houghton Mifflin Harcourt.

Kazdin, A. E. (2013). *The everyday parenting toolkit: The Kazdin method for easy, step-by-step lasting change for you and your child.* Boston, MA: Mariner.

Webster-Stratton, C., Mostyn, D., & Marie, J. S. (2005). *The Incredible Years: A trouble-shooting guide for parents of children aged 2-8 years.* Seattle, WA: Incredible Years.

8

CHAPTER

Treatment component #2: Effective commands and consistent consequences including rewards

The second main treatment component is effective commands and consistent consequences, including rewards. In a nutshell, it consists of giving effective commands and providing consistent consequences for them, including rewards, response cost, and natural and logical consequences. In regard to Chapter 6's, Overview of evidence-based treatment components for oppositional defiant disorder, evidence-based treatment components, it includes the following treatment components:

- tangible rewards
- *commands*
- monitoring
- response cost
- goal setting

The Clinician's Guide to Oppositional Defiant Disorder. DOI: https://doi.org/10.1016/B978-0-12-815682-7.00008-2

- *stimulus control*
- natural or logical consequences
- behavioral contracting
- functional analysis

It is heavily involved in all behavioral management training programs. Effective commands and consistent consequences can reverse coercive cycles by eliminating the need for repeated requests and threats, as well as decreasing reliance on punishment. Such strategies will increase parental consistency and follow-through. Further, increased use of rewards, to the extent possible, should facilitate a warmer relationship at home and help improve caregiver–child attachment. It should be noted that information in this chapter comes from the online and text resources cited at the end of this chapter.

Effective commands and consequences overview

Overall, there is a structured process for issuing effective commands and following through with consistent consequences that will greatly enhance parenting effectiveness, as shown in Table 8.1. Key to this is limiting commands so one can follow through consistently each time. Parents should provide a transitional warning and make sure the child is listening. Then, they should issue an effective command, allow a few seconds for compliance, ignore any attitude, and praise any move toward compliance. If there is no move toward compliance, then they should reissue the command with a warning as to the consequence for noncompliance. Again, they should wait, praise any compliance, and ignore any attitude. If there is no compliance, move immediately to the consequence. For consequences, parents have many options: rewards, natural consequences, or response cost. After consistent enforcement of noncompliance, the parent should see dramatic progress such that they will be able to increasingly fade out reward systems and avoid conflicts around commands.

TABLE 8.1 Effective commands and consequences overview.

1. Provide a transitional warning
2. Issue an effective command
3. Come up with a consequence
   a. Rewards
   b. Response cost
   c. Natural consequences
   d. Logical consequences

Transitional warnings

Parents should be encouraged to set their child up for success by giving what is called a transitional warning. A transitional warning lets the child know that they are about to be asked to change activities. Providing such warnings requires some thinking ahead. However, it will pay dividends by heading off problems before they arise.

Parents should be encouraged to make sure to have the child's attention when they give them the warning. Parents should tap the child on the shoulder, make eye contact with them, and let them know that, in about 5 minutes, they will be asked to wrap up their play and get ready to leave. Doing this instead of just telling them that right now they need to get ready to leave will avoid many tantrums that would otherwise almost certainly occur. Also, parents need to make sure their child is paying attention. If the child is zoned out watching television, he/she may not even hear the parent. Tapping them on the shoulder or making sure to make eye contact when the transitional warning is given is very important.

Effective commands

Limiting commands is also critical because the parent will be enforcing each and every instance of noncompliance. This will take a lot of time. So, clinicians should encourage parents to ask themselves if they are going to have time and be willing to enforce a consequence for every instance of noncompliance before they ever give a command. This is a big focus of Ross Greene's book *The Explosive Child*. He advocates for picking your battles by greatly reducing the number of commands issued.

In addition, parents should be encouraged to carefully phrase their commands. First of all, they should not ask children to comply. They should tell them to comply. They should issue commands as statements (e.g., "Pick up your toys"), not questions (e.g., "Can you pick up your toys?"). And they should not use the term "let's" unless they are serious about helping. If giving a direct command feels rude or unnatural, it is fine to tack "please" onto the front of the command (e.g., "please pick up your toys").

Finally, parents should try to give small, simple instructions for big tasks like cleaning up. That makes it easier for the child to quickly comply, is easier to remember and less daunting, and provides more opportunities to praise compliance. So, rather than asking a child to pick up all of their toys, it probably makes more sense to ask them to put their LEGOs in the box. Then, when that is complete, ask them to put their books on the bookshelf. And so on.

Parents should try to avoid chain commands (e.g., "put your LEGOs in the box, your books on the bookshelf, and your stuffed animals and balls in the toy chest"). Chain commands are often too much for young children to remember. Related to this, parents should make sure each command is developmentally appropriate. They should use positive terms, telling their child what to do rather than what not to do. So, they should say, "Pick up your shoes and put them in the closet" rather than "Do not leave your shoes out." The child may know that they are not supposed to leave their shoes out, but they may be unsure where they should put their shoes. So, parents should make it easy and tell them what they should *do*. This can be particularly challenging for salient misbehaviors like aggression. Sometimes, it is easiest for parents to think of what they want to see instead. So, "No running in the house" becomes "Walk please! Or, if you need to run, go outside."

Parents should try to issue commands in a neutral tone of voice. The child may always have problems with compliance, but issuing commands harshly in a negative tone only sets the stage for problems. Finally, choices can be helpful, if they are an option. For example, parents can say, "You can put all your toys in the toy box or sweep them into your closet" or "You can wear this outfit or that outfit, but I need you to get dressed. If you are not dressed by the time I get back, then I will choose for you."

So, to summarize, as discussed shown in Table 8.2, tips for issuing commands include:

- Make sure there is time to provide a consequence; otherwise, don't issue a command.
- Give a transitional warning first if the child is doing something else.
- Make sure the child is paying attention.
- Do not phrase as a question.
- Only give one specific command at a time; in other words, keep it simple.
- Use positive terms ("do" vs "do not" or "stop").

Consequences

After an effective command has been issued, the parent should wait a few seconds. The parent may be anticipating noncompliance, but they should try to remember that the child is being asked to switch gears. Give the child at least 5 seconds to start to comply. If the child makes any move toward complying, the parent should praise the child immediately! If the child has a bad attitude, moves slowly, or complains, the parent should ignore it and very specifically praise the compliance (so the child knows the parent is not praising the bad attitude).

While the parent is waiting on the child to comply, they need to come up with a consequence for noncompliance. The best consequences are:

- immediate
- meaningful

This part is the trickiest because it involves thinking on one's feet. This is where reward systems and response cost can be very helpful.

TABLE 8.2 Effective commands.
How to give effective commands
Guidelines for effective commands
1. *Make sure the child is paying attention to you.* Make eye contact. Reduce all distractions by turning off television, music, and computer. 2. *Make sure you mean it!* Never give a command you will not see to completion or threaten a consequence you will not give. 3. *Do not present the command as a question or favor.* 4. *Only give one command at a time.* 5. *Tell your child what he or she can do.* Be specific. Avoid unclear or limited statements, such as "please behave" or "stop it." 6. *Use transitional warnings when appropriate.* Some commands may be more effective when preceded by a transitional warning. (Example: "In 5 min it will be time to turn off the television.")
Steps to effective commands
Offer direction: specific, one step
Example: "Please take your plate to the sink."
Wait 5 s, then provide "if–then" warning
Example: "*If* you take your plate to the sink, *then* you can have dessert" (logical consequence)
When at all possible, frame consequence *positively*
Example: "If you do ... then ..." (something your child likes)
Wait 5 more seconds, and then follow through with stated consequence. Consequences that are *immediate* and *meaningful* are best.
Example command
Please keep the toys on the floor.
If your child complies, provide immediate, specific praise. If not, then provide a warning statement, such as "if you don't keep the toys on the floor, then they will have to be put away."

Rewards

Both rewards and response cost are based on behavioral theory. Behavioral theory really divides parenting strategies into two main categories. The first and most effective strategy is reinforcement, which is just a fancy term for any strategy the parent uses to increase a behavior they like. Use of rewards such as praise, tokens, stickers, or privileges is a *positive* reinforcement strategy, meaning something the parent gives the child that makes it more likely for them to repeat a good behavior. Parents should be informed that this typically underutilized strategy is actually the most powerful and effective strategy for changing a child's (or anyone's) behavior. In contrast, response cost is a punishment which is a behavior used to decrease a misbehavior. Specifically, response cost is a *negative* punishment strategy, meaning the parent takes something away to decrease an undesirable behavior. A parent could choose to take away tokens, stickers, or a privilege. However, punishment of any kind is not as effective as positive reinforcement, or use of rewards, and this is something parents should keep in mind.

Parents should be informed that there are many different options when it comes to setting up reward systems, and creativity is helpful, but not necessary. First of all, rewards can be very simple; a smile, labelled praise, physical affection, or an extra privilege (e.g., choice of snack) works just as well as anything fancier. However, parents can set up the reward system in an obvious place or in an easily accountable manner. Many parents like to put their reward tracking system in a prominent place, such as on the refrigerator or next to the front door or child's room door. For these types of charts, a parent can use stickers or tally marks. For some examples of possible systems for both younger and older children, see Tables 8.3 and 8.4, respectively.

However, a parent does not have to have a manifest chart system like this. The parent can just carry around a notebook in which they log points, or have a jug into which the child places some tangible sign of the reward (e.g., a poker chip or a coin). Alternatively, they can use a smartphone app like Privilege Points. The important point is to have a system that is easily accessible and can be viewed by the child on demand. A system that the parent has a difficult time remembering to use defeats the purpose. Obviously, more tangible systems work better for younger children. That is, while the notebook tracking system works well for most children over age 6, it is often less appealing for most kids under 6 because they have a more difficult time understanding it.

When getting started, parents should be encouraged to chart only one target behavior. This gives both the parent and child time to adjust to carefully tracking a specific behavior. A second important point in setting up a good reward system is to establish very specific, positively framed behavior goals. For example, if bedtime is a problem, the parent should choose one easy-to-measure positive behavior to target, perhaps getting and staying in bed after 8 p.m.

TABLE 8.3 Reward/Chore chart for a young child.

Reward	Cost
Choice of dessert	2
Stay up 10 min past bedtime	3
Screen time: 30 extra minutes	5
Rent a movie	10
Have a friend over	20
Have a sleepover	30
Buy a new toy	40
Chores	**Points**
Brush teeth	2
Asking nicely using manners	2
Getting up on time with only 1 reminder	2
Make bed	4
Clean room	10
Help fold clothes	10

TABLE 8.4 Reward/chore chart for adolescents.

Reward	Cost
Choice of dessert	2
Stay up 30 min past bedtime	3
Screen time: 30 extra minutes	5
Go to see a movie	10
Have a friend over	20
Stay out 30 min past curfew	30
Buy a video game/pair of shoes	60
Chores	**Points**
Take out garbage	2
Bath	2
Getting up on time with only 1 reminder	2
Being polite to adults	4
Folding and putting away clothes	10
Clean room	20

Third, the parent should choose how many points the child can earn for particular target behaviors. For example, a parent might choose to award up to two points for behavior for bedtime: one for getting in bed and one for staying in bed. That will also allow the child to earn up to two points (and, later, once you introduce response cost, allow the child to lose one of the two points for getting out of bed after bedtime). The system should be designed to allow the child to cash in their points for prizes as soon as possible. Obviously, nighttime is a challenge, but the child should be able to cash in points across the day without having to wait more than an hour or two if at all possible.

Fourth, there should be a number of different prizes and privileges priced at a range of values. See the samples in Tables 8.3 and 8.4. Here is where knowing the child well will really help. The parent will want to have some small items or privileges that can be earned for each positive behavior (e.g., a sticker, extra story at bedtime), others that require a day or two of saving points (e.g., small prizes such as a matchbox car; 10 minutes extra TV time), and larger items that take about a week to earn (e.g., having a friend over; trip to the skating rink). In fact, as the parent gets started, they can leave off the big items entirely, but as the child starts to develop mastery of initial targeted behaviors, the parent can add additional target behaviors. Even then, the chart should list just a few behaviors (four at most) that are being targeted. The parent can then add chores to this system by using chore cards that list the number of points earned for particular chores completed, with more points awarded for more onerous chores. So, in total, that would allow for at most about eight behavioral goals (four target behaviors and four chores) with a similar number of prizes being earned. The parent can make it simpler than that, and should, when they are just starting out.

The parent will gradually be able to fade out giving rewards for behaviors by spacing out the rewards. So, for example, instead of always giving the child a point or two for staying in bed at night, once the child has been successfully earning points for this behavior for a week or two, the parent can start giving points for 2 days in a row, 5 days in a row, or a week in a row. Around this time, the parent can also start using response cost, or subtracting points for not completing relevant tasks in a timely fashion. This differs from what parents did previously because now children are able to lose points instead of just earning them. At this point, parents can also charge points for specific misbehaviors, such as noncompliance or other serious issues such as aggression.

For both the reward system and response cost, have parents pick a neutral time to introduce the idea to their child. The parent should not be doing it in reaction to either positive or negative behavior. They should just inform the child of the reward system and talk to them about the target behaviors and the opportunity to earn points. The parent will introduce loss of points later on, once the child has seen some successful goal completion and been able to accrue a number of points.

The reward system and response cost can come in handy with giving consequences for noncompliance with effective commands. If the parent is having problems coming up with a consequence in the moment, they can add the option of giving points as a reward or threatening a loss of points (i.e., response cost). The parent can always do this no matter what else is going on.

Natural and logical consequences

Another idea is to allow natural consequences, or consequences that would happen naturally for misbehavior. For example, if the parent wants the child to shower or to get dressed, reminding the child that they may be teased by peers if they do not may be the most effective consequence. Maybe the child needs to learn that their grade suffers when they do not complete or turn in homework. However, if a few instances of not turning in work or dressing appropriately do not teach the child a lesson, the parent should add additional, ideally logical consequences to make sure the message hits home. For example, a logical consequence for a child having trouble getting dressed in time for school would be to be wake them up earlier in the morning. A logical consequence for not completing homework would be less screen time, or screen time delayed until after completion of homework.

Summary

Overall, there is a structured process for issuing effective commands and following through on consequences for commands that will greatly enhance parenting effectiveness. Key to this is limiting commands so the parent can follow through consistently each time. Then, parents should provide a transitional warning and make sure the child is listening. Next, parents should issue an effective command, allow a few seconds for compliance, ignore any attitude, and praise any move toward compliance. If there is no move toward compliance, parents should then reissue the command with a warning as to the consequence for noncompliance. Again, they should wait, praise any compliance, and ignore any attitude. If there is no compliance, they should move immediately to the consequence. For consequences, parents have many options: rewards, response cost, and natural and logical consequences. After consistent enforcement, the parent should see dramatic progress such that they will increasingly be able to fade out reward systems and avoid conflicts.

Case example

Frederick

Frederick is a 10-year-old African American male. His mother presented with him to the emergency room when his school called her to come and pick him up during the middle of the day after he threatened to "gut" another 10-year-old boy in his class. The school reported that the provocation for this incident was that Frederick became angry when the other boy asked him to share his colored pencil. More concerning, Frederick was found to have had a knife hidden in his schoolbag and indicated that he planned to use it on the other boy, so that the other boy would "get what was coming to him." The school has suspended Frederick until his mother obtains treatment for him. Frederick has a history of problems with peers. He has few friends and his peers report being scared of him. Frederick frequently, graphically threatens his peers following minor disagreements, telling them he will "cut them open," he "wants to explore their insides," and he will "show them their hearts." He is known to hold a grudge and will wait for a peer following a disagreement after school, threatening them and saying he will hurt them. Frederick lives with his mother, who is single. His biological father has been in jail for armed robbery since Frederick was born. His mother is a mortician with little family in the area. Frederick often spends his afternoons largely unsupervised at the morgue. Frederick's mother acknowledges that she is sometimes scared of him. He reportedly does not listen to her, often argues with her, and she is at a loss as to how to discipline him. Frederick's mother indicated that he has always been difficult to parent. She is worried because his school is insisting that she seek some kind of treatment for Frederick; otherwise, they have said they will expel him.

Conceptualization: Frederick is exhibiting oppositional defiant disorder with high callous–unemotional traits. Frederick may have a genetic predisposition toward conduct problems and callous–unemotional traits in particular given that his father is currently serving time in jail for armed robbery, and Frederick is described as vindictive and engaging in proactive or instrumental forms of aggression that are premeditated. This genetic predisposition may particularly increase his risk for conduct problems given family stressors such as an absent father and little social support. In addition, Frederick's mother spends long hours at work, which means she has little time to supervise him. His exposure to dead bodies seems to be increasing his callousness and detachment toward others. Finally, Frederick does not get along with his peers and is isolated at school. Perhaps most critically, Frederick and his mother do not have a warm and loving relationship, and he is likely insecurely attached. She acknowledges that she is sometimes scared of him and is at a loss as to how to discipline him.

Personalization of treatment tips: Given the severity of Frederick's current behaviors and the family's lack of social support, an intensive, community-level intervention is likely to be best. It will be critical to involve the school and neighborhood to provide increased monitoring of Frederick's behavior while his mother is working and to facilitate peer friendships. Frederick's mother will also need consultation about how to build more warmth and affection into their relationship. The use of a reward system to reinforce appropriate behaviors will be critical, given the presence of callous–unemotional traits. Frederick will need to be assessed for conduct disorder.

Ideal treatment

Multisystemic therapy

Back-up treatment possibilities

Enhanced Positive Parenting Program

Useful treatment components

Praise

Differential reinforcement

Relationship/Rapport building

Tangible rewards!!!

Transitional warning

Rewards are particularly useful for young children and children with high callous–unemotional traits. For example, use of a good reward system would be key for Frederick's case. When introducing effective commands and consistent consequences, including rewards, to Frederick's mother, I would say something like:

> *First of all, set your child up for success by giving them what we call a transitional warning. A transitional warning lets your child know that you are about to ask them to change activities. Providing such warnings requires some thinking ahead on your part as the parent. However, it will pay dividends by heading off problems before they arise.*

Sometimes, parents have a difficult time understanding why they should do their child the courtesy of giving them notice. I always use an example from work. I ask parents how they would feel if their boss came by their office and told them, "Meeting. My office. Now!" What would their initial reaction be?

Parents always cringe. That's exactly it. If that is the adult reaction, with our superior self-control skills, how do we expect children with far inferior emotion regulation skills to react when we do almost exactly the same thing to them?

The nice thing about children though is that their sense of time moves a lot more slowly than ours. You know how Christmas normally feels like it takes forever to arrive for children? But, for parents, it is always here before we feel like we have had the proper time to prepare? Because of this, you only need to give children a few minutes to prepare for a change, even though adults might want at least 30 minutes advance warning.

It is important to make sure to have the child's attention when you give them the warning. Tap them on the shoulder, make eye contact with them, and let them know that, in about 5 minutes, they will be asked to wrap up their play and get ready to leave. Doing this instead of just telling them that right now they need to get ready to leave will avoid many tantrums. Just like the parent at work, the child likely had some plans for their play. For example, they may have wanted to finish building their tower. Giving them the opportunity to adjust their expectations will avoid a tantrum that otherwise is almost inevitable. Also, parents need to make sure their child is paying attention. If the child is zoned out watching television, he/she may not even hear you. Tapping them on the shoulder or making eye contact when the transitional warning is given is very important. A warning they did not hear will not help you in any way.

Effective commands

I also spend a lot of time talking to parents about limiting commands. I stress that this is particularly important because the parent will be enforcing each and every instance of noncompliance. This will take a lot of time. So, I tell parents that, before they issue a command, they should ask themselves if they are going to have time and be willing to enforce a consequence for every instance of noncompliance. Things like getting dressed and picking up may be things they can forgo for now. If the child goes to school in his/her pajamas, that may not be a major problem. Likewise, it may actually be faster for the parent to pick up after the child compared with following through with some consequence. However, coming when called in a busy parking lot is an important safety issue that merits the time and energy of consequences for noncompliance. I always tell parents that if in doubt, particularly initially, do not give a command. That will give extra weight to the few commands you *have* given.

In addition, parents should carefully phrase their commands, as described in Table 8.2. First of all, they should not ask children to comply. They should tell them to comply. This is more difficult than it sounds. As adults, we often politely ask people to do things. But with kids, this is a mistake because children are very literal and may actually think they have a choice—and careless phrasing can set you up for a battle of wills. So do not say, "Can you pick up your toys?" Instead, say, "Pick up your toys." Or, if that seems too rude, you can say, "Please pick up your toys." It is also not usually appropriate to say, "Let's clean up your toys." Not unless the parent is really serious about helping about helping the child clean up.

Also, parents are notoriously too vague with children. The prior scenario is a great example of this. What do I mean by clean up your toys? All toys in the toy box? All neatly ordered? All brushed into a big pile in the corner of the room? I should specify because the child may have a very different idea of what picking up his/her toys means.

Finally, it is best to give small, simple instructions for a big task like cleaning up one by one. That makes it easier for the child to quickly comply, is easier to remember and less daunting, and provides more opportunities to praise compliance. So, rather than asking a child to pick up all their toys, it probably makes more sense to ask them to put their LEGOs in the box. Then, when that is complete, ask them to put their books on the bookshelf. And so on.

Another common problem for parents is chain commands. You may wonder why you cannot just issue all of the prior commands in one string such as "Put your LEGOs in the box, put your books on the bookshelf, and put your stuffed animals and balls in the toy chest." The reason a parent should not do that is because it is too much for a young child to remember.

Make sure each command is developmentally appropriate. Does the child understand? Use positive terms; tell your child what to do rather than what not to do. So, say, "Pick up your shoes and put them in the closet" rather than "Do not leave your shoes out." The child may know that they are not supposed to leave their shoes out, but they may be unsure where they should put their shoes. So, make it easy and tell them what they should *do*. This can be particularly challenging for salient misbehaviors like aggression. I like to have some stock phrases on hand such as "Keep your hands to yourself" (or even better: "Keep your arms at your sides or crossed"). And sometimes it is easiest to think of what you want to see instead. So, "No running in the house" becomes "Walk please! Or, if you need to run, go outside."

Finally, some parents like to provide explanations because they think it will provide their child some incentive to comply. For example, "I need you to pick up your toys because Grandma is coming to visit soon, and she likes a clean house." Unfortunately, for young children, explanations often distract from the message. Hearing that Grandma is coming soon may lead to such excitement that your child runs off and forgets all about cleaning. It is better to save the explanation for another time. Further, changing the behavior actually communicates your message better. Think about it from an adult perspective. Ever tried eating healthier or exercising more because your doctor said it would be good for you? Or did you find it worked better to try to make a few small changes on your own, and then, after you noticed positive health effects (e.g., losing weight, feeling better), you felt motivated to continue making changes? Behavior change works better than verbal explanations for children, just like adults!

Try to issue commands in a neutral tone of voice. The child may always have problems with compliance, but issuing commands harshly in a negative tone only sets the stage for further problems. Finally, choices can be helpful if that is an option. So, for example, if you can, give the child a choice. For example: "You can put all your toys in the toy box or sweep them into your closet." Or "You can wear this outfit or that outfit, but I need you to get dressed. If you are not dressed by the time I get back, then I will choose for you."

So, to summarize, tips for issuing commands:

- Make sure there is time to provide a consequence; otherwise, don't issue a command.
- Give a transitional warning first if the child is doing something else.
- Make sure the child is paying attention.
- Do not phrase as a question.
- Only give one specific command at a time; in other words, keep it simple.
- Use positive terms ("do" vs "do not" or "stop").

Yes, this is more work and requires more monitoring for the parent, but it also dramatically increases the likelihood that the child will comply. And, again, this is why the parent should consider beforehand whether the command is really necessary in the first place. It will take just as much or more of the parent's time (vs the child's time) to monitor for compliance and reward or punish appropriately.

Consequences

So, the parent has thought carefully about whether the command is necessary, followed all these rules, and issued a command. Congratulations! Now what?

First of all, wait a few seconds. The parent may be anticipating noncompliance, but again, remember that the child is being asked to switch gears. Give them at least 5 seconds to start to comply. The parent probably knows what it feels like to have a boss breathing down their neck or expecting immediate compliance. Be a good boss to the child.

If the child makes any move toward complying, praise immediately! What happens if the child has a bad attitude, moves slowly, or complains? Think about the last chapter. Yes, that's right: you need to ignore it and very specifically praise the compliance (so your child knows you're not praising their bad attitude).

But here is where the really tricky part comes in. What do you do if, after 5 seconds, the child has made no progress toward complying? This is where the parent needs to be able to think on their feet. They need to find a consequence. The best consequences are:

- immediate
- meaningful

So, if the parent wants the child to finish eating their nutritious meal instead of just playing around with it, I would say: "I need you to please finish eating most of what is on your plate." If there is no progress, then I would say, "If you do not finish eating most of what is on your plate, then you will lose your opportunity to have dessert."

See? The fact that the consequence happens immediately after they eat gives them an incentive to finish quickly and is meaningfully related to their decision not to eat their meal. If they choose not to eat their healthy food, then they are not allowed to eat sweets.

I know with my kids this is an ideal consequence because my kids will eat almost anything, barring their absolute least favorite food (tomatoes), if they can eat ice cream afterward. Of course, it helps that I keep their favorite flavors stocked, and I make sure they know I always have new yummy treats around.

In this example, finding an immediate, meaningful consequence was relatively easy because I have structured salient rewards around mealtime (because eating a full, nutritious meal is a chronic challenge with my kids). You can do the same by building in rewards at difficult times of the day. If getting ready in the morning is a challenge, consider letting your child pick out their breakfast cereal or allowing them to earn a few minutes of screen time before leaving the house, to give them motivation to move quickly in the morning. If bath time is a problem, consider making screen time or dessert contingent on them getting ready for bed. Building rewards in strategically will facilitate those times of day.

Rewards and response cost

However, there are many times when it is difficult to come up with a good consequence that can happen right away. Bedtime is usually a good example. This is where reward systems and response cost can be very helpful.

It can be helpful to explain behavioral theory to parents at this point. Both rewards and response cost are based on behavioral theory. Behavioral theory really divides parenting strategies into two main categories. The first and most effective strategy is reinforcement, which is just a fancy term for any strategy the parent uses to increase a behavior they like. Use of rewards such as praise, tokens, stickers, or privileges is a *positive* reinforcement strategy, meaning something the parent gives the child that makes it more likely for them to repeat a good behavior. This typically underutilized strategy is actually the most powerful and effective strategy for changing a child's (or anyone's) behavior. A raise for doing a good job at work is a pretty powerful incentive, right? Same principle. In contrast, response cost is a punishment, which is a behavior used to decrease a misbehavior. Specifically, response cost is a *negative* punishment strategy, meaning the parent takes something away. A parent could choose to take away tokens, stickers, or a privilege. However, punishment of any kind is not as effective as positive reinforcement, or use of rewards, and this is something to keep in mind.

Rewards can be as simple as use of labelled praise, physical affection, or a privilege. There are also many different options when it comes to setting up reward systems, and creativity is helpful, but not necessary. Here are the fundamentals:

First of all, set up the reward system in an obvious place or in an easily accountable manner. Many parents like to put their reward tracking system in a prominent place, like on the refrigerator or next to the front door or child's room door. For these types of charts, a parent can use stickers or tally marks. For some examples for both younger and older children, see Tables 8.3 and 8.4 respectively.

However, a parent does not have to have a manifest chart system like this. The parent can just carry around a notebook in which they log points or have a jug into which the child places some tangible sign of the reward (e.g., a poker chip or a coin). Alternatively, they can use a smartphone application like Privilege Points. The important point is to have a system that is easily accessible and can be viewed by the child on demand. A system that the parent has a difficult time remembering to use defeats the point of it. However, obviously, more tangible systems work better for younger children. That is, while the notebook tracking system works well for most children over age 6, it is often less appealing for most kids under 6 because they have a more difficult time understanding it.

When getting started, the chart should include only one target behavior. This gives both the parent and child time to adjust to carefully tracking a specific behavior. Hence, a second important point in setting up a good reward system: establish set very specific, positively framed behavior goals. Is bedtime a problem? Choose one easy-to-measure positive behavior to target: perhaps getting and staying in bed after 8 p.m. Is cleaning their room a problem? Set a very clear goal of picking up all toys and putting them in the toy chest before 8 p.m.

Third, the parent should choose how many points the child can earn for particular target behavior(s). I might award up to two points for behavior at bedtime: one for getting in bed and one for staying in bed. That will also allow the child to earn up to two points (and, later, once you introduce response cost, it will allow the child to lose one of the two points for getting out of bed after bedtime). The system should be designed to allow children to cash in points for prizes as quickly as possible. Obviously, nighttime is a challenge, but the child should be able to cash in points in across the day without having to wait more than an hour or two if at all possible.

Fourth, there should be a number of different prizes and privileges priced at a range of values. See the samples in Tables 8.3 and 8.4. Here is where knowing the child well will really help. The parent will want to have some small items or privileges that can be earned for each positive behavior (e.g., a sticker, extra story at bedtime), others that require a day or two of saving points (e.g., small prizes such as a matchbox car; 10 minutes extra TV time), and larger items that take about a week to earn (e.g., having a friend over; a trip to the skating rink). In fact, as the parent gets started, they can leave off the big items entirely, but as the child starts to develop mastery of initial targeted behaviors, the parent can add additional target behaviors. Even then, the chart should list just a few behaviors (four at most) that are being targeted. The parent can then add chores to this system by using chore cards that list the number of points earned for particular chores completed, with more points awarded for more onerous chores. So, in total, that would allow for at most about eight behavioral goals (four target behaviors and four chores) with a similar number of prizes being earned. The parent can make it simpler than that, and should, when they are just starting out.

The parent will gradually be able to fade out giving rewards for behaviors by spacing out the rewards. So, for example, instead of always giving the child a point or two for staying in bed at night, once the child has been successfully earning points for this behavior for a week or two, the parent can start giving points for 2 days in a row, 5 days in a row, or a week in a row. Around this time, the parent can also start using response cost, or subtracting points for not completing relevant tasks in a timely fashion. This differs from what parents did previously because now children are able to lose points instead of just earning them. At this point, parents can also charge points for specific misbehaviors, such as noncompliance or other serious issues such as aggression.

With both the reward system and response cost, have parents pick a neutral time to introduce the idea to their child. The parent should not be doing it in reaction to either positive or negative behavior. They should just inform the child of the reward system and talk to them about the target behaviors and the opportunity to earn points. The parent will introduce loss of points later on, once the child has seen some successful goal completion and been able to accrue a number of points.

The reward system and response cost can come in handy with giving consequences for noncompliance with effective commands. If the parent is having problems coming up with a consequence in the moment, they can add the option of giving points as a reward or threatening a loss of points (i.e., response cost). The parent can always do this no matter what else is going on.

Natural and logical consequences

Another idea is to allow natural consequences, or consequences that would happen naturally for misbehavior. For example, if the parent wants the child to shower or to get dressed, reminding the child that they may be teased by peers if they do not may be the most effective consequence. Maybe the child needs to learn that their grade suffers when they do not complete or turn in homework. However, if a few instances of not turning in work or dressing appropriately do not teach the child a lesson, the parent should add additional, ideally logical consequences to make sure the message hits home. For example, a logical consequence for a child having trouble getting dressed in time for school would be to be woken up earlier in the morning. A logical consequence for not completing homework would be less screen time, or screen time that is contingent on finishing homework first.

Review

So, to review, the parent should be issuing an effective command to a child who is prepared and listening, making sure they are ready to dish out consequences, allow a few seconds for compliance, ignore any attitude, and praise any move toward compliance. If there is no move toward compliance, they should reissue the command with a warning as to the consequence for noncompliance. Again, wait, praise any compliance, and ignore any attitude. If there is no compliance, move immediately to the consequence. This will require as much hard work by the parent as the child, perhaps more so, given the need to stay calm, think quickly, and follow through consistently. But know that after consistent enforcement, the parent should see dramatic progress such that they will increasingly be able to fade out reward systems and avoid conflicts. Of course, then the parent will likely be moving on to new target behaviors. But such is the life of a parent.

Challenges

By far, the biggest challenge is being consistent about following through on a consequence. Because, let me tell you, if a parent ever gives a command and then instead does the task themselves, all they are doing is teaching their child that there is always a chance the parent may not follow through and they can get out of doing undesirable tasks entirely. And for many children, this is enough to lead to noncompliance. So, I tell parents to do what they need to do, such as cutting down on commands, so they can *always* give consequences for noncompliance. As a related point, if the parent finds their child is habitually slow to comply, the parent should ask themselves what they might be doing to facilitate this delay. Is the parent nagging or asking repeatedly? Is the parent asking nicely several times before yelling? Both of these behaviors teach the child to wait until the parent is frustrated before complying. So the parent should pay attention to their own behavior both before and after the command to make sure they are not inadvertently teaching their child bad habits. Here is where the ABC chart in Chapter 4, The Importance and ease of assessment of ODD, can be helpful.

The second biggest challenge is getting the consequence or reward right for the particular child. If the child shrugs when the parent gives a consequence or a reward, the parent has not gotten it right for that particular child yet. The parent should see a pained expression (for a consequence) or a small smile (for a reward) typically. Do not worry; it takes some trial and error to get it right. In my experience, parents usually err on the side of not being strict enough in this area. If you find yourself thinking, "oh, I couldn't take X away; it would lead to World War 3," you have probably hit on just the right thing. And likewise, if you're thinking, I couldn't *not* give my child X; I have been promising it to him/her forever; again, you are probably hitting on just the right thing. Remember—you are not being a monster; you are making your child earn their privileges, and that is something they will thank you for later. The real world for adults works just the same way.

A note on rewards and bribes, given parents often conflate rewards and bribes and are concerned about feeling like they need to "bribe" their child for good behavior. A bribe is a reward that is given in advance of positive behavior. For example, if a parent gives their child some chocolate and tells the child that they now expect them to behave well at church, that is a bribe. If instead the parent tells them that they can have some chocolate after church, but only if they behave well during church (meaning staying quiet the entire time), that is a reward. Do not bribe; only reward child behavior. Rewards are actually how the world works so by using rewards, parents are only preparing children for the real world. Rewards, in the form of salary, raises, etc., are—after all—the reason most adults go to work. If an adult was not rewarded with pay, no one would work, right? This is the same for children.

However, parents often forget that the only things they really *need* to provide their children are shelter, food, clothes, and medical care. All the extras (e.g., TV, video games, snacks, nice room decorations, etc.) are just basically unnecessary, and often unearned, rewards. Make your child work for those rewards and privileges with their good behavior.

Finally, there is no need to always rely on monetary or even food rewards. Children will work just as hard for social rewards, like praise or extra privileges. Yes, children will work for being able to stay up later and get extra screen time, but they will also work for getting to unlock the car door and getting to physically pick out their cereal at the store. These social rewards are often easier to hand out in the moment, such as in a public setting or at difficult times of day (e.g., at night just before bedtime).

The more immediate the consequence, the more effective it is. So, if the parent chooses to take a toy away, they should do so immediately. Taking a phone away 2 days later is not effective. But this leads to some obvious issues. What is a parent supposed to do for problems at school or in public places? Or what happens with behaviors just before bedtime?

The end of the day may be the most challenging time because there is little chance left to reward and because both parents and children are tired. For that reason, I try to keep commands to a minimum at that time of day. Perhaps the best nighttime reward I have come up with is an extra bedtime story, or getting to stay up an extra 10 minutes. However, it also works well to try to build in a reward early in the morning, maybe a special breakfast treat, getting to sleep in a few extra minutes, or getting to bring a favorite toy or flower to school with them.

Obviously, it is important to be consistent across parents and other caregivers, to the extent possible. If there are known disagreements that cannot be resolved (e.g., between home and grandparents' house), then it can be good to explicitly note that with the child. For example, "I know you receive treats when you whine at Grandma's house, but remember, that does not work here at home."

Communication with the child's teacher(s) is essential. Better yet, the parent should get a sense of the child's specific problem behavior (e.g., gets out of chair), reframe as the opposite (e.g., keeping butt in chair), and work with the teacher to send home ratings (such as 0 for unsuccessful, 1 for tried but imperfect, and 2 for great work). Even just a three-point (e.g., red, yellow, green) system can work. You can just convert that into 0 points for poor behavior, 1 for trying, and 2 for great work.

For public places, first of all, try to set the child up for success by telling them what the parent needs to see (vs does not want to see) before you are out and about. So, if the parent and child are going to the grocery store, the parent should not just tell the child "don't be bad" or "be good." The parent should be more specific, such as by telling the child "stay where I can see you" or "use your inside voice." Let the child know that if they can do that, they can earn points, pick out their own cereal, choose a piece of candy in the checkout aisle, etc. Preferably do this just beforehand so it is front and center for the child during the outing.

Sometimes, I see parents struggle with setting a behavior goal that is reasonable for their child. The parent should not necessarily be aiming for what they want to see from their child, at least not initially. Instead, they should be aiming for progress. They should try to pick a goal that the child can accomplish with hard work and not something that is either impossible or too easy. If the parent chooses something impossible, the child will not even try. If the parent chooses something too easy, the child will be earning reward after reward with little to no effort and balk at future challenges. For example, the parent may not want to set a goal of the child keeping their room clean. They may want to set a goal of having them put their shoes in their closet. Or making their bed. Or putting their clothes away.

Finally, getting the child's input as to their behavioral goals, that is, asking the child what they want to work on, is always helpful for increasing their motivation. If the parent has numerous behavioral goals (perhaps too many), why not ask the child what they would like to work on first? That will enlist their good will, enhance their motivation, and perhaps even gain valuable insight into what behaviors are particularly problematic for them. The parent can even write up a behavioral contract for the child to sign to make it more official.

Hopefully, this chapter has provided some good ideas for ways to expand your discipline toolbox. Having more options and choices is always useful. Figuring out what works best for your family, however, almost always involves some trial and error.

Conclusion

Overall, there is a structured process for issuing and following through on consequences for commands that will greatly enhance parenting effectiveness. Key to this is limiting commands so that you can follow through consistently each time. First of all, provide a transitional warning and make sure the child is listening. Then, issue an effective command, allow a few seconds for compliance, ignore any attitude, and praise any move toward compliance. If there is no move toward compliance, then reissue the command with a warning as to the consequence for noncompliance. Again, wait, praise any compliance, and ignore any attitude. If there is no compliance, move immediately to the consequence. For consequences, parents have many options: rewards, natural consequences, or response cost. After consistent enforcement, the parent should see dramatic progress such that they will be able to fade out reward systems and avoid conflicts.

Further reading

Online resources:

Privilege Points application

Parenting check up: https://www.parentingcheckup.org/

Brief behavioral intervention materials: https://www.mededportal.org/publication/10376/

Text resources:

Barkley, R. A., & Benton, C. M. (2013). *Your defiant child: Eight steps to better behavior.* Guilford Press.

Forehand, R., & Long, N. (2002). *Parenting the strong-willed child: The clinically proven five-week program for parents of two- to six-year-olds* (revised and updated). New York: McGraw-Hill.

Greene, R. W. (1999). *The explosive child.* HarperCollins World.

Kazdin, A. E. (2009). *The Kazdin method for parenting the defiant child.* Houghton Mifflin Harcourt.

Kazdin, A. E. (2013). *The everyday parenting toolkit: The Kazdin method for easy, step-by-step lasting change for you and your child.* Boston, MA: Mariner.

Webster-Stratton, C., Mostyn, D., & Marie, J. S. (2005). *The Incredible Years: A trouble-shooting guide for parents of children aged 2-8 years.* Seattle, WA: Incredible Years.

9

CHAPTER

Treatment component #3: Time-out

The third main treatment component is time-out. In a nutshell, it consists of removing the child from a warm, positive environment, which then serves as a negative punishment strategy. In regard to Chapter 6's, Overview of evidence-based treatment components for oppositional defiant disorder, it only includes one: time-out. It can be used for a few misbehaviors at a time, including potentially noncompliance and breaking of house rules, including serious misbehavior such as aggression, repeated offenses, and noncompletion of longer tasks. It is critical that time-out should be used sparingly, administered in a calm fashion, and connected with positive attention to those behaviors one wants to see. In this way, it can help short-circuit coercive cycles. Like the previous two chapters, this chapter is particularly important for working with young children. Information in this chapter comes from the online and text resources cited at the end of this chapter.

Time-out overview

Time-out is a negative punishment strategy, meaning it takes the child away from a positive, fun environment to decrease a misbehavior. That is why it is

The Clinician's Guide to Oppositional Defiant Disorder. DOI: https://doi.org/10.1016/B978-0-12-815682-7.00009-4

TABLE 9.1 Time-out overview.

1. Limit to 1–2 serious misbehaviors
2. Determine logistics
3. Explain to child beforehand
4. Matter-of-factly enforce
5. Monitor, but do not engage during time-out
6. Give child a second chance to comply afterward

so critical to start with the differential attention principles of Chapter 7, Treatment component #1: Differential attention, before seeking to implement time-out. Time-out will *not* work if the environment is not already largely positive.

Limit use

As shown in Table 9.1, it is best to encourage the parent to limit use of punishment, including time-outs, to a few misbehaviors, particularly at first. They should start with one or two serious misbehaviors. It is best to use for serious, relatively infrequent behaviors such as aggression, lying, running off, or noncompliance, but its use should be limited to the worst one or two of these infractions. If the parent is trying to use time-out several times every day, that is too often and is likely to be unsuccessful, both because it is too punitive and because it is almost impossible to be consistent in implementation that often.

Logistics

As shown in Table 9.2, determining the logistics of time-out takes some forethought on the part of the parent. The parent should set up time-out in an easily monitored location that is neither too fun nor potentially dangerous. A stationary chair (far away from anything breakable or easy-to-access toys) that is easy for the parent to comfortably monitor is ideal. The location should be a little bit isolated, but the parent should be able to see it at all times during time-out.

Explain beforehand

Setting up time-out is something that requires some forethought, so the parent should not spring it on the child for the first time right after misbehavior. Likely, both the parent and the child will be angry at that point, and in-depth explanations will have the opposite of their intended effect; they will reward the behavior the parent is trying to eliminate. The parent should pick a

TABLE 9.2 Time-out guidelines.

Guidelines for time-out
If done correctly, time-out is a positive way to promote new learning. When you use time-out, you remove the child from time in enriched activities for a short period immediately after the child has misbehaved. You direct the child to or place the child in a chair or on the floor with a *brief* statement identifying "time-out for . . . ." Provide no attention until the child has self-calmed and is removed from time-out. Time-out works well to decrease challenging behaviors such as noncompliance and aggression if combined with positive reinforcement.
Steps:
1. Before using time-out, decide where the time-out chair/area will be. It should be free from any potentially dangerous objects (outlets) and out of reach of shelves and furniture. It should be in a place where the child cannot watch television or play with toys. 2. Identify behaviors that you will use for time-out (example: hitting). 3. Before you begin using time-out, explain to the child where the time-out chair is, which behaviors will have time-out as a consequence, and how to get out of time-out (self-calm). 4. Keys to effective use of time-out are *immediacy* and *consistency*. The child should be placed in time-out each time the challenging behavior occurs. 5. Following the challenging behavior, clearly tell the child what he or she did and send or guide the child to time-out. For example, "you hit Johnny; time-out." Say this phrase calmly and only once. Do not reason, negotiate, or give long explanations. Remove any toys in the child's hands. If the child does not go willingly, take the child to time-out, using as little physical guidance as necessary. Do not make eye contact with the child, argue with, or reason with the child while they are in time-out. *Use self-talk to remain calm* while the child is in time-out. 6. The first few times you use time-out, your child may scream, cry, kick, etc. The child may also try to leave time-out before you have told him/her to do so. *Do not* allow the child to leave time-out. As long as the child is seated in the chair or floor, ignore their tantrum. If the child leaves the chair, return him/her to the chair without talking. The child will soon learn that you will *always* put him/her back in the chair. 7. Time-out is over when the child has remained seated and calm. Find a way to give the child positive attention as soon as possible.

neutral time to introduce the concept of time-out to the child, and then explain exactly what behaviors will lead to time-out (e.g., aggression). Further, they should inform the child as to the location of the time-out chair and explain that when they are sent to time-out, they will be required to sit in that chair quietly until they are told they can leave it.

Matter-of-factly enforce

After providing that explanation, the parent should wait until the child engages in the specified behaviors, matter-of-factly label the behavior, and tell them that they need to go to time-out. They should do it as briefly and calmly as possible. For example: "You hit, so go to time-out." It is important that the response be both immediate and consistent.

Monitor

It is important that the parent ignore any attitude. The rule is to give the child 1 minute in the chair per year of age. However, a parent needs to require at least 30 seconds of silence before allowing the child to leave the chair. If the child leaves the chair before the time is up, the parent should return them to the chair and restart their time. Parents should not use a timer. The parent should be the boss, so they should let the child out of time-out when the parent has decided enough time has passed. That means the parent can let the child out a little early or a little later as they deem fit and as is convenient. The parent should monitor the child for the duration of time-out.

Second chance afterward

The parent should give positive attention to the child as soon as possible afterward. If the child was sent to time-out for noncompliance, the parent will want to reissue the command as soon as the child returns from the chair. Time-out does not excuse the child from complying with the parental request. If the child complies at this point, feel free to praise the compliance.

Summary

Because time-out is a negative punishment strategy, it should be used relatively sparingly. The parent should start with 1–2 serious misbehaviors. The parent should determine a safe, not fun location where they can monitor, and the child should be informed about the procedure before it is actually needed. When misbehavior occurs, the parent should then calmly institute the procedure. They should monitor, but not engage with the child during time-out. Once the child is out of time-out, they should be given a second chance to comply, and the parent should praise compliance or other behaviors as soon as possible.

Case example

Luis

Luis is a 4-year-old Latino male. He was referred by his pediatrician for an evaluation after his parents presented complaining about Luis' aggression. Luis only uses one- to two-word phrases to communicate and is difficult to understand. His parents speak Spanish at home and both work long hours at minimum wage jobs. They have five kids total, ages 1, 4, 8, 10, and 12. Luis' parents report that he was born 1 month premature, weighing 4 lb and 3 oz. Luis' mother had severe hypertension toward the end of her pregnancy. Although his motor milestones were reported to be on time, Luis did not say his first words until age 3. He is still not potty trained and sleeps in bed with his parents. Luis' parents complain that he becomes angry and aggressive with minimal provocation. Luis will hit, kick, bite, and throw a tantrum if he does not get his way. He frequently does things that he knows his parents find annoying (such as yelling and running away at the supermarket). He does not comply with adult commands, yelling no and running away. He once ran away in a store parking lot and was almost hit by a car. His parents were worried that social services would be called. Luis' parents are concerned about him starting school next year, given they cannot currently leave him at home with even a babysitter due to his severe misbehavior.

Conceptualization: Luis is exhibiting oppositional defiant disorder in the context of speech and language problems and other delays with independent sleep and elimination problems. Luis is the youngest in a large family. His parents are under economic and personal stress, working long hours to provide for the family. Luis was also exposed to a number of prenatal risk factors, including stress during pregnancy, hypertension, prematurity, and low birth weight. He also experienced developmental delays, particularly with language. The high stress at home, large number of siblings, his parents' limited time, and Luis' language delays have led to coercive cycles between Luis and his parents. He may have difficulty communicating his needs and understanding parental requests. He may also have difficulty obtaining parental attention using appropriate strategies. Therefore he often resorts to aggression, tantrums, and noncompliance. He has been delayed with potty training and refuses to sleep independently.

Personalization of treatment tips: Given the number of family stressors, a family level intervention with a focus on behavioral skills and addressing sleep and elimination issues would probably be best. Speech and language evaluation and treatment with consideration of the family's bilingualism will also be critical. A consultation with a pediatrician regarding elimination issues will be important. Attention-deficit/Hyperactivity disorder will also need to be considered for impulsive behaviors.

Parent–child interaction therapy or enhanced Positive Parenting Program (Triple P)

Parent management training Oregon model

Standard Triple P

Helping the noncompliant child

Praise

Differential reinforcement

Relationship/rapport building

Tangible rewards

Commands

Monitoring

Response cost

Goal setting

Stimulus control

Natural or logical consequences

Behavioral contracting

Functional analysis

Time-out

Along with differential attention, which was described two chapter ago, time-out would be a critical tool to use with Luis. When introducing time-out to Luis' parents, I would first discuss the pitfalls of punishment.

> *Punishment is not usually effective by itself. It must be combined with a reward to show the child what to do. Further, punishment often models aggression; if you get angry and yell or spank and hit your child, you are only modeling behaviors you do not want to see them do. Excessive punishment also leads to negative interactions that diminish your influence and leads your child to try to avoid you. Finally, such an approach often only leads to transient decreases in your child's misbehavior while they are around you rather than a lasting change in different situations.*

I would explain that time-out is a negative punishment strategy, meaning that it takes the child away from a positive, fun environment to decrease a misbehavior. That is, punishments are usually less effective at shaping behavior compared with reinforcement strategies such as rewards.

Just think of it this way: Are you more motivated at work when you think it is possible to get a raise, or when you are trying to avoid being reprimanded? Ever felt like sneaking around and/or cutting corners to avoid being reprimanded? That is exactly the same way children respond. Given that parents are typically trying to change child behavior, rather than teach children to be sneaky, it is best to rely on rewards as opposed to punishment to the extent possible.

Limit use

For these reasons, it is best to limit use of punishment, including time-outs, to a few misbehaviors, particularly at first. Remember that we want the child to get more positive attention than negative attention, and we want the home environment and parent–child relationship to be warm, because that is healthier for the child and because it will make punishment more effective. We also want to be sure that the parent is being consistent in how they implement time-out. Basically, we do not want parents to overuse time-out.

For example, a parent can use time-out for noncompliance if that is one of their most major concerns. In that case, the parent should send the child to time-out for noncompliance. Then, when the child gets out of time-out, the parent should reissue the command immediately (which may necessitate additional time-outs until the child complies). It is also usually good to use time-out for serious violations such as aggression or dangerous behaviors (like running off). The parent might want to use time-out for other violations of house rules (stealing, cursing, lying, etc.). The parent could also use time-out for repeated offenses; for example, if they have fined the child twice, and the behavior does not improve. Or, the parent can use time-out for non-completion of longer tasks (e.g., not cleaning room or finishing homework). I usually recommend that parents start with one or two target misbehaviors, preferably those that only happen relatively infrequently (a few times a week), so parents have a chance to practice before ramping up to use time-out for more common misbehaviors such as noncompliance. For example, in Luis' case, I would recommend his parents initially begin using time-out for aggression and running off.

Logistics

Determining the logistics of time-out takes some forethought. The clinician should discuss in detail with the parent the logistics of their time-out procedure. The parent should set up time-out in an easily monitored location that is neither too fun nor potentially dangerous. So, time-out in a bedroom is often not ideal because it is difficult to monitor and has too many toys. Time-out in the kitchen may not be ideal because of all the glassware. I typically recommend a stationary hardback chair that is placed in a relatively empty corner of the living area. An ideal location is far away from anything breakable or easy-to-access toys, and is easy for the parent to comfortably monitor. The chair should be sturdy, stationary, and boring. It should be a little bit isolated, but the parent should be able to see it at all times during time-out.

Explain beforehand

Setting up time-out is something that requires some forethought, so the parent should not spring it on the child for the first time right after misbehavior. Likely, both the parent and the child will be angry at that point, and in-depth explanations will have the opposite of their intended effect; they will reward the behavior the parent is trying to eliminate. The parent should pick a neutral time to introduce the concept of time-out to the child, and then explain exactly what behaviors will lead to time-out (e.g., aggression). Further, they should inform the child as to the location of the time-out chair and explain that when they are sent to time-out, they will be required to sit in that chair quietly until they are told they can leave it.

Matter-of-factly enforce

After providing that explanation, parents should wait until the child engages in the specified behaviors, matter-of-factly label the behavior, and tell them that they need to go to time-out. Do it as briefly and calmly as possible. For example: "You hit so go to time-out." It is important that the response be both immediate and consistent. It does not work to tell the child they will be put in time-out later. It also does no good to argue with the child about going to time-out or to engage in in-depth explanations about why they need to go to time-out. Finally, it does not do any good to yell. The parent can guide the child to time-out, but they do not want to get into a physical struggle with the child. All of that reinforces the misbehavior by giving it too much attention.

Monitor

Importantly, ignore any attitude. The rule is to give the child 1 minute in the chair per year of age. However, a parent needs to require at least 30 seconds of silence before the child is allowed to leave the chair. If the child leaves the chair before time, return them to the chair and restart their time. Do not use a timer. The parent should be the boss so the parent should let the child out of time-out when the parent decides enough time has passed. That means the parent can let the child out a little early or a little later as they deem fit and as is convenient. Because the parent should be monitoring the child for the duration of time-out, this is just as time-consuming for the parent as the child. That is why I recommend using time-out sparingly, particularly at first.

Second chance afterward

The parent should give positive attention to the child as soon as possible afterward. If the child was sent to time-out for noncompliance, the parent will want to reissue the command as soon as the child returns from the chair. Time-out does not excuse the child from complying with the parental request. If the child complies at this point, feel free to praise the compliance.

How to handle possible problems

As shown in Table 9.3, the biggest potential problem with time-out is the child refusing to stay in the chair. If this happens, the parent can try guiding the child gently back to the chair and restarting the time. If that does not work because the child continues to get up, the parent can impose a very stiff fine or privilege loss (e.g., no screen time for the rest of day). Other options require one-on-one work with a professional; there are safe holds you can consider or more isolated options (like a locked room). However, you would need to consult with someone about these other approaches.

What happens if time-out is needed in a public location such as a grocery store? It is best to set up a reward system beforehand for such times, as discussed in the last chapter. However, it is also helpful to have a plan for time-out, particularly for handling dangerous or aggressive behaviors. I usually try to pick a potential time-out location as I enter a new place. It may be a relatively deserted aisle of the grocery store, the cry room at church, or the family car at another child's birthday party. Then, if needed, the child would have to sit in that location for the same specified period of time-out while you supervise. Make sure the location is safe. For example, in the car, a parent would need to make sure to have it well-ventilated and keep the keys on their person.

Finally, how does a parent handle endless time-outs for noncompliance? For example, what happens if the child will not comply, goes to time-out, comes out, and still will not comply? The parent can continue to use time-outs, perhaps shortening the time-outs a little, or eventually—after the parent reaches their limit with time-outs—they can impose a stiff fine or privilege loss as described above.

Many parents wonder about other, harsher parenting strategies, such as grounding, spanking, and other variations on these techniques. In sum, those discipline strategies are not recommended. For harsh punishments like grounding, research demonstrates that they are not effective. Remember, to be effective, a consequence has to be immediate. Grounding the child for a month is not immediate; any effectiveness of this approach will be worn out by end of the first evening. Not to mention, it is a nightmare to enforce! The parent is almost sure to be inconsistent in the enforcement of a month-long grounding.

Physical discipline is also not recommended, but for different reasons. Namely, physical discipline strategies are usually utilized out of anger, and they model poor coping (like hitting when angry). In addition, physical discipline like spanking is a punishment. As mentioned at the beginning of the

TABLE 9.3 Time-out troubleshooting.

Things to check when time-out is not working
1. Be sure you are not warning the child more than once before sending him/her to time-out. Warnings only teach the child that he/she can be aggressive one more time.
2. All adults who are responsible for caring for the child should be using time-out. All adults should agree on what behaviors lead to time-out.
3. To make time-out effective, positive attention must be available when child is not in time-out.
4. Your child may tell you that time-out does not bother them. Do not fall for this trick! Your child is trying to convince you that time-out does not work. You should notice over time that the difficult behaviors for which you use time-out occur less often.
5. Remember to expect an initial increase in the targeted behaviors, which will rapidly decrease.
6. *Ignore* all behaviors that occur in time-out as long as the child is safe and remains in time-out.
7. Make sure the child does not have access to distractions like the dog, a younger sibling, the television, or a view out the window.
8. When your child is in time-out *remember*: Do not look at him/her. Do not talk to him/her. Do not act angry or worried. Do use self-talk to remain calm. Do find something to do while your child is in time-out.

chapter, all punishment strategies, including time-out, are less effective than reward strategies. In addition, these punishment strategies are usually overutilized, particularly relative to more positive reinforcement strategies. That is why therapeutic approaches try to shift parents away from use of punishment and toward increased use of reinforcement strategies. Overall, the best thing parents can do for children while disciplining them is to (try to) stay calm and model consistent follow-through. It is often true that the punishment will not fit the crime. But that is okay because the child is still learning.

I cannot stress enough how this technique will not work if there is not a largely positive home environment in place. It will also not work if it is overused (i.e., if the family is using it more than about three times a day). The whole basis of this punishment is removing children from fun, warmth, and positive time. If that is not the child's predominant experience in the home, then time-out will end up being a reward, not a punishment, and this will indirectly reinforce misbehaviors. That is why we often teach this punishment strategy last, or nearly last, in treatment. It should be a last resort and used only for serious misbehaviors.

Conclusion

Because time-out is a negative punishment strategy, it should be used relatively sparingly. Start with 1–2 serious misbehaviors. The parent should predetermine a safe, not fun location that they can monitor and inform their child about the procedure before it is actually needed. When misbehavior occurs, calmly institute the procedure. Monitor, but do not engage with your child during time-out. Once the child is out of time-out, give them a second chance to comply and praise compliance or other behaviors afterward as soon as possible.

Further reading

Online resources:

Parenting check up: https://www.parentingcheckup.org/

Brief behavioral intervention materials: https://www.mededportal.org/publication/10376/

Text resources:

Barkley, R. A., & Benton, C. M. (2013). *Your defiant child: Eight steps to better behavior.* Guilford Press.

Forehand, R., & Long, N. (2002). *Parenting the strong-willed child: The clinically proven five-week program for parents of two- to six-year-olds* (revised and updated). New York: McGraw-Hill.

Kazdin, A. E. (2009). *The Kazdin method for parenting the defiant child.* Houghton Mifflin Harcourt.

Kazdin, A. E. (2013). *The everyday parenting toolkit: The Kazdin method for easy, step-by-step lasting change for you and your child*. Boston, MA: Mariner.

Webster-Stratton, C., Mostyn, D., & Marie, J. S. (2005). *The Incredible Years: A trouble-shooting guide for parents of children aged 2-8 years*. Seattle, WA: Incredible Years.

10

CHAPTER

Treatment component #4: Cognitive skills

The fourth main treatment component for addressing disruptive behavior problems and oppositional defiant disorder (ODD) is cognitive skills. In a nutshell, this consists of anger identification, perspective taking, and problem-solving around strategies about how to manage anger. In regard to Chapter 6's, Overview of evidence-based treatment components for oppositional defiant disorder, evidence-based treatment components, it includes the following treatment components:

- cognitive
- self-monitoring

These skills are heavily involved in all cognitive therapies.

Cognitive skills teach children and adolescents how to cope with anger, accurately appraise and generate alternate appraisals of problem situations through perspective taking, generate more and different possible solutions to the problem, and evaluate the likely and actual consequences of their behavior. These skills facilitate social information processing across numerous situations and can improve child and adolescent relationships with parents, peers, and teachers. Cognitive skill training is often particularly useful for working with adolescents. Of course, it should be noted that cognitive skills

The Clinician's Guide to Oppositional Defiant Disorder. DOI: https://doi.org/10.1016/B978-0-12-815682-7.00010-0

TABLE 10.1 Cognitive skills overview.

1. Awareness of anger
   a. Awareness of angry feelings
   b. Awareness of anger triggers
   c. Awareness of anger expression
2. Behavioral strategies for managing anger
   a. Behavioral strategies
   b. Distraction
   c. Deep breathing
3. Cognitive strategies for managing anger
   a. Coping statements
   b. Seeing others' perspective
   c. Avoiding jumping to conclusion

are much easier for adolescents to learn if parents have been using and modeling them. It should be noted that information in this chapter comes from the text resources cited at the end of this chapter.

Cognitive skills overview

As shown in Table 10.1, teaching adolescents cognitive skills progresses through several major stages. First, the therapist teaches the adolescent to be aware of their anger through knowing their physiological cues (e.g., racing heart), their typical expression of anger (e.g., yelling), and their typical triggers (e.g., someone telling them no). Next, adolescents learn strategies for managing anger in the moment using behavioral strategies (e.g., walking away), coping statements (e.g., I will get through this), deep breathing, and distraction. Finally, adolescents learn cognitive strategies for managing anger such as perspective taking, avoidance of jumping to conclusions, and cognitive modification.

Anger awareness

The first step toward teaching adolescents to deal with anger using cognitive strategies is to make sure they increase their awareness of when they are becoming angry. Using a worksheet and the examples recorded in Table 10.2, review their physiological anger cues such as racing heart, rapid breathing, shaking, feeling flushed, and sweating. Explain to them that it is helpful to identify levels of anger, from mild irritation to extreme, dangerous anger. For example, it is helpful for them to be able to identify cues of their own mild irritation (e.g., rolling their eyes) so they can try to take proactive steps to manage their anger. Have adolescents identify common triggers for their anger, for example, being told no or being teased by a sibling. Have the adolescent notice and ask for feedback about how they express anger. Do

TABLE 10.2 Anger log.

	Monday	Tuesday	Wednesday	Thursday	Friday	Saturday	Sunday
a.m.							
Early p.m.							
Late p.m.							

Rate your angriest moment during each time block using a scale from 1 (not angry at all) to 10 (furious). For any rating over 5, please note the situation.

they roll their eyes, frown, clench their fists, become flushed, cry, or yell? Being aware of these expression habits again can provide the adolescent with valuable clues that they are becoming angry before they get too angry. Knowing these cues can also help them to take action to manage their anger before they upset other people with negative expressions, such as yelling, that can make difficult situations worse.

Behavioral strategies for managing anger

There are a number of behavioral strategies adolescents can use to decrease their anger levels. Behavioral strategies can be useful initially. However, for extreme anger, deep breathing and/or distraction are also sometimes particularly helpful.

First, go over some behavioral strategies for dealing with anger. As shown in Table 10.3, these can include:

- ignoring
- walking away
- telling someone
- talking about it
- compromising
- telling yourself it is not worth it

Also, have the adolescent come up with a list of distraction techniques, or fun activities he/she can engage in when they are extremely angry and need to cool down. This list should be personalized to and by the adolescent (and can be added to Table 10.3), but some examples might include:

- talking to a friend
- exercising
- drawing
- listening to music
- playing a game
- watching television
- playing with a pet

Finally, for managing severe anger, use of techniques like deep breathing can be helpful. A sample script is shown in Table 10.4. Another helpful strategy is visualizing a calm place (e.g., the beach) or thinking back to a calming memory (e.g., last family vacation).

In sum, adolescents should use behavioral strategies for addressing anger. When dealing with severe anger, distraction and/or deep breathing are particularly useful.

Cognitive strategies for managing anger

In tandem with behavioral strategies, adolescents should be increasingly encouraged to try to engage in cognitive strategies for managing anger. Use

TABLE 10.3 Things I can do when angry.

- Ignore it
- Walk away
- Tell someone
- Talk about it
- Compromise
- Tell myself it is not worth it
- Go on a run
- ________________________
- ________________________
- ________________________
- ________________________
- ________________________
- ________________________
- ________________________
- ________________________
- ________________________
- ________________________
- ________________________
- ________________________
- ________________________
- ________________________
- ________________________
- ________________________
- ________________________
- ________________________
- ________________________
- ________________________
- ________________________
- ________________________
- ________________________
- ________________________
- ________________________
- ________________________
- ________________________
- ________________________
- ________________________
- ________________________

TABLE 10.4 Deep breathing script.
Find a comfortable, quiet spot to sit or lie down. Make yourself comfortable and feel your limbs loosen. Feel free to close your eyes if you want. Take a breath. Now, let's focus on making your breaths deeper and slower.
Breathe in slowly through your nose, feeling your chest and belly expand as you fill your lungs. You are an expanding balloon, being inflated. Now, breathe out slowly. Feel yourself deflating. Let's count while we do it.
Breathe in ... 1—2—3. Breathe out ... 1—2—3. Breathe in ... 1—2—3. Breathe out ... 1—2—3.
Put your hand on your belly and feel your balloon inflating and deflating.
Breathe in ... 1—2—3. Breathe out ... 1—2—3. Breathe in ... 1—2—3. Breathe out ... 1—2—3.
Let's try to slow your breathing down now. We'll count to 4 this time.
Breathe in ... 1—2—3—4. Breathe out ... 1—2—3—4. Breathe in ... 1—2—3—4. Breathe out ... 1—2—3—4.
Feel all your tensions and troubles melting away.
Breathe in ... 1—2—3—4. Breathe out ... 1—2—3—4. Breathe in ... 1—2—3—4. Breathe out ... 1—2—3—4.
Slow it down one final time. Let's count to 5 this time if we can.
Breathe in ... 1—2—3—4—5. Breathe out ... 1—2—3—4—5. Breathe in ... 1—2—3—4—5. Breathe out ... 1—2—3—4—5.
Feel yourself relaxed enough to drop off to sleep. Your worries are gone and you are totally relaxed and stress free.
OK, take another minute to enjoy this feeling, and, when you are ready, open your eyes.

of coping statements can be helpful. As shown in Table 10.5, some common coping statements include:

- It's not important.
- It's not worth getting worked up over.
- It will be okay.
- I'm bigger than this.
- I'm not going to let them upset me.
- They don't know what they are talking about.
- I'm not going to get into trouble over this.
- I'm going to wait to respond.
- Other people like me.
- I am fine.
- This will get better.
- I am trying my best.

Having adolescents note, record, or discuss recent anger-inducing events can be helpful to ground conversations about use of cognitive strategies, as shown in Table 10.6. When reviewing this worksheet of anger-inducing events and reactions and thoughts, adolescents should be encouraged to try to view the other person's perspective. Sometimes, therapists can help the adolescent get a jump start on this by being more readily able to see the adult or parent perspective and pointing it out as an alternative.

When reviewing these instances, it is also helpful to encourage adolescents to try to refrain from jumping to conclusions. Sometimes, other people's intentions are ambiguous, and it is better for everyone involved to wait before making a judgment. There are a number of different intentions adolescents should at least consider. These include:

- trying to be helpful
- trying to be hurtful
- it was an accident
- it was unclear

Adolescents should be encouraged to use their coping statements or come up with other modified cognitions as appropriate to help them defuse. Sometimes, waiting to rush to judgment is all it takes, but other times, use of more balanced thoughts and/or coping statements is also needed.

Summary

To reduce anger in difficult interpersonal situations, there are a number of useful cognitive strategies adolescents can try. Adolescents should work on becoming aware of when they are starting to get angry, including identifying physiological cues and common triggers and knowing their own anger expression. Next, adolescents should try to take proactive behavioral

TABLE 10.5 Coping statements.

- It's not important.
- It's not worth getting worked up over.
- It will be okay.
- I'm bigger than this.
- I'm not going to let them upset me.
- They don't know what they are talking about.
- I'm not going to get into trouble over this.
- I'm going to wait to respond.
- Other people like me.
- I am fine.
- This will get better.
- I am trying my best.

TABLE 10.6 Cognitive worksheet for managing anger.

Day/ situation	Rate anger (1–10)	Original thought	Behavioral strategy	Cognitive strategy/ coping statement	Rerate anger (1–10)	Outcome
Example: Friday Parents wouldn't let me go out	*9*	*They are so unfair! They hate me!*	*Went on a run*	*Tried to see their perspective/ it's not that important*	*5*	*Invited a friend over instead*

measures to cool down, including use of behavioral strategies like walking away, distraction, and deep breathing. Finally, cognitive strategies should be attempted to manage anger including using coping statements, seeing others' perspectives, avoiding jumping to conclusions, and modifying cognition.

Case example

Anna

Anna is a 15-year-old Caucasian female whose parents present with concerns about possible drug use, sexting, and promiscuous sex. Anna has been diagnosed with depression and has been taking antidepressants since age 13. She was described as irritable and easily annoyed most of the time. She acknowledges frequent marijuana use with friends and being sexually active with several males. She has been grounded for the last 2 weeks after she sent a naked picture to one of these males, and her parents were informed by a friend's mother who saw the picture on her daughter's Snapchat. Anna acknowledges that her current friend group has not been the best influence. She complains that the girls are all catty and talk about her behind her back. She reports engaging in sexting or sex, impulsivity, without a lot of forethought about the consequences, or while under the influence of alcohol. She indicated that she has no desire to listen to her parents and often argues with them about curfews and rules. She justified her behavior by reporting that she was bullied extensively in grade school and feels the need to fit in with her peers whatever the cost.

Conceptualization: Anna exhibits ODD in the context of a preexisting depression diagnosis. She is also at risk for emerging substance use problems with marijuana and alcohol. She has a history of peer problems including bullying through covert aggression (e.g., rumors). Through these experiences, she seems to have developed faulty social information processing in that she almost always attributes hostile intentions to her peers, and she impulsively engages in inappropriate reactions such as substance use and sexting. She furthermore does not seem to have learned to evaluate the negative consequences of her actions. Her parents, to date, have been largely ineffective at monitoring or disciplining her to obtain desired behaviors.

Personalization of treatment tips: Given Anna's depression and the prominent role peers play in her problems, a social learning approach would probably be most effective. It will also be important to involve Anna's parents in the treatment to facilitate a more effective problem-solving approach to setting rules and consequences for her. Better monitoring of Anna's behavior, including use of substances, will be critical. Assessment for attention-deficit/hyperactivity disorder for Anna's impulsive behaviors may also be helpful. A psychiatric consultation regarding the effectiveness of Anna's antidepressant at its current dosage for managing depressive symptomatology will also be important.

Ideal treatment

Problem-solving skills training

Back-up treatment possibilities

Cognitive-behavioral therapy
Assertiveness training
Rational–emotive mental health program

Useful treatment components

Cognitive
Self-monitoring
Problem-solving
Communication skills
Family therapy
Modeling

Anger awareness

When describing cognitive skills to Anna, I would ask her to log her angry moments using something like the anger log in Table 10.2. When reviewing the log, I would say something like the following:

> *It is normal to have different feelings, even anger, regularly. Let's discuss how you've been feeling inside when you are angry. What are some cues that you might be angry?*

Anna might indicate that she feels tense and irritable when she gets angry. We would discuss other common signs of anger such as racing heart, rapid breathing, shaking, feeling flushed, and sweating. We would also discuss the fact that there are different levels of anger, and how important it is to be aware of one's level of anger. For example, one might be mildly irritated, moderately frustrated, or even incensed. Becoming aware of even mild irritation is helpful as it is easier to intervene at mild levels of anger rather than waiting until one is furious.

I would ask her what kinds of situations are almost guaranteed to make her angry and note any commonalities between situations she has logged. These are known as "triggers." I would explain to her that it is helpful to know one's triggers because that can help a person be prepared to deal with their anger. I might share that, for me, some situations that almost always lead me to become angry are people driving slowly in the fast lane and picky eaters. I would explain that it is helpful for me to know this because, when I get in a situation where I have to deal with these issues, I can use alternate strategies to help keep my cool.

I would tell Anna that, even though anger is a normal emotion that everyone experiences, it can be difficult to express anger. I would ask her what she thinks people see when she is angry. A frown? Clenched fists? Flushed skin? Tears? Yelling? I would ask her which of these reactions are helpful and which are not. I would ask her if there ways she could work on improving her expression of anger. I might even provide her with a personal example about how I used to cry when I got really angry, but I have since learned to speak up assertively as soon as I recognize that I am starting to feel tense so I can try to improve the situation before I become upset enough to tear up.

Behavioral strategies

Anna and I would next review different strategies for coping with anger. I would explain that it is helpful to be aware of all the different ways of coping with anger so one can choose which strategy works best for oneself in any given situation. Some common behavioral strategies for dealing with anger include:

- ignoring
- walking away
- telling someone
- talking about it
- compromising
- telling yourself it is not worth it

Then, I would encourage Anna to tell me about a recent situation from her anger log so we could discuss strategies that worked and did not work in that situation. Next, we would brainstorm other strategies she might have tried. Our conversation might go somewhat like the following:

Anna:	"Some guy catcalled me. I yelled at him, and he just got louder."
Therapist:	"Can you think of anything else you could have done?"
Anna:	"Well, I could have ignored him, but he needed to be told off."
Therapist:	"Is there anything else you could have done?"
Anna:	"Well, I guess I could have told a teacher. Mr. Anderson was right there."

Anna might say that she sometimes becomes too angry to be able to do anything other than react. In this case, we would discuss that this is why recognizing small signs of anger can be helpful. However, we would also review strategies that can be used to help one cool off and become calmer. Deep breathing is a good strategy to use when one gets really angry. We would discuss how the nice thing about deep breathing is that it can be done anywhere and without anyone else knowing. Another helpful strategy is visualizing a calm place (e.g., the beach) or thinking back to a calming memory (e.g., last family vacation). We would practice doing both in session to see which Anna likes most and then I would have her go home and practice daily, preferably at night as she is trying to fall asleep (at first). Next, I would have her try to start noticing when her anger levels increase.

Anna and I would also discuss how distraction, when possible, can help you cool down. I would have Anna make her own list of engaging activities that she could use to distract herself, as shown in Table 10.3. Some examples I might provide to get her started include:

- talking to a friend
- exercising
- drawing
- listening to music
- playing a game
- watching television
- playing with a pet

I would also stress that it can be helpful to get some physical distance from whatever is causing the anger, if at all possible.

Cognitive strategies

I would stress to Anna that it is important to be aware of what she is thinking in these situations so that she can change any inaccurate or unhelpful thoughts that are interfering with effectively coping with anger. First, I would review coping statements a person can use in a stressful situation. Some of them resonate with particular adolescents more than others. Common coping statements are shown in Table 10.5, and adolescents can circle the ones they like or add to them. Some common examples include:

- It's not important.
- It's not worth getting worked up over.
- It will be okay.
- I'm bigger than this.
- I'm not going to let them upset me.
- They don't know what they are talking about.
- I'm not going to get into trouble over this.
- I'm going to wait to respond.
- Other people like me.
- I am fine.
- This will get better.
- I am trying my best.

I would point out to Anna the coping statements that I find most helpful and perhaps discuss situations in which I have used them. I would also have Anna review recent anger-provoking situations, like those described above, and think about what coping statements might have been useful in those situations.

I would encourage Anna to log and to review with me recent situations in which she became really angry using a worksheet like the one shown in Table 10.6. We would then discuss what she was thinking about at the time.

Anna: "So, I was in class, and my teacher told us our assignment was due, but I hadn't been in class to receive it. When he got to me to collect it, I reminded him I had been absent and asked if I could turn it in the next day, but he said no because it was only extra credit. I was thinking, this teacher hates me and is always so unfair to me."

Therapist: "So, yes, when we have thoughts like 'that's so unfair; that teacher is really out to get me,' it just makes us angrier, right? What if instead you thought, oh well, it's just one assignment and only extra credit. I will try to get in on extra credit later in the semester. Would that help to decrease your anger?"

Anna: (shrugging) "Maybe."

Therapist: "Let's try another one."

Anna: "Well, when Phoebe told me she was too busy to hang out, and I found out later she went to a party with a group of other people, I was thinking, I knew she didn't like me! She just made up an excuse not to hang out!"

Therapist: "Yes, exactly. So that kind of thought, that she doesn't like you and lied in order not to hang out, would also make me angry and hurt. But what if she *was* busy and then her plans changed last minute, so she decided to go to the party? Or what if she wanted to invite you to the party, but there wasn't any extra room in the car or someone else in the group didn't want you to come? In that case, it would probably be premature to get angry until you find out what happened."

Anna: "Maybe. I didn't think about those possibilities. But I really think that maybe she just didn't want to hang out with me."

Therapist: "Yes, well, that is certainly a possibility. The point is to try not to rush to judgment, especially in ambiguous situations."

At this point, I would point out to Anna that we often jump to negative conclusion that may or may not be true. And even if those negative conclusion are true, it may not be very helpful to think of things in a negative way because it will make you unnecessarily upset and, in any case, it will not lead to any constructive action. So sometimes, it is more helpful to try to hold off on rushing to a negative judgment or, otherwise, try to change how we think about things. One way to do this is to use coping statements.

We would also talk about another strategy that can be helpful for controlling anger: trying to see the other person's perspective. An example of how important this can be is shown in Fig. 10.1. I would show Anna this picture and ask her what she sees—it is possible to see either an hourglass or two faces. I would point out that what she initially saw probably makes it difficult to see the alternative.

Then, I would point out that this is a good example of how blind spots work. If a person has one negative experience with another person, then those bad feelings can influence how they see that person and what motives they ascribe to their actions every time they interact with them after that. It

FIGURE 10.1 Illusion. *Reproduced from Nevit Dilmen [CC BY-SA 3.0 (https://creativecommons.org/licenses/by-sa/3.0)] via Wikimedia Commons.*

can even make it difficult to see the positive things that they do. So, blind spots happen when individuals let past feelings interfere with their perception of the present. For example, after a teenager has a bad experience with a teacher, they tend to think the teacher is always out to get them, right?

I would use Anna's own example. That is, when Anna's teacher gave her that extra credit assignment, she thought he was being unfair and assigning extra work; she thought this because of her blind spot. Such an interpretation of events just fueled her anger further. However, it was just as likely, or perhaps more likely, that he was giving her a unique opportunity to bring up her grade. If she had been able to step back a moment and look at the situation from a different perspective, she might have been able to consider an alternative explanation that would have decreased her anger and improved her response to her teacher's suggestion.

For this reason, I would tell Anna that it can be very helpful to consider numerous intentions people can have to determine if one might be jumping to the conclusion that someone is out to get them. Possible different intentions include:

- trying to be helpful
- trying to be hurtful
- it was an accident
- it was unclear

She should consider all possible intentions in a given situation and try to give other people the benefit of the doubt. If in doubt about a person's intention, or it is unclear, it may be most helpful just to admit that the intention is unclear rather than jumping to a negative conclusion. This could help defuse the situation and allow one to collect more information before one decides how to respond.

I would suggest that the goal is to have more cool cognitions about the situation, whether that is trying to see the other person's perspective, avoiding jumping to conclusions, or using coping statements. Even though such strategies may not be instantly effective, practicing them will create more constructive cognitive habits that will decrease anger gradually over time. I would tell Anna, for example, that although she may still be tempted to think people are being unfair to her when she becomes angry, she will gradually learn to respond or even replace such thoughts with more calming thoughts, for example, that the person is just enforcing a rule or that she can work around the problem regardless of the person's intention.

Summary

Discussion of cognitive skills for managing anger can be very helpful for adolescents. They should be encouraged to increase their awareness of when they are starting to become angry, including identifying physiological cues and common triggers, as well as knowing their own anger expression. Next, they should try to utilize proactive behavioral measures to cool down, including behavioral strategies like walking away, coping statements, deep breathing, and distraction. Finally, they should try to use cognitive strategies for managing anger including seeing others' perspectives, avoiding jumping to conclusions, and modifying cognition. We will discuss more about how to take action to address difficult interpersonal situations in the next chapter.

Further reading

Online resources:

https://copingskillsforkids.com/managing-anger/

Text resources:

Barkley, R. A., & Robin, A. L. (2014). *Defiant teens: A clinician's manual for assessment and family intervention*. Guilford Publications.

Larson, J., & Lochman, J. E. (2010). *Helping schoolchildren cope with anger: A cognitive-behavioral intervention*. Guilford Press.

Lochman, J. E., Wells, K., & Lenhart, L. A. (2008). *Coping power: Child group facilitator's guide* (Vol. 2). Oxford University Press.

Webster-Stratton, C., Mostyn, D., & Marie, J. S. (2005). *The Incredible Years: A trouble-shooting guide for parents of children aged 2-8 years*. Seattle, WA: Incredible Years.

Wells, K., Lochman, J. E., & Lenhart, L. (2008). *Coping power: Parent group facilitator's guide*. Oxford University Press.

Wells, K., Lochman, J. E., & Lenhart, L. (2008). *Coping power: Parent group program workbook*. Oxford University Press.

11

CHAPTER

Treatment component #5: Problem-solving

The fifth main treatment component for addressing disruptive behavior problems and oppositional defiant disorder (ODD) is problem-solving. In a nutshell, this involves teaching parents and children or adolescents problem-solving and communication skills. In regard to Chapter 6's, Overview of evidence-based treatment components for oppositional defiant disorder, it includes the following treatment components:

- problem-solving
- communication skills
- family therapy
- modeling

These skills are heavily involved in cognitive therapies and are particularly important for use with adolescents. Problem-solving teaches parents and adolescents how to utilize perspective taking, generate more and different possible solutions to the problem, agree on a compromise, and evaluate the outcome. It is also important for improving social information processing, both in and outside the home environment. It should be noted that information in this chapter comes from the text resources cited at the end of this chapter.

The Clinician's Guide to Oppositional Defiant Disorder. DOI: https://doi.org/10.1016/B978-0-12-815682-7.00011-2

TABLE 11.1 Problem-solving skills overview.

1. Is there a rule that can be negotiated?
2. If so, use PICC model
   a. Problem identification
   b. Identification of all possible solutions
   c. Consider the consequences
   d. Choose the best solution and evaluate its outcome
3. Use proper etiquette
4. Keep in mind possible solutions such as compromise
5. Manage unreasonable beliefs
6. Monitor outcomes

Problem-solving skills overview

Problem-solving becomes particularly important during adolescence, when parents and adolescents begin negotiating rules. As shown in Table 11.1, problem-solving is a process consisting of several steps: problem identification, identification of all the choices, thinking about the consequences of each choice, and choosing a solution and evaluating its outcome. Therapists should review this process and etiquette associated with problem-solving, which entails focusing matter-of-factly on the pros and cons of different solutions and not losing one's temper. Families may often find it helpful to consider alternative solutions such as a compromise. Therapists should review and teach families to avoid, to the extent possible, unreasonable beliefs like expecting perfection or believing that rules will ruin one's life. Finally, monitoring and reevaluating decisions periodically is important for good problem-solving.

Problem-solving process

Therapists should begin by discussing with parents how important it becomes to start negotiating rules once children reach early adolescence. Help parents proactively identify some family issues that can be negotiated (e.g., curfew). There is a problem-solving process one can teach families, as shown in Table 11.2. First, identify the problem (P). Next, identify (I) all the choices. Then, think about the consequences (C) of each choice. Finally, choose (C) a solution and evaluate its outcome. Or, in other words, ask:

- What is the problem?
- What are some solutions?
- What are the consequences?
- What is the best solution?
- Am I using my plan?
- How did I do?

TABLE 11.2 Steps to better problem-solving.

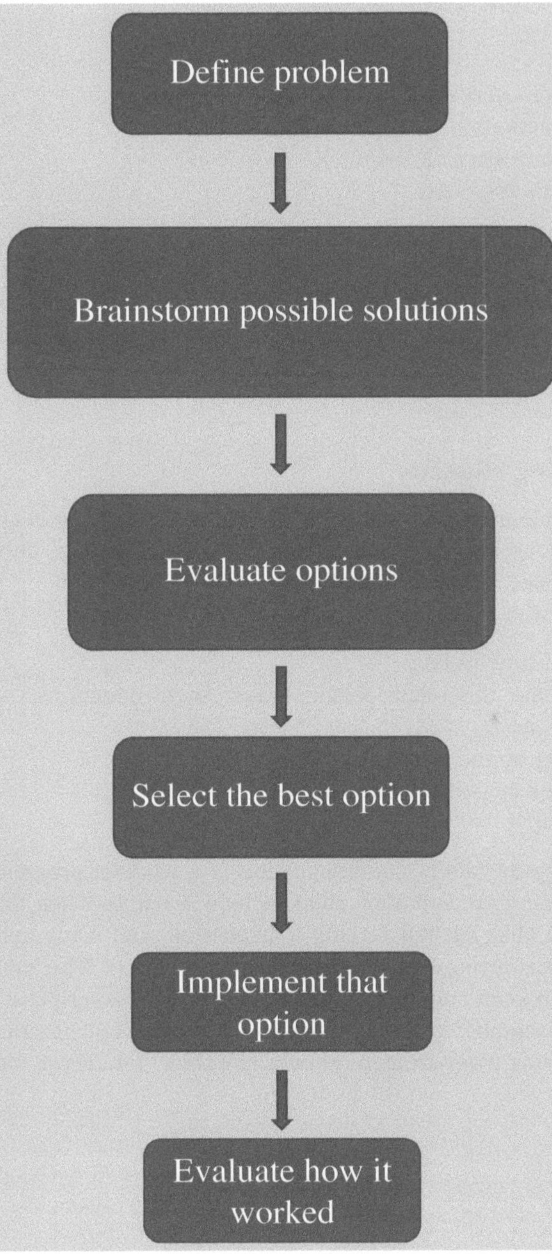

Encourage parents to have a number of possible alternative solutions in mind at the start of problem-solving. Here are some possible solutions that cut across many different circumstances:

- seek help
- assert yourself verbally
- take direct action
- compromise or bargain
- avoid or wait until later

Families should be encouraged to be strategic about how they engage in problem-solving. They can use a contract, as shown in Table 11.3. They should be encouraged to periodically discuss how the process is going and how well their chosen solution is working, revisiting and revising it as necessary.

Problem-solving etiquette

Following problem-solving etiquette is critical to this process, given that these negotiations can very easily and very quickly turn into arguments. Review guidelines with families to make sure problem-solving remains cordial and respectful:

- Find a good time to talk.
- Do not blame the other person, guess their intentions, or use broad generalizations.
- Do not bring up old issues.
- Do not attack or put down the person.
- Be persistent!!!

Stress that good family communication is a work in progress. Some tips that can help improve communication include listening when the teenager is in the mood to talk, but not forcing a discussion, and using active listening to encourage the teenager to express his/her opinion. The most important thing is to try to keep communication lines open whenever possible.

There are a number of communication strategies that families should be encouraged to stay away from, as shown in Table 11.4. These include:

- insulting
- criticizing
- interrupting
- disengaging
- yelling
- lecturing
- commanding

TABLE 11.3 Problem-solving worksheet.

Problem-Solving Worksheet

We agree on the following definition of the problem:

____

____

____

Possible choices:	Consequences of the choices:
____________________	____________________
____________________	____________________
____________________	____________________
____________________	____________________
____________________	____________________
____________________	____________________
____________________	____________________

The solution we have chosen is:

____

____

____

____

We will implement this solution for week(s) and then talk about how it is working.

Signature of Child:

____

Signature of Parent:

____

____

99

TABLE 11.4 Communication habits.

What to do	What not to do
State the problem neutrally	Blame
Ask for the other person's perspective	Criticize
Stay calm	Name call
Note positives and negatives	Interrupt
Consider alternative solutions	Get defensive
Focus on own feelings	Lecture
Talk in a normal tone	Be sarcastic or belittle others' concerns
Make eye contact	Stonewall
Find points of agreement when possible	Command
Summarize concerns	Yell
Use respectful, polite language	Drag others into argument
Admit to past mistakes, misunderstandings	Not be able to move on
Stay on topic	Bring up old fights
Ask to take a break from conversation if needed	Curse, get violent

However, families can and should work on replacing these negative communication strategies with positive ones, also shown in Table 11.4. More positive communication strategies include:

- matter-of-factly stating the issue
- taking turns
- politely disagreeing
- noting the positive and negative aspects of the situation
- saying how you feel
- taking responsibility
- asking nicely

Proactively talk to families about how to handle situations in which emotions flare, as they undoubtedly will. Above all else, it is important to encourage everyone to honestly express how they feel without being hurtful to others. That is, family members should be encouraged to try to calmly state the issue, say how they feel, and take turns. Everyone should try to use a normal tone of voice and be polite and respectful when disagreeing. If they can see the other person's perspective, they should summarize it. They should try to accept responsibility for any past issues, as appropriate, and lay out positive and negative aspects or concerns related to the situation.

Parents can and should be encouraged to use many of the strategies discussed in Chapter 10, Treatment component #4: Cognitive skills. They should also watch out for unreasonable beliefs, shown in Table 11.5. These include, from the parent's perspective:

- the expectation for perfection or total obedience
- ruination
- malicious intent
- indulgence

To go into more detail, teenagers are not going to behave perfectly all the time. Having high expectations is great, but getting angry for anything less than perfection or total obedience is setting the parent and teenager up for failure. Likewise, equating a mistake with the teenager ruining his/her life is excessive. A mistake is just a mistake, perhaps better termed a learning experience. Expecting that every misbehavior is done out of malicious intent, or just to get on the parent's nerves, is likewise unlikely to be accurate and is a negative place from which to start a constructive conversation. So, the parent should try to give the teenager the benefit of the doubt. Finally, it is not healthy for the parents to expect that teenagers should be appreciative for everything the parents buy them, or that they can buy a teenager off through indulgence. Limit setting is sometimes the best way to show love.

TABLE 11.5 Identifying unreasonable beliefs.

Unreasonable belief	Example	More reasonable belief
Parents		
Perfectionism	He should always complete his schoolwork and turn it in on time	Turning in complete homework most of the time is a big accomplishment for him
Ruination	She's home late so she must be having unprotected sex and drinking, which will lead to pregnancy and living with us forever	She lost track of time and will be punished accordingly
Malicious intent	He got in that car accident to get back at me	It was an accident and we will talk about steps to try to decrease his risk
Appreciation/indulgence	She should appreciate all her new clothes because buying these new clothes is how I show my love	She should say thank you and earn some of her clothes allowance from her chores, but she knows I love her regardless of what I buy her
Adolescents		
Unfairness/ruination	My parents are ruining my life by making me come home by curfew	Other kids have rules to follow too—my parents are trying to look out for me
Autonomy	I should have complete freedom	No one is completely free; some rules are good
Love/appreciation	Getting my way/stuff is a sign my parents love me	My parents love me, and sometimes rules reflect that love better than freedom—stuff does not equate love; ditto sex

Source: Adapted from Barkley, R. A., & Robin, A. L. (2014). *Defiant teens: A clinician's manual for assessment and family intervention.* Guilford Publications.

Adolescents should also try to identify their own unreasonable beliefs. On the adolescent's side, shown in Table 11.5, unreasonable expectations often include:

- unfairness
- ruination
- autonomy
- love/appreciation

Teenagers often express the idea that their parents' rules are totally unfair and will ruin their lives. Of course, the reverse is often closer to the case. But a conversation or statement about the purpose of the rule can often be helpful. If the teenager thinks the rule is going to ruin his/her life, this might be a great time to get his/her perspective and concerns and see if a compromise might be possible. Alternatively, reviewing the purpose of the rule from the parent's perspective may help. Teenagers often expect and demand total freedom, which is inappropriate. Explaining that gaining freedom is a privilege to be earned may be helpful. Finally, some teenagers think that getting their way is a sign of love from their parents, when often the opposite is the case. Again, providing an explanation can be helpful.

Finally, it is important for parents to monitor both the success of the problem-solving process and its outcome. Clinicians should encourage families to discuss how their problem-solving went. Are there any ways the family can improve their communication and etiquette? How did the solution they chose work? Do they need to make any adjustments?

Summary

Problem-solving becomes particularly important during adolescence, when parents and teenagers begin negotiating rules. Therapists should review the problem-solving process with families, as it consists of several steps: problem identification, identification of all the choices, thinking about the consequences of each choice, and choosing a solution and evaluating its outcome. The importance of maintaining good problem-solving etiquette should be stressed. For example, families should focus on the pros and cons of different solutions and not losing their tempers. It is often helpful to consider alternative solutions such as a compromise. Critically, families should be encouraged to try to avoid unreasonable beliefs like expecting perfection or believing that rules will ruin one's life. Finally, it is essential to monitor and reevaluate decisions periodically.

Case example

Anna

Anna is a 15-year-old Caucasian female whose parents present with concerns about possible drug use, sexting, and promiscuous sex. Anna has been diagnosed with depression and has been taking antidepressants since age 13. She was described as irritable and easily annoyed most of the time. She acknowledges frequent marijuana use with friends and being sexually active with several males. She has been grounded for the last 2 weeks after she sent a naked picture to one of these males, and her parents were informed by a friend's mother, who saw the picture on her daughter's Snapchat. Anna acknowledges that her current friend group has not been the best influence. She complains that the girls are all catty and talk about her behind her back. She reports engaging in sexting or sex and impulsivity, without a lot of forethought about the consequences, or while under the influence of alcohol. She indicated that she has no desire to listen to her parents and often argues with them about curfews and rules. She justified her behavior by reporting that she was bullied extensively in grade school and feels the need to fit in with her peers whatever the cost.

Conceptualization: Anna exhibits ODD in the context of a preexisting depression diagnosis. She is also at risk for emerging substance use problems with marijuana and alcohol. She has a history of peer problems including bullying through covert aggression (e.g., rumors). Through these experiences, she seems to have developed faulty social information processing in that she almost always attributes hostile intentions to her peers, and she impulsively engages in inappropriate reactions such as substance use and sexting. She furthermore does not seem to have learned to evaluate the negative consequences of her actions. Her parents, to date, have been largely ineffective at monitoring or disciplining her to obtain desired behaviors.

Personalization of treatment tips: Given Anna's depression and the prominent role peers are playing in her problems, a social learning approach would probably be most effective. It will also be important to involve Anna's parents in the treatment to facilitate a more effective problem-solving approach to setting rules and consequences for her. Better monitoring of Anna's behavior, including use of substances, will be critical. Assessment for attention-deficit/hyperactivity disorder for Anna's impulsive behaviors may also be helpful. A psychiatric consultation regarding the effectiveness of Anna's antidepressant at its current dosage for managing depressive symptomatology will also be important.

Ideal treatment

PSST

Back-up treatment possibilities

CBT
Assertiveness training
REMH

Useful treatment components

Cognitive
Self-monitoring
Problem-solving
Communication skills
Family therapy
Modeling

Problem-solving process

When describing problem-solving to Anna and her parents, I would say something like:

> *Now that Anna is getting older, it is important to involve her more in decisions. Although, for example, you might have wanted Anna to be home by dark as a child, you typically have to become more flexible about rules such as these as children become adolescents. Can you think of other rules that might need to be negotiated like this?*

Usually, families can easily come up with additional rules. Some common ones include bedtime, friends with whom the child is allowed to hang out, time spent away from home, amount of screen time, and privacy, just to name a few. It is normal and adaptive for families to begin to negotiate with rules like these. Having a negotiation strategy can be very helpful, perhaps just as much for parents as for teenagers!

Remind the family that, despite the fact that it can be intimidating, it is important to engage in proactive problem-solving in difficult family and other interpersonal situations. When you run into a problem, what should you do? In general, problem-solving can be broken down into several distinct steps. First, identify the problem (P). Next, identify (I) all the choices. Then, think about the consequences (C) of each choice. Finally, choose (C) a solution and evaluate its outcome. Or, in other words, ask:

- What is the problem?
- What are some solutions?
- What are the consequences?
- What is the best solution?
- Am I using my plan?
- How did I do?

First, break the problem down into solvable steps. Then, brainstorm possible solutions and evaluate their consequences. Ask yourself, what might happen if I do this? What might happen if I do *that* instead? Think about potential consequences. Is there a clear, best choice? If there is not, how does one choose? One strategy is to focus on your long-term goal. Will this help you get there? Finally, remember to evaluate how the decision worked out. It may be helpful to try out another solution.

I remind families that it can also be helpful to have a number of different possible solutions in mind at the start. Here are some possible solutions that cut across many different circumstances:

- seek help
- assert yourself verbally
- take direct action
- compromise or bargain
- avoid or wait until later

Problem-solving etiquette

I stress to families that in the problem-solving process, it is important to think ahead instead of just reacting to the problem as it arises. There are some general rules for problem-solving etiquette, which are helpful for families and in other difficult interpersonal situations. I remind parents that they should model calm, respectful problem-solving for their adolescent to emulate. If parents lose their temper, teenagers are almost guaranteed to!

Here are some guidelines to make sure problem-solving remains cordial and respectful:

- Find a good time to talk.
- Do not blame the other person, guess their intentions, or use broad generalizations.
- Do not bring up old issues.
- Do not attack or put down the person.
- Be persistent!!!

If you run into an obstacle, don't worry. Go back to the drawing board and try a different way of handling the problem. Remember to focus on resolving the problem, not on assigning blame.

The model of problem-solving described above can be used to discuss family rule changes. A schematic of this is shown in Table 11.2. I would tell the family:

> *In the problem identification step, it will be important for both you and Anna to try to be empathetic and think of the other's perspective. For example, with curfew, what are the parental concerns? What are Anna's concerns? It is important here not to name call, blame, or use put-downs. Use "I" language,*

or—in other words—own your perspective. If you are upset, do not name call, but rather indicate how you are feeling; for example, "I am feeling upset because I do not feel heard right now." Discuss and share ideas for solutions. Entertain any ideas, at least initially. Then, review the solutions and discuss whether they will really work by thinking of their outcomes. Everyone should weigh in on whether they like a given solution. This will rule out some ideas entirely (like curfew at dark and no curfew at all). Next, decide on the best solution, the one most agreeable to everyone, if possible. If there is more than one solution, you are lucky and can choose which one to try first. If no solution is agreeable to everyone, then you will have to negotiate and compromise; for example, a curfew that progressively gets later and later following compliance. Then, implement your choice and evaluate the results.

The family must figure out how they will evaluate the outcome. What constitutes a good outcome? How will the outcome be monitored? Will reminders be given? What are the consequences for noncompliance? Are any difficulties anticipated? It will be important to set up a family time to review how things are going. Should this happen weekly? Monthly? Where and when? One can also use a possible family contract that notes different solutions and outcomes in writing, as shown in Table 11.3.

I always remind families that good family communication is a work in progress. Some tips that can help improve communication include listening when the teenager is in the mood to talk, but not forcing a discussion, and using active listening to encourage the teenager to express his/her opinion. The most important thing is to try to keep communication lines open whenever possible.

There are some communication strategies that families should try to stay away from; I review those shown in Table 11.4. These include:

- insulting
- criticizing
- interrupting
- disengaging
- yelling
- lecturing
- commanding

However, families can and should work on replacing these negative communication strategies with positive ones, also shown in Table 11.4. More positive communication strategies I discuss with families include:

- matter-of-factly stating the issue
- taking turns
- politely disagreeing
- noting the positive and negative aspects of the situation
- saying how you feel
- taking responsibility
- asking nicely

I also proactively talk to families about how to handle situations in which emotions flare, as they undoubtedly will. Then, it is helpful for everyone in the family to use coping strategies. For example, it can be helpful to take a hike or count to 10 and then try again later. Above all else, it is important that one learns how to honestly express feelings without being hurtful to others. That is, a family member should be able to calmly state the issue, say how they feel, and take turns listening to another family member do the same. Use a normal tone of voice and be polite and respectful when disagreeing. If you can see the other person's perspective, summarize it. Accept responsibility for any past issues, as appropriate, and lay out positive and negative aspects or concerns related to the situation.

Parents can and should use many of the strategies discussed in Chapter 10, Treatment component #4: Cognitive skills. They should also watch out for unreasonable beliefs, shown in Table 11.5. These include, from the parent's perspective:

- the expectation for perfection or total obedience
- ruination
- malicious intent
- indulgence

I discuss these in detail with families. Teenagers are not going to behave perfectly all the time. Having high expectations is great, but getting angry for anything less than perfection or total obedience is setting the parent and teenager up for failure. Likewise, equating a mistake with the teenager ruining his/her life is excessive. A mistake is just a mistake, perhaps better termed a learning experience. Expecting that every misbehavior is done out of malicious intent, or just to get on the parent's nerves, is likewise unlikely to be accurate and is a negative place from which to start a constructive conversation. So, the parent should try to give the teenager the benefit of the doubt. Finally, it is not healthy for the parents to expect that teenagers should be appreciative for everything the parents buy them, or that they can buy a teenager off through indulgence. Limit setting is sometimes the best way to show love.

On the adolescent's side, shown in Table 11.5, unreasonable expectations often include:

- unfairness
- ruination
- autonomy
- love/appreciation

I also review these in detail with adolescents. Teenagers often express the idea that their parents' rules are totally unfair and will ruin their lives. Of course, the reverse is often closer to the case. But a conversation or statement about the purpose of the rule can often be helpful. If the teenager thinks the rule is going to ruin his/her life, this might be a great time to get his/her perspective and concerns and see if a compromise might be possible. Alternatively, reviewing the purpose of the rule from the parent's perspective may help. Teenagers often expect and demand total freedom, which is inappropriate. Explaining that gaining freedom is a privilege to be earned may be helpful. Finally, some teenagers think that getting their way is a sign of love from their parents, when often the opposite is the case. Again, providing an explanation can be helpful.

I discuss how monitoring is essential. But how it is done can and should be discussed. Family values should be kept in mind as a family and teenager negotiate new freedoms. Try to find time to remind teenagers of their values or talk to them about their values. Parents should know that rebellious teenager behavior is normal. Try to look for the positive, even if it is just that you hope your teenager learned something from a negative experience and will not make that same mistake again. Finally, be sure to find support from others, and know it is normal to worry or be angry. If parents find themselves spending a lot of time worrying or being angry, they should schedule a time to worry and then try to let it go. They should be counseled not to let the stress of having a teenager take over their life. They should practice modeling taking care of themselves by doing fun or nice things. They may need to be reminded that parenting is a hard and thankless job! In sum, adolescence is a trying time, full of growing pains for both parents and adolescents. Growth and movement in the right direction is success!

Summary

To summarize, problem-solving becomes particularly important during adolescence, when parents and adolescents begin negotiating rules. Problem-solving consists of several steps: problem identification, identification of all the choices, thinking about the consequences of each choice, and choosing a solution and evaluating its outcome. It is important to maintain good problem-solving etiquette by focusing on the pros and cons of different solutions and not losing your temper. It is also helpful to consider alternative solutions such as a compromise. Finally, it is critical to try avoid unreasonable beliefs like expecting perfection or believing that rules will ruin one's life. And it is essential to monitor and reevaluate decisions periodically.

Further reading

Text resources:

Barkley, R. A., & Robin, A. L. (2014). *Defiant teens: A clinician's manual for assessment and family intervention*. Guilford Publications.

Faber, A., & Mazlish, E. (2012). *How to talk so kids will listen & listen so kids will talk*. Simon and Schuster.

Lochman, J. E., Wells, K., & Lenhart, L. A. (2008). *Coping power: Child group facilitator's guide* (Vol. 2). Oxford University Press.

Webster-Stratton, C., Mostyn, D., & Marie, J. S. (2005). *The Incredible Years: A troubleshooting guide for parents of children aged 2–8 years*. Seattle, WA: Incredible Years.

Wells, K., Lochman, J. E., & Lenhart, L. (2008a). *Coping power: Parent group facilitator's guide*. Oxford University Press.

Wells, K., Lochman, J. E., & Lenhart, L. (2008b). *Coping power: Parent group program workbook*. Oxford University Press.

12

CHAPTER

Related treatment issues: how to address sleep, toilet training, social skills, and learning problems and when to consider medication for comorbid disorders

The last main treatment component targets behaviors that commonly cooccur with oppositional defiant disorder (ODD) including problems sleeping independently, toilet training problems, problems with peers, and learning problems. In regard to Chapter 6's, Overview of evidence-based treatment

The Clinician's Guide to Oppositional Defiant Disorder. DOI: https://doi.org/10.1016/B978-0-12-815682-7.00012-4

components for oppositional defiant disorder, it includes the following treatment components:

- social skills training
- educational support

Resources for the following sections are listed at chapter's end. Given ODD's relatively high rates of comorbidity, or cooccurrence, with other disorders, such multipronged approaches are often useful. These ideas are elucidated quite well in Luis' and Anna's cases, as they both have multiple cooccurring problems.

For Luis' difficulties with independent sleep and toilet training, a behavioral approach for addressing sleep and toilet training issues would be highly effective if a physician has already ruled out medical problems. Suggestions on how to utilize such approaches for sleep and toilet training problems are detailed below.

Luis

Luis, our 4-year-old Latino male, has preschool ODD given that he often loses his temper, is frequently angry, often refuses to comply with adult requests, and deliberately annoys others. An important diagnostic consideration in his case would be disruptive mood dysregulation disorder. If his temper outbursts occur three or more times each week, and his mood is persistently angry or irritable between these outbursts, then he might be better diagnosed with disruptive mood dysregulation disorder (vs ODD). Yet, clearly, language problems are an important issue in this case and need to be formally evaluated, as this will affect both diagnosis and treatment; that is, Luis' language problems may be leading to his aggressive temper outbursts. Luis' parents' use of Spanish at home and his prematurity will be important to consider in such an evaluation. Other diagnostic and treatment concerns include Luis' elimination (or potty-training) problems and his problems sleeping independently. These issues can also be addressed during treatment. Finally, looking into additional avenues of social support for Luis' parents will be important.

Possible cooccurring problems

- disruptive mood dysregulation disorder
- language problems
- *potty-training problems*
- *independent sleep problems*

Other considerations

- bilingualism
- prematurity

Behavioral strategies for addressing problems with independent sleep

Behavioral strategies for addressing problems with independent sleep focus on setting up a positive environment around bedtime, tracking sleep, and eliminating cues for sleep. First, parents must the stage for a good night's sleep by making sure the child's room is pleasant, and there is a good routine in place for bedtime. Next, they should track the child's sleep to make sure that they are getting enough sleep, but are not going to bed too early. Finally, parents should eliminate themselves as a bedtime cue by making sure they are out of the room when the child falls asleep.

When working with families with children like Luis, who are experiencing problems with independent sleep, it is important to talk to them about how to set the stage for sleep, as described in Table 12.1. When I work with families, I ask them to make sure the child's room is a pleasant, relaxing place. What that means will differ from child to child and family to family, but some things to consider include:

- a nightlight
- white noise or wave machine
- humidifier
- a lamp
- stuffed animals or dolls
- favorite blanket
- books
- posters or pictures

It is also important to have a consistent bedtime routine. Bedtime should be at the same time every night, and parents should warn the child that bedtime is approaching. It is ideal to plan relaxing activities in the routine leading up to bedtime, such as a bath. Planning pleasant activities that precede bedtime, such as story time, can motivate the child to complete the bedtime routine and get into bed in a timely fashion.

The parent should not stay in the child's bed until he/she is asleep. The idea is to get the child relaxed and ready to go to sleep, but the parent does not want the child to have to rely on their physical presence to be able to fall asleep; this is what usually leads to middle-of-the-night awakenings and children climbing into parents' beds. Naptimes should be set up in the same manner. It can also be helpful if the parent uses a sticker or reward system to reinforce the child for going to sleep on their own.

The parent should track the child's sleep. What time does he/she fall asleep? What time does he/she wake up? If the child is consistently taking a long time to fall asleep or waking up too early, the parent may want to push the child's bedtime back to make sure they are actually tired and not being forced to stay in bed longer than the amount of sleep they actually need. Lying in bed when one is not tired is actually counterproductive and can

TABLE 12.1 Setting the stage for independent sleep.

Setting the stage for independent sleeping
1. Young children are developing a sense of ownership and a desire for privacy. They need a place they can call their own. With this in mind, be sure to consult with and involve your child in the following recommendations.
2. Your child spends a great deal of his or her time in their room. Be sure the room is kept neat and clean so that it is more desirable to be in. Responsibility for keeping the room clean will vary depending on the individual child's age and abilities.
3. A nightlight or small light within the child's reach may allow your child to feel "safer" and more secure during the night.
4. Pictures or posters selected by the child will further reinforce that this is your child's own room and a place to be enjoyed.
5. Use of a quiet fan or humidifier often allows for some "white noise" to fill your child's room so that noise and conversation going on in the rest of the house are drowned out.
6. Place possessions around your child's bed so it becomes sort of a "mini-home" to which he or she will enjoy returning each night.
7. Have a bedside table or shelf stocked with your child's books available.
8. Remember, you are trying to make your child's room a pleasant, relaxing place for playing and going to sleep.
9. In addition to making the child's room an enticing environment, you want to make getting there enjoyable too. Give your child plenty of notice that bedtime is approaching. A predictable, consistent bedtime routine is very important in allowing children to transition to bedtime.
10. Set aside time to do something special with your child before bed. Avoid any activities that will excite your child at this time. You might both enjoy a discussion, quiet play, or story reading. Be sure to let your child know that your special time together will not extend beyond the time you and he or she have agreed upon.

make it more difficult to fall asleep. There are published guidelines about how much sleep children need at different ages, but—given substantial individual differences among children—the best guide to how much sleep any particular child needs is individual parental tracking of child sleep. Once a parent has determined how much sleep their child needs to feel well rested (in other words, how much time they actually sleep before waking up well rested in the morning), then the parent should set the child's bedtime accordingly. If in doubt, I find it helps to push the bedtime back slightly, at least temporarily, so the child will have an easy time falling asleep at bedtime; the parent can gradually move the bedtime up once they have established a satisfactory bedtime routine.

Once an appropriate bedtime has been set, the parent should only check on the child briefly at bedtime. They should also only check in on the child briefly in the middle of the night after wakening before matter-of-factly returning the child to their own bed. If the parent allows the child to get in bed with them or they get into bed with the child, they are teaching the child that the child needs the parent to be able to fall asleep, and problems with independent sleep will continue. A structured approach to keep and return children to bed is more comprehensively covered in Table 12.2.

It is important that children learn to fall asleep on their own eventually. To do this, the family may have to go through a difficult night or two of crying until the child learns to fall asleep on his/her own. Once the child learns to fall asleep independently, they should eventually stop having problems with getting out of bed in the middle of the night. The child will return to sleep much easier following awakenings if they do not require the parent's presence to fall asleep in the first place. However, the parents should carefully plan when they start independent sleep training (e.g., on the weekend or over a holiday) in case it takes a long time for the child to fall asleep and/or he/she is up out of bed or crying for periods of time while learning.

For this reason, everyone must really be ready for the child to sleep independently. If parents or other family members like the child being in bed with them, that is fine. Whatever works best for the family is the goal here. However, in this case of families who enjoy cosleeping, they should wait to begin this approach until they are ready to follow through so they do not cause problems with their child's independent sleep later on. Inconsistency or differing expectations across family members will just cause the child unnecessary confusion.

In sum, as shown in Table 12.3, set the stage for a good night's sleep by making sure the child's room is pleasant, and there is a good routine in place for bedtime. Track the child's sleep to make sure they are getting enough sleep, but are not going to bed too early. Finally, eliminate yourself as a bedtime cue by making sure you are out of the room when they fall asleep.

TABLE 12.2 Helping your child learn to stay in bed.

Helping your child learn to stay in bed

The goal is to have your child fall asleep with you not in the room, and you can use the door as a controlled way of enforcing this. The chart below shows the number of minutes that you should keep your child's door closed if she will not stay in bed at bedtime or after nighttime wakings. Use the following guidelines:

- Let your child know that having the door open is something he can earn if he stays in his bed quietly. If he gets out, then the door will close briefly as a consequence.
- Keep the door closed for the number of minutes listed, even if your child goes back to bed sooner. However, you may talk to him through the door (minimally) and tell him how much time remains.
- When you open the door, if your child is still awake, speak to her briefly if she is in bed, offer encouragement, and then leave. If she is still out of bed, restate the rules, put her back in bed (if it can be done easily), and shut the door for the next amount of time listed.
- Remember, the door is to enforce the goal of having your child fall asleep without you, not to punish or scare him. So, reassure him by talking through the door and do not threaten or scream. He will learn that having the door open is entirely under his control.
- If your child wakes during the night and won't stay in bed, begin the door-closing schedule at the minimum time for that day and again work up to the maximum.
- Use the same routine at naptime, but if she has not fallen asleep after 1 h, end the naptime.
- The numbers of minutes listed are the ones that most families find workable. If these amounts of time seem too long, they can be reduced as long as the times increase progressively.

Number of minutes to close the door if your child will not stay in bed

		If your child continues to get out of bed			
Day	**First closing**	**Second closing**	**Third closing**	**Fourth closing**	**Subsequent closings**
1	1/4	1/2	1	2	3
2	1/2	1	2	3	5
3	1	2	3	5	7
4	2	3	5	7	10
5	3	5	7	10	12

(Continued)

TABLE 12.2 (Continued)

Number of minutes to close the door if your child will not stay in bed

		If your child continues to get out of bed			
Day	**First closing**	**Second closing**	**Third closing**	**Fourth closing**	**Subsequent closings**
6	5	7	10	12	15
7	7	10	12	15	20

If your child cries for you in the middle of the night

The goal is to have your child fall asleep by himself without you in the room. The chart below shows the number of minutes to wait before going in if your child is crying at bedtime or after nighttime wakings. Use the following guidelines:

- Each time you go in to him, spend only 2–3 min. You are going in briefly to reassure him (and yourself); you are not going in to help him fall asleep.
- The first night your child wakes during the night, begin at the minimum waiting schedule for that day and work up to the maximum.
- Use the same schedule for naps, but if he has not fallen asleep after 1 h, end the naptime.
- The minutes listed to wait are the ones that most families find workable. If they seem too long, the wait times can be reduced as long as the times increase progressively.

Number of minutes to wait before briefly going in to your child

		If your child is still crying		
Day	**At first wait**	**Second wait**	**Third wait**	**Subsequent waits**
1	3	5	10	10
2	5	10	12	12
3	10	12	15	15
4	12	15	17	17
5	15	17	20	20
6	17	20	25	25
7	20	25	30	30

Source: Based on Ferber, R. (2006). *Solve your child's sleep problems.* New York: Simon & Schuster.

TABLE 12.3 Independent sleep training overview.
1. Set the stage for sleep
2. Establish a routine
3. Track sleep
4. Eliminate self as cue for sleep

Behavioral strategies for addressing problems with toilet training

It is not uncommon for children with disruptive behavior problems, like Luis, to also have problems with toilet training. To successful conduct toilet training, parents should first assess if their child is ready. Then, they should track their child's elimination patterns. Next, they should get rid of the diaper and set them up for success with toys. Last, but not least, parents should praise enthusiastically any attempts or successes on the toilet!

When working with families, I ask parents to determine—first and foremost—whether their child is ready to train. Most specialists recommend toilet training between ages 20 and 30 months. However, just like with sleep requirements, there is a lot of individual variability. Therefore, here are some signs that the child might be ready to train:

- can communicate his/her needs
- can repeat simple phrases
- retreats to a private spot to have a bowel movement
- can pull down pants
- is interested in potty-related stuff

Signs of toilet training readiness are detailed in Table 12.4. The other issue the parent should assess, perhaps most importantly, is whether they themselves are ready to begin the hard work of potty training. That is critical because it is hard work—perhaps more so for parents than for children!

First, the parents will need to keep track of the child's urination patterns and bowel movements. This is easiest if the parent starts potty training with an initial period of the child staying undressed from the waist down. This will also speed up the process of training. But this will require the parent to devote a day, or ideally several days, to being totally available to watch the child, keep the toilet close, and place the child on it as soon as the parent notices them starting to go. Doing this will help the parent notice patterns faster and speed up the child's learning curve as they associate the feeling of going with moving to the toilet. The parents should praise attempts or any success. The key is to get the child moving in the right direction and to notice patterns in when the child goes and signals they might be ready to go. So, for example, a parent might notice that their child always tends to have a bowel movement midday, and that he/she tends to get quiet, move to a private location, and turn red while going.

TABLE 12.4 Toilet training readiness.

Toilet training readiness
Most children have the muscle control to regulate themselves between 18 months and 3 years of age. Children with disabilities or certain medical problems may not have this ability until a later age. More important than any other factor is the level of readiness.
Readiness signals: Your child may be ready to start toilet training if she:
• has predictable, regular, soft, formed bowel movements • can pull own pants up, is able to help dress self • imitates others' bathroom habits (e.g., likes to watch you go to the bathroom, wants to wear underwear) • indicates by words, facial expression, or posture that she is urinating or having a bowel movement (e.g., grunting, squatting, letting you know) • has words for stool and urine • is able to follow simple instructions • can tell you she has to urinate/bowel movement before it happens • does not like the feeling of being in a dirty diaper • has "dry" pants for at least 2–3 h or is dry after naps • demonstrates a desire for independence • can walk and sit down • asks to use the toilet or potty chair, "big kid pants," pull-ups, or underwear
Pretoilet training
Prepares your child for toilet training and will make the process easier for you. You can begin this process when your child is around 15 months or older and should continue until your child demonstrates some of the readiness signals listed above. If your child is ready to begin toilet training, spend at least a week practicing pretoilet training skills so that your child becomes familiar with the process.
• *Name urine and bowel movements:* When your child has a dirty diaper, mention what has happened using words that you have chosen (e.g., "you have poop in your diaper").
Toilet training
There are several steps involved in toilet training. Keep in mind that your child should feel comfortable with each step before moving on to the next.
Step 1: Keep track of when your child urinates and has bowel movements so that you identify her elimination pattern. Continue to obtain this information while implementing steps 2 and 3. *Step 2:* Begin to introduce the potty to your child. Place a potty chair in the bathroom and wait for your child to inquire about it. This gives your child a sense of control and

(*Continued*)

TABLE 12.4 (Continued)

lets him initiate the training. This also avoids negative comments such as, "No, I don't wanna see potty." Using a special child potty is not necessary; you could also use a smaller child seat on top of the regular toilet seat. If you do that, make sure there is a step stool for your child's feet.

Step 3: Have your child sit on the potty a few times a day with her clothes on. This will get your child in the habit of sitting on the potty. Encourage your child to sit on the potty. You can do this by providing a special activity to do (playing with a favorite toy or game) or giving a special treat such as stickers for sitting on the potty. Only allow that desirable activity to occur when your child sits on the potty. This will keep your child from being tense and bored.

Step 4: Encourage your child to sit on the potty a few times a day with her pants and diaper off. Try to place your child on the potty close to the time she usually urinates or has a bowel movement (you will know this from step 1). A natural time to do this may be around bath time, when your child's clothing is already off. Or, try this about 10–15 min after a meal. Don't have your child sit too long (no longer than 5 min at the most). If your child urinates or has a bowel movement while on the potty, make a huge deal and give lots of praise and attention (hugs, kisses, clapping, verbal compliments, positive reinforcement of urination or bowel movement).

Step 5: During the toilet training period, allow your child to take over the toileting procedure. This includes letting your child push pants and underwear down, get on the toilet, get the correct amount of toilet paper, wipe clean from front to back, put toilet paper into the toilet, get off the toilet, pull pants and underwear up, flush toilet, and wash and dry hands. When your child performs any of these tasks, remember to give lots of praise and positive attention.

Step 6: Leave your child's diaper off for a block of time each day (at least 30 min). During this time, explain to your child that big boys and girls go "peepee and poopoo" in the potty. Show your child where the potty is and tell her to sit on it when she has to go. Remember to tell your child that you will help him and take him to the bathroom whenever he wants. Occasionally remind your child that it is there if she needs it. If your child asks to use the potty, *make sure to drop everything and get your child to the potty.* If your child is successful, give lots of positive reinforcement and praise your child. If he tries but does not go, still praise for trying. When your child has an accident (which virtually all children do) don't punish her or get angry.

Step 7: Transition your child into pull-ups, training pants, and then underwear. First, have your child wear pull-ups or training pants all the time instead of diapers. Remember, it may take a few months before your child can go a couple of days without having an accident. Once your child has mastered this, allow her to wear underwear instead.

Once the parent gets a feel for the child's signals, and the child has had some success in at least moving in the direction of the toilet when they are going, the parent can put the child in clothes, either "commando" style or in training pants. However, once the parent moves to this phase, they need to be ready to put the child on the potty at strategic times of the day to try to go, based on what they now know about the child's elimination schedule. The parent should try to make this time as pleasant as possible for their child by letting them pick out their potty and/or training pants and/or keeping some favorite toys and books by the toilet for entertainment purposes while they are trying to go. When there are accidents, the parent should matter-of-factly point this out, and then have the child help clean up. Be sure not to shame the child! Attention and praise are key. Remember, this is a process, and accidents will happen.

Nighttime training can happen in tandem with daytime training. However, parents can also wait for the child to start consolidating their urine, a natural process once they start daytime training. If the parent chooses to wait for consolidation, then the child should have a number of dry diapers at night before beginning nighttime training. If the parent starts nighttime and daytime training at the same time, without waiting for consolidation to occur, and the child has not had dry diapers at night, the parent will need to wake up about twice a night to bring the child to the potty. Typically, it is recommended that the parent try to bring the child to the potty around 10 p.m. and 2 a.m. Also, the parent should restrict the child's fluids for a few hours before bedtime. It is okay to allow the child some small amount of water, but the child should not have any big cups of fluids just before bed.

Just like with daytime training, there are bound to be accidents overnight, perhaps even more likely than during the daytime. However, for recurrent nighttime accidents over an extended period, use of a bedwetting alarm can be very effective. For recurrent daytime or nighttime urine or bowel accidents, it is important to rule out any medical issues (such as constipation due to dietary issues). This is particularly important if the child regresses after successful toilet training.

In sum, as shown in Table 12.5, once the child is showing signs that they are ready to train, monitor the child's output. Then, once the parent is ready to closely monitor the child and put them on the toilet at particular times, begin putting them on the potty with toys. Praise, praise, praise any successes!

TABLE 12.5 Toilet training overview.

1. Assess signs of readiness to train
2. Track elimination patterns
3. Trade in diaper for clothes and make toilet a fun place
4. Reward attempts and successes!

Social skills training for interpersonal problems

Likewise, it is very common for children and adolescents with disruptive behavior problems to have problems getting along with peers. Social skills training for social skills problems will be helpful for many of these individuals, including Anna.

Anna

Anna is our 15-year-old Caucasian female whose parents presented with concerns about possible drug use, sexting, and promiscuous sex. Anna, as you will remember, has already been diagnosed and successfully treated for depression with antidepressants. However, she still appears to be exhibiting enough significant difficulties to be diagnosed with ODD as well. She is often irritable and easily annoyed, and argues with or defies adult requests. Other diagnostic considerations include substance use disorder. Bullying, safe sex, and healthy peer and romantic relationships will also all need to be addressed in treatment.

Possible cooccurring problems

- Substance use disorders

Other considerations

- *Bullying*
- *Sexual and romantic relationships*
- *Peer relationships*

As shown in Table 12.6, early and even later monitoring and coaching can be helpful. How to handle bullying should be discussed explicitly. As children reach adolescence, it can be helpful to reaffirm personal values.

When working with families and adolescents, I stress that monitoring is of key importance. For younger children, monitoring helps the parent be knowledgeable about the child's strengths and weaknesses. For

TABLE 12.6 Social skills training.

1. Monitor!
2. Coach
3. Handling bullies
    a. Ignore
    b. Be assertive
4. Help set personal goals

TABLE 12.7 Refusal skills.

• Say no thanks • Make an excuse • Leave the situation • Change the subject • Suggest a better idea • Find other kids to hang out with

adolescents, monitoring provides first-hand information about the quality of the adolescent's friendships (as well as provides information about their peer group, a powerful influence on teenagers!). In younger children, the parent should explicitly coach weak social behaviors (e.g., taking turns) by providing explicit verbal and nonverbal instruction during structured play opportunities. For older children and adolescents, like Anna, the parent can teach the problem-solving skills covered in the last chapter, but they should especially help the adolescent use those skills in social situations (such as when resolving conflicts). Parents should also remember to model social skills to children and adolescents through their personal interactions with them, as well as through their interactions with other adults.

Parents can teach children and adolescents how to handle bullies through use of ignoring and/or assertiveness skills. Remind children and adolescents that bullies are bound to lose interest if they do not respond to them. Explicitly teach children and adolescents assertiveness skills by teaching them key phrases they can use. For example, a parent could teach a child or adolescent to say, "if you keep calling me names, I am going to tell an adult" or "no one cares what you think."

Parents should also reaffirm personal goals (e.g., no smoking) with their adolescent as a protection against peer pressure. Use of avoidance skills such as making excuses can also be helpful. For example, a child or adolescent could say, "my mother won't let me" or "I have to go home." Finally, assertiveness skills can be helpful and should be explicitly taught in regard to these types of situations. For example, a child or adolescent could be taught to say, "I don't want to do that." See Table 12.7 for other key phrases.

Educational support for learning problems

Children with disruptive behavior problems often also have learning problems and need substantial educational support. Parents should be sure to have a good home/school communication system in place. Advocate for the child through consideration of accommodations, modifications, and therapies. Explicit coaching in academic skills such as organization may also be helpful.

When I work with families, I stress that it is of primary importance to have consistent school/home communication. With electronic learning systems, this is getting easier and easier. However, the parent can also use a daily note with a few specific behavioral goals that can be rated by the teacher.

It is important to advocate for children. Know that children have rights to a good education regardless of their individual learning style or any behavioral or emotional problems. This is codified in federal law by the Individuals with Disabilities Education Improvement Act and section 504 of the Rehabilitation Act of 1973. If a child qualifies for services, the parent can ask for accommodations (e.g., extra time for tests, seating nearer the front of the classroom with fewer distractions, frequent reminders/check ins) and/or modifications (e.g., less homework, use of a computer, voice recorder, copies of notes, oral testing). See the list in Table 12.8.

It is usually best to start by trying to work with the teacher before moving up the administrative ladder. Try to form a team with the teacher. The parent should express appreciation for what the teacher does and ask how they can be helpful. Also, know what resources school can provide. If the child attends public school, speech and language therapy for speech problems is likely available. Public school systems also often provide physical and occupational therapy for problems with gross or fine motor skills such as riding a bike or handwriting, respectively. If the child's school does not offer these services, private services can also be obtained.

Finally, it can be helpful to explicitly teach the child academic strategies. Have a mandatory homework time in a quiet, structured environment (such as at a desk) at a set time of day. Make fun activities such as screen time contingent on successful completion of work. Children can benefit from explicit instruction in organization. For example, keeping an assignment log and one folder for completed homework to turn in can be a useful strategy, particularly for individuals who struggle with organization. Teach the child to review their work and to reward themselves with a brief break or a small snack for finishing tasks. For children with learning problems, consider hiring a tutor. Having someone else work with the child on difficult tasks (such as reading) can greatly improve the parent–child relationship and provide the parent with more time to help the child with other issues.

In sum, as shown in Table 12.9, be sure to have a good home/school communication system in place. Advocate for the child through consideration of accommodations, modifications, and therapies. Explicit coaching in academic skills such as organization may also be helpful.

TABLE 12.8 List of accommodations and modifications.

• Low distraction location • Frequent reminders • Multimodal instruction • Frequent, positive reinforcement • Provide opportunities to move around classroom or fidget • Frequent breaks • Extended time • Assistance with homework at school • Shortened assignments • Technological assistance (e.g., computer, calculator, voice recorder) • Provide copies of notes • Read aloud • Graphic organizer

TABLE 12.9 Educational support.

1. Have a good school/home communication system
2. Advocate for your child
   a. Accommodations
   b. Modifications
   c. Therapies
3. Coach in organizational skills

Medication for comorbid disorders

For ODD alone, medication is only recommended as an adjunctive treatment, not as the main intervention. However, in situations where a child or adolescent is facing multiple comorbid, or cooccurring, problems such as depression—like in Anna's case—medication can be helpful. For example, current guidelines suggest that, for ODD comorbid with attention-deficit/hyperactivity disorder (ADHD), psychostimulants may be useful for treating ADHD. For severe conduct problems, mood stabilizers may be effective for decreasing severe aggression. Finally, for aggression in the context of intellectual disability or pervasive developmental disorders like autism, antipsychotics may be useful. Of course, the nature of the presenting problems will dictate the type of medication(s) considered. Pediatricians or psychiatrists can be useful consultants in this endeavor. For complicated cases, a psychiatrist is a particularly helpful resource.

In sum, medication is not currently recommended for ODD alone. For comorbid problems, a consultation with a psychiatrist is highly recommended.

Conclusion

In sum, a variety of additional interventions can be useful for treating ODD with its common cooccurring issues, including—depending on the age of the child and their presenting issues—behavioral treatment for independent sleep and toilet training problems, as well as social skills training and educational support. Medication is solely recommended as an adjunctive treatment for ODD at this point, but can be useful for addressing comorbid disorders such as ADHD and depression.

Further reading

Online resources:

General healthy parenting tips: www.5adayparenting.org

Essential information for parenting toddlers and preschoolers: https://www.cdc.gov/parents/essentials/index.html

General parenting skills for addressing tricky child behaviors (such as tantrums): https://www.zerotothree.org/resources?q = &topic = challenging-behaviors&type = &rformat = &age_range =

Information on general development and socialization, including how to handle aggression: https://www.healthychildren.org/English/ages-stages/toddler/Pages/Aggressive-Behavior.aspx

Information for pediatricians and parents about child health issues with listed resources: https://brightfutures.aap.org/families/Pages/Resources-for-Families.aspx

Parenting support groups: http://parentsanonymous.org/

Current practice parameters for assessment and treatment of ODD in children and adolescents: https://www.jaacap.org/article/S0890-8567(09)61969-9/fulltext

Text resources:

Barkley, R. A., & Robin, A. L. (2014). *Defiant teens: A clinician's manual for assessment and family intervention*. Guilford Publications.

Bloomquist, M. L. *Skills training for struggling kids: Promoting your child's behavioral, emotional, academic, and social development*. New York: Guilford.

Clowacki, J. (2015). *Oh crap! Potty training: Everything modern parents need to do it once and do it right*. New York: Touchstone.

Ferber, R. (2006). *Solve your child's sleep problems*. New York: Simon & Schuster.

Mercer, R. (2011). *Seven steps to nighttime dryness: A practical guide for parents of children with bedwetting* (2nd ed.). Ashton, MD: Brookeville Media.

Webster-Stratton, C., Mostyn, D., & Marie, J. S. (2005). *The Incredible Years: A troubleshooting guide for parents of children aged 2-8 years*. Seattle, WA: Incredible Years.

Index

Note: Page numbers followed by "*f*" and "*t*" refer to figures and tables, respectively.

P

R

S

T

FSC
www.fsc.org
MIX
Papier | Fördert gute Waldnutzung
FSC® C083411

Kolibri 360 GmbH
Ferdinand-Jühlke-Straße 7
99095 Erfurt, Deutschland
produktsicherheit@kolibri360.de